FROM IMAGE TO LIKENESS

A Jungian Path in the Gospel Journey

W. Harold Grant
Magdala Thompson
Thomas E. Clarke

paulist press 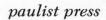 *new york/ramsey*

Library of Congress
Catalog Card Number: 83-60377

ISBN: 0-8091-2552-8

Published by Paulist Press
545 Island Road, Ramsey, N.J. 07446

Printed and bound in the
United States of America

Contents

Acknowledgements   v

Preface   1

CHAPTER 1   God's Image We Bear
(*Wholeness/Holiness*)   5

CHAPTER 2   A Gift To Be Simple
(*Sensing/Simplicity*)   29

CHAPTER 3   The Truth That Makes Us Free
(*Thinking/Justice*)   68

CHAPTER 4   With a Joyful Heart
(*Feeling/Gratitude*)   107

CHAPTER 5   Eye Has Not Seen
(*Intuiting/Hope*)   144

CHAPTER 6   Fullness of Love
(*Individuation/Charity*)   178

EPILOGUE   "The Way Has Come to Thee"   208

APPENDIX A   Resources   212

APPENDIX B   Patterns of Type Development   215

Biographical Data   249

ACKNOWLEDGEMENTS

We wish at the outset to express our gratitude to the many people, too numerous for mentioning by name, who have contributed in any way to the preparation of this book. Our most important indebtedness is to the late Isabel Briggs Myers, who developed the Myers-Briggs Type Indicator (MBTI) over a period of decades, and so provided a practical instrument for utilizing Carl Jung's insights into personality types.

Others are worthy of special mention:

Those who on one or more occasions were members of the team for the retreat/workshops (R/W) from which this book originated: Sister Eleanor Augur, R.S.M.; Sister Marie Foley, R.S.M.; Sister Janice Futrell, O.S.B.; Sister Elizabeth Ann Linehan, R.S.M.; Sister Mary Aquin O'Neill, R.S.M.

The directors and staffs of the centers which welcomed us and shared their hospitality: the generalate of the Sisters of Mercy of the Union, Bethesda, Maryland; Blessed Trinity Shrine Retreat, Holy Trinity, Alabama; Mercy Center, St. Louis, Missouri; Salve Regina College, Newport, Rhode Island; Mercy Center, Madison, Connecticut; Cabrini Contact Center, Des Plaines, Illinois; Loyola Retreat House, Guelph, Ontario; Bon Secours Spiritual Center, Marriottsville, Maryland.

All the participants of all the programs—some six hundred laypersons, sisters, brothers, clergy.

Those who read the first draft of this book and assisted us with their suggestions: Sister Janice Futrell, O.S.B.; Raphael Jordan; George Wilson, S.J.

Biblical quotations and references, unless otherwise noted, are from *The Jerusalem Bible* (Garden City N.Y.: Doubleday, 1966). We have done our best to make use of inclusive language in our own remarks, but have left unchanged the text of English translations of the Bible.

Preface

This book represents a stage on a journey. For almost a decade the three of us have been conducting retreat/workshops (R/W) based on the Gospel as illuminated through the Jungian personality types. The Myers-Briggs Type Indicator (MBTI) has been the instrument employed in these programs for helping participants to identify their types. Several hundred people have thereby been strengthened toward human and Christian growth, and their positive response has assisted us in developing both ourselves and this educational and pastoral vehicle. At this point in our journey, we want to share our experience with a wider circle, with readers who will walk with us chapter by chapter, as we describe in both behavioral and religious language one way of envisaging the human call.

Like the R/W itself, this book invites to a kind of "learn by doing" set of exercises. To the best of our ability we will provide accurate information, clarifying analyses, stimulating reflections and suggestions. But all of these will be aimed at assisting readers, individually and in groups, to exercise themselves in the various human and Christian behaviors which we will be describing. One of our basic convictions is that the best way to grow in a desired virtue is to practice it with the help of models, whether these models be verbal descriptions or persons—fictional, historical or living. From the very beginning, then, we encourage our readers to take an active and participatory posture toward what we say. It is they—not we—who will speak the real message, not as print on paper, but as a lived experience of growth. Practice makes perfect, or at least it keeps us moving toward perfection or wholeness. "Arise and walk" is the perennial message of Jesus to all who seek to develop God's image in their lives.

God's image! That is the central model and motif we have

chosen for expressing the Gospel vision of human life. As we will elaborate, the very first chapter of the Bible epitomizes what it means to be human by having God say, "Let us make man in our own image, in the likeness of ourselves" (Gen 1:26).

With some of the Fathers of the Church, we have been struck with the dynamic and developmental aspect of God's human creation. Going beyond the literal sense of this key text, they saw "image" as expressing the *potential* of the human for becoming, in a sense, divine; "likeness" stood for the *fulfillment*, the actualization of that potential, the term of growth. In this sense, then, human development is a journey from the image of God toward likeness to God.

What drew us toward this model was, in large part, the fact that Carl Jung in his analytical psychology also made much of the God-image (and Christ-image). In his clinically grounded theory, these terms relate to the *Self*, whose disclosure and liberation are the goal of the process of *individuation*. Jung did not identify the God-image with the Self, but did assert that the two could not be *clinically* (empirically) differentiated. For him the Christ-image was *symbol* of the Self.

The title of our book thus invites the reader both to *marvel* at the greatness of our human endowment—our creation according to God's image—and to *yearn* for the fulfillment of our human destiny, the time when "we shall be like him because we shall see him as he really is" (1 Jn 3:2).

Along with this primary model, the journey from image to likeness, the reader will encounter three other major models, which will be more fully explained in the first chapter, but which it will be helpful to identify here. The *second* major model is that of the Jungian personality types, and more specifically of the four "functions"—two "perceiving" functions, namely "sensing" and "intuiting," and two "judging" functions, namely "thinking" and "feeling." All four functions admit of exercise in two distinct "attitudes," which Jung designates as "extraversion" and "introversion." It will be a recurring feature of this book to take these Jungian functions and, by *a method of correlation,* link them with biblical, theological and spiritual themes.

Chapter 1 will lay out a basic understanding of the four functions and sketch the broad lines of the method of correlation with the Gospel. Its focus, therefore, will be our human potential, God's image in us, viewed from both behavioral and religious standpoints. Chapters 2 to 5 will journey successively through each of the four functions and their corresponding Gospel motifs, offering description, analysis, reflection, and some specific exercises by which growth in several key virtues is fostered. Chapter 6 in its turn will center on the goal of the journey, the fullness of Godlikeness—what Jung calls "individuation" and what is most importantly expressed in the Gospel by the simple term "love."

The *third* major model is really a developmental perspective on the second. It views the functions and attitudes on the basis of a *developmental typology.* Here we offer, with some support from our dealing with several hundred people in the context of the R/W, and from experience with several thousand students in two universities, the model of *four successive stages of development* between the ages of six and fifty. This model, which is a distinctive feature of our R/W and of the present book, was originated by Harold Grant. Admittedly it calls for further testing by experience. Compared with much else that we shall be saying, it is less able to appeal to explicit support within the Jungian tradition. We offer it here because we have found it to be a framework which encourages people to regard their personality not statically but dynamically, within the context of the human "life-cycle." Throughout this volume we shall use both the MBTI code and one which we ourselves have devised to designate each of the sixteen Jungian types. Appendix B will offer a summary view of how the two codes are to be correlated.

A *fourth* major model, which will also be elaborated in Chapter 1, attempts to situate the human potential and its fulfillment within the framework of *solitude/friendship/society,* a language which we borrow from Thoreau's *Walden.* This model proposes that we regard each of the functions and virtues and their development not only as exercised by individuals, but also within analogous aspects of human relationships and of society and culture. Together with the three preceding models, this fourth one can foster a holistic approach to our humanity and also to the Gospel in its encounter with that humanity.

Here, then, are our four basic models: (1) the journey from image to likeness; (2) the four Jungian functions and their exercise in extraverted and introverted attitudes, correlated with kindred facets of the Gospel; (3) a developmental typology which predicates four stages of growth toward wholeness; (4) the triad of solitude, friendship and society as expressive of the human reality which is called to develop from image to likeness. This identification of the four models will, we trust, suffice for now. Only at the end of the first chapter do we expect the reader to have a firm grasp on them; and the entire book will be needed for a full appreciation of how they interweave with one another.

Finally, we offer a few simple *exercises* aimed at disposing the reader for setting out on the journey with us:

1. *An exercise of wonder.* Read *Psalm 8,* which exegetes describe as an echo of the account of creation in Chapter 1 of Genesis, or *Psalm 139,* especially verse 14, which in one translation reads, "I thank you for the wonder of my being." With or without words, marvel at the gift of being human, of being created according to God's image, of being called to grow into Godlikeness.

2. *A reflective review.* What do the authors hope that I will gain by reading this book? How do they suggest that I go about the reading? How is the book structured? What is my initial understanding of the models being offered? What previous experience and understanding do I bring to the reading? What are my own hopes?

3. *A commitment.* How much time and energy do I want to invest in reading this book and exercising myself according to its suggestions? Is there someone else—even several people—whom I would like to invite to share the journey with me?

CHAPTER 1
God's Image We Bear

Wholeness/Holiness

"My ways are not your ways" (Is 55:8). Sin sets limits to our human dreams of greatness and would seduce us into the blasphemous thought that "if God is, I am not; if I am, God is not." But ours is a God not of limits but of fullness and fulfillment, who calls us not to death but to an ever fuller life (Jn 10:10). Our very power to aspire to greatness is already a realization of God's great aspiration for us. God never stops dreaming of the unlimited growth of the divine image in us toward divine likeness. "You shall be like gods" (Gen 3:5). The serpent's deception was not in sowing the dream of divinization but in suggesting that we pursue it in isolation, outside of a gift-relationship with God. The Gospel and the model of development which we propose here share a deep awareness that there is evil—darkness—in human life. But they also share the conviction that in spite of evil, and even to some degree through it, human beings can grow without limit toward God-likeness. It is this capacity to journey from image to likeness that we want to explore now in the Gospel, with the help of a typology of human development.

I. CREATED ACCORDING TO GOD'S IMAGE

There are countless images, symbols, models of the human potential to be found in Scripture. We choose here to describe it primarily in terms of the *image of God* theme, together with related themes: *holiness, perfection, wholeness, fullness, glory.* Then we lay out the broad features of our developmental typology, and we try to show how it can enlighten and be

5

enlightened by what our Christian faith tells us about human destiny.

The story begins in the very first chapter of the Bible. Since we cannot linger here on the many significant details of this biblical keynoting of human dignity, we would encourage the reader to explore the entire passage of Genesis 1:1–2:4, which is a liturgical account of the creation. Its peak moment comes with the creation of human beings, male and female, in God's image and likeness. They are called to increase and multiply and fill the earth, to exercise stewardship with regard to it and all its inhabitants.

In a Christian reading which situates the passage within the context of the whole Bible and of its ongoing interpretation in the Church, what are, for our purposes, some of the key fruits? First, human beings in their radical constitution reflect the very image of God. Whenever we see a human being, or husband and wife, or members of a human society struggling to shape a distinctive world for themselves, we are being shown something about God. Second, just to be human is a call or an imperative to grow, to let God's image in myself, in us, in our world, develop into Godlikeness. Third, being human involves human relationship, and most basically the relationship of man and woman: "male and female he created them." Fourth, being human involves responsible stewardship toward the rest of creation, through work and the ordering of life on earth.

In all of this we can already see in germ the three basic dimensions of what it means to be human, according to the fourth major model of which we have spoken in the Preface. God's image is found in *each* person as an individual person— hence the dimension of *solitude*. But persons are also persons in relationship with other persons—hence the dimension of *friendship* symbolically contained in the male/female language of the account. And, finally, persons in relationship with other persons act and interact within the world. They act upon and are influenced by the world of *nature*, and out of it create the world of *society*, which in its turn tends to shape them in their persons and relationships. When Thoreau wrote in *Wal-*

den about having three chairs in his cabin, one for solitude, one for friendship, and one for society, his striking metaphor was pointing to our integral human call to grow from God-image toward Godlikeness. The Gospel, as we shall see, speaks to us about all three.

It is good news indeed to hear of our richness by creation. But that original gift of beauty has been disfigured by what Christians call original sin. Whatever myths and symbols one has recourse to for acknowledging the presence of radical evil in the world, and whatever stammering efforts we make toward rational expression of our disfigurement, human experience confirms what our faith teaches on the dark mystery of sin and evil. Precisely insofar as we are under the domination of sin, our human lives no longer mirror the beauty of God. Our capacity for finding God through interiority and solitude is replaced by self-hatred, narcissism, anxiety. Our aptitude for human communion yields to alienation and hostility toward the neighbor. And instead of creating a human city which anticipates the heavenly city, we become the prey of massive societal evils, a nightmare existence. When one reflects on those frightful twentieth century experiences which have become symbolic of our plight—Dachau and Hiroshima and Jonestown, among others—one does not have to be in the Judaeo-Christian tradition to assent to the reality of original sin. Where, one might ask, is God's image in our world today?

But the Christian story contains a third stage of development, *redemption* or restoration, which we might term the good news after the bad news. It is such good news that the Church, in an ecstatic and hyperbolic moment of the Easter celebration, acclaims the tragic moment of fall as a "happy fault" (*O felix culpa*). In the second Adam—Jesus—and the second Eve—the Church (typified by Mary)—there has taken place not an annulment of our disfigurement but rather its *transfiguration.* Darkness itself, sings the Church, is now made beautiful by the light that has come to shine in it. That light is a human being, Jesus Christ, the second and ultimate Adam, the one who *is* the image of God. His incarnation, his life, death and resurrection, and the consequent gift of the Spirit have more wonderfully, more powerfully, re-established our ability to grow from God-image to Godlikeness, in our individual existence, in our relationships, and in our creation of society and history.

We would encourage the reader at this point to do what we do not here have the space to do, namely explore in the New Testament, and particularly in Paul, some of the facets of the image theme in its Christological aspects. Here are some of the key passages: Romans 8:29; 1 Corinthians 15:49; 2 Corinthians 2:12—4:6; Philippians 2:5–11; Colossians 1:15; 3:10; Hebrews 1:3. Out of such passages there emerges a view of the drama of salvation through Christ Jesus which can be expressed somewhat as follows.

The disfigurement of our humanity through the fall was permitted by God only in view of its ultimate transfiguration. Human beings, made according to God's image, were to be restored to or rather recreated beyond the original beauty with which they reflected God. This has been accomplished by God's own Word and Son, who *is* the image of the unseen God (Col 1:15; Heb 1:3). The manner of this re-creation is wonderful beyond the power of words to express. It has taken place by the "marvelous exchange" (*admirabile commercium*). The sinless One takes on the form or image of our enslaved humanity in order to give us a share in his own perfect reflection of the beauty of God (Phil 2:7; see 2 Cor 5:21). The glory of God shining on the face of Christ Jesus becomes, as we Christians gaze upon it, the source of our imaging of that glory on our own faces, in our own lives (2 Cor 3:18; 4:6). This takes place not only by our conscious imitation of the example of Jesus in our lives, but especially by the transfiguring action of the Holy Spirit who has been poured forth into our hearts by the risen Lord Jesus (2 Cor 3:18; Rom 5:5; Gal 4:4).

One point, already mentioned in passing, needs accenting, especially in view of the typology we will be exhibiting. The call to divinization is simultaneously a call to humanization, and this latter term must be understood as inclusive of the darkness of our human condition. Paul speaks very daringly of the degree to which Christ Jesus plunged himself into the human condition: "For our sake God made the sinless one into sin, so that in him we might become the goodness of God" (2 Cor 5:21). It is not by escaping from darkness and negativity that we disciples of the second Adam will come to Godlikeness, but by acknowledging and, in a sense, embracing them. Whatever speculative difficulties may be involved in Jung's desire to bring the concept of evil into the Godhead itself, the psychological insight which he sought to express finds a counterpart in Christian faith; sin itself does not escape the alchemy of God's Spirit working our eternal transfiguration. When the time comes to speak of how the saving crucifixion of Christ Jesus finds its counterpart in a typology of human development, we shall be recalling this aspect of our faith. The grain of wheat does indeed have to die in being sown; the journey does lead to crossroads where it is the "foolish" choice which keeps us on the path to the kingdom.

Although the primary model we are working with here is the journey from image to likeness, no single idea is able to capture the entire mystery of our human call. Throughout this book as throughout the Scriptures themselves, a wide variety of ideas, often interwoven with one another, will be employed. At this point, then, we wish to invite the reader to reflect on several other themes which are closely linked with the image of God. In each case we shall give a few leads for biblical prayer and reflection.

The Call to Holiness

The call to holiness is identical with the call to grow toward Godlikeness, especially because God is presented as the model for human holiness. "It is I, Yahweh, who brought you out of Egypt to be your God; you therefore must be holy because I am holy" (Lev 11:45). Within the Old Testament, the concept of God's holiness, as reference point and norm for human holiness, underwent considerable development, which we may generally describe as one of interiorization. This characterization of God is linked with other descriptions of the God of the covenant, and especially with the concept of divine justice, a much more comprehensive and rich conception than is contained in our commonplace understanding of justice today. In any case, the moral and spiritual integrity to which humans are to aspire has no lesser model than the all holy God.

In the New Testament, Jesus himself is acknowledged as "the holy one of God" (Jn 6:69), and Christians are called as his disciples to be holy. "Be holy in all you do, since it is the Holy One who has called you, and Scripture says: 'Be holy, for I am holy'" (1 Pet 1:15). So conscious were early Christians of their call to holiness and of their having been made holy through baptism that "holy ones" or "saints" became a common way of addressing the Christian communities. Nothing unworthy of those who are saints and who are called to aspire to ever greater holiness should appear in the conduct of Christians (Eph 5:3; Col 3:12). In short, holiness is one primary way of specifying the likeness to God which has already begun in us and which we are to develop under the inner guidance of God as *Holy* Spirit.

Perfection

Another specification of the term of our growth is the concept of perfection. Understandably, but we think unfortunately, perfection and striving for perfection has a rather poor press nowadays. There is more than one reason for this. Especially as a reaction against perfectionism and against a perennial spiritual form of the work-ethic called Pelagianism, many people are wary of any language which appears to suggest lifting oneself by one's bootstraps, or a "grunt and groan" approach to prayer and asceticism. It is not uncommon today to contrast perfection and wholeness, as Carl Jung himself did.

We believe that these reactions are understandable. But the New Testament treatment of perfection and of human efforts to grow toward it has no such negative connotations. In the Sermon on the Mount, Jesus himself proposed to his disciples the idea of human perfection in imitation of the divine perfection: "In a word you must be made perfect as your heavenly Father is perfect" (Mt 5:48, New American Bible).

He also held out to the rich young man the basic condition—
total renunciation of goods in favor of the poor—for achieving
the perfection which is identical with entering into life (Mt
19:21).

Paul also holds out to early Christians the goal of perfection. A magnificent passage in Ephesians presents as the term
of the building up of the body of Christ "the perfect Man"
(Eph 4:13), which figure appears to be Christ Jesus himself,
archetype of the new humanity, and at the same time we
ourselves, "fully mature with the fullness of Christ himself."
There is, too, the passage where Paul presents himself as
racing toward the goal and the prize, perfect knowledge of
and communion with Christ Jesus. He is not yet perfect, he
says, but, forgetting what is behind, he presses forward eagerly
(Phil 3:12–14). Paul's famous hymn to charity likewise envis-
ages perfection as the goal of life (1 Cor 13:10). Finally, the
Letter to the Hebrews, as it seeks to revive the hopes and
aspirations of a discouraged Christian community, reminds it
of the example of God's own Son, who had to learn obedience
by suffering, who had himself to *become* perfect, that he might
be the one who "leads us in our faith, and brings it to perfection" (Heb 12:2; see 2:10–18; 4:12–16; 5:1–10).

Aspiring to perfection and struggling to grow toward it
through a sustained and disciplined shaping of one's life are far
from being a Pelagian enterprise. These purposes are quite
compatible with—in fact comprise both the fruit of and disposition for—a trusting reliance on God's grace. No one, perhaps,
in our day has more eloquently described the interplay of
divine grace and human freedom, trust in God's mercy and
vigorous doing of the truth in love, than Dietrich Bonhoeffer.
Only the one who believes obeys, he says, and only the one
who obeys believes. Believing here refers to the element of
trust and receptivity, the acknowledgement of the need of
God's grace; obedience is the faithful carrying out of God's
will. "Costly grace" (in contrast to "cheap grace") is the phrase
that Bonhoeffer uses to crystallize this genuinely Christian and
highly paradoxical attitude.[1] Later, in dealing with the typology of human development, we shall come to speak of the

rhythm of receptivity and response, and so shall be hearing an echo of Bonhoeffer's dictum in behavioral terms.

Fullness/Wholeness

Even after the foregoing apologia for the language of perfection, some may look for an alternative image. They may be attracted, then, to the notion of fullness, which is not far removed from the notion of wholeness. This latter term is attractive to many today, especially in circles influenced by Jung, and more generally among those who see the need for an holistic approach to life. Terms like fullness and wholeness, just in the speaking, enlarge our spirits and our aspirations. They suggest the image of the circle or sphere, which is a primary symbol of perfection in dreams, myths and fantasy. Let us simply point the reader toward a possible exploration of the theme of fullness in the New Testament. The prologue of John is a familiar instance. God's Incarnate Word is "full of grace and truth" (or "gracious love and faithfulness"), and, says the author, "from his fullness we have, all of us, received" (Jn 1:14, 16).

This communication of the fullness of Christ Jesus to the community of his disciples finds a rich counterpart in the "captivity letters" of the Pauline corpus. It is in the fullness of time, says the Letter to the Ephesians, that the universe is to find again its unity and completion in Christ (Eph 1:10). This is to take place through the Church, which is both the body of Christ and the fullness (*pleroma*) of the one who fills the whole creation (1:23). And the fulfillment of the Christian vocation, ultimately, will come when, "knowing the love of Christ, which is beyond all knowledge, you are filled with the utter fullness of God" (3:19). The Letter to the Colossians speaks in the same vein, with accent on the person of Jesus Christ, but precisely as he is head of the Church and of the whole creation. "God wanted all fullness [the Jerusalem Bible says 'perfection'] to be found in him" (Col 1:19), and so "in his body (or: 'in him . . . bodily') lives the fullness of divinity, and in him you too find your own fulfillment" (2:9).

Fullness and fulfillment, then, are both the promise and the challenge of the Gospel. Today something of a reaction is taking place against what is seen as the presence of a certain narcissism in some of the movements which espouse human development. That there is narcissism in our society, in part an excessive reaction to the threat of absorption by technologism, stands beyond dispute. But this danger should not divert anyone from honoring the deep human yearning, planted in our hearts by God, to come to wholeness and fulfillment. If we keep listening to the Gospel and have a sound behavioral grasp on what is involved in human growth, we need not fear that the search for holiness, perfection, fullness, will make us self-centered in the pejorative sense. Love of self and of the neighbor grow in direct, not in inverse, proportion. We shall have further occasion to comment on the inseparability of the two.

Glory

A final biblical companion of the notion of image is the term "glory." The reader who has followed our invitation to explore the passages in 2 Corinthians and Hebrews will have picked up this connection. In the Old Testament, words like *kabod* and *shekinah* were used to describe the brightness which manifested God's presence, especially in the tent of the covenant and later in the temple. In the New Testament, God's glory in this sense is Christ Jesus himself, and his radiance is communicated to the community of his disciples. "We saw his glory" (Jn 1:14) describes a *transforming* or *transfiguring* Christian experience. The Fourth Gospel returns several times to this theme of glory, notably at Cana, where the disciples have their first experience of his glory (2:11), and in the priestly prayer of Jesus at the Last Supper (17:1–5). The accounts of the transfiguration are other high points of this theme (Mt 17:1–9; Mk 9:2–10; Lk 9:28–36; 2 Pet 1:16–18).

It is appropriate to mention this theme of glory here because the typological model of human development which we shall be presenting depends for its efficacy on the experience of a *transforming enlightenment.* What distinguishes human development from the growth of merely material organisms—plants and animals—is that it takes place by way of consciousness, knowledge and freedom. The image of shining glory and the concept of enlightenment both suggest a knowledge gained through the presence of God, experienced with a certain intimacy or immediacy, and resulting in a conversion or transformation of our human attitudes and behaviors. This is the transfiguring knowledge of glory that lets the image of God grow toward greater and greater likeness.

II. A TYPOLOGY OF HUMAN DEVELOPMENT

With this rudimentary sketch of how the Christian story portrays the journey from God-image to Godlikeness, let us now begin to describe how a model of human development inspired by Carl Jung's theory of psychological types can assist that journey. We say "inspired by" and not "according to" Jung, since we shall often be proceeding beyond what Jung and his disciples have had to say about growth. Also, our use of his insights and terminology will be largely confined to those which deal with personality types, and so we will be only incidentally concerned with some of his other major contributions, for example, those on dreams, archetypes, the collective unconscious, and the like. Readers who may have engaged in Jungian analysis as clients or therapists and even many who have made use of such Jungian instruments as the Gray-Wheelwright Psychological Type Questionnaire or MBTI may be disappointed to find that certain aspects of personal development are here treated cursorily or not at all. Nor are we pursuing what would truly be a massive undertaking, the correlation of each of the sixteen MBTI types with biblical, theological and spiritual themes which have an affinity with them.

Our aim is more modest: a general indication, with some examples, of how a developmental typology may be interwoven with some themes and vehicles of spirituality in a way which facilitates integral human growth. Readers who may wish to pursue what they find here more deeply or more broadly will find some suggested readings and resources in Appendix A.

Psychic Energy

Let us begin with a notion which was basic for Jung, the notion of psychic energy. As a material organism or giant industrial complex depends essentially on the flow of physical energy among its diverse components, so the human system is shaped by the character and quality of its psychic energy. Jung was not the first or the only major thinker to grasp the central importance of this metaphor in our age. Back at the turn of the century Henry Adams, brooding over what modernity had lost in the transition from the Middle Ages and pondering what might be ahead of us, meditated profoundly on "the Virgin and the dynamo" as two very diverse symbols of energy, one religious and the other secular. While Jung was developing his own views Pierre Teilhard de Chardin, from a quite different vantage point, was beginning to construct a synthetic vision in which the notion of energy was crucial.

Thanks especially to Jung, we appreciate better today that between the conscious and the unconscious levels within each person, in the hidden and the overt dimensions of how people relate to one another, and in the powerful forces which shape society and culture, psychic energies are constantly flowing. In each instance, it is the quality of this flow of energy which measures the health of humanity. It is remarkable, let us note in passing, how much the language of Paul is filled with terms which express the presence of divine force, power and energy in the world through the sending of the Spirit by the risen Jesus (1 Cor 1:18, 24; 2:4–5; Eph 1:15–23; Phil 2:12–13). The spiritual task, from this viewpoint, is to find ways in which the immense psychic resources of our humanity can be disclosed and set free to be the carriers of the very power of God at work in our midst.

Varieties of Preferred Behaviors

Both clinical and ordinary experience led Jung and others
to see that psychic energy does not flow uniformly in all
human beings. Early in life and throughout their days on earth,
people manifest diverse spontaneous *preferences* in dealing
with life. These preferences do not predetermine people to a
fated existence, but they profoundly affect the way in which
we will freely develop, especially in interaction with other
people in the human environment. Let us now identify these
different preferences.

Extraversion/Introversion

Jung distinguished, first of all, two contrasting "attitudes,"
extraversion (E) and *introversion* (I). This important discovery,
now part of ordinary language, has formed the basis of countless jokes and cartoons. But let us beware of misleading stereotypes about extraverts being people who talk a lot, and
introverts being people who are shy or timid. It is better, in
fact, to avoid such simplistic statements as "I'm an extravert,"
and "I'm an introvert." All of us demonstrate both extraverted
and introverted behavior and need both attitudes if we are to
answer life's challenges.

What is the meaning of these two terms? Let us say that
extraversion is occurring when *the flow of psychic energy* in
an individual or in a group is outward, toward the external
object, and that introversion is taking place when the flow of
psychic energy is directed inward, toward the subject. When a
preference for E is being exercised, the individual or group is
being "charged" by engagement with outer reality, in persons
or objects, in nature or society; we are enjoying the world,
society, other people. When a preference for I is being exercised, the "charging" and enjoyment comes by way of movement toward the interior, toward the conscious subject. It is
worth saying again: *all* of us are gifted, as part of God's image
in us, with the *ability* to exercise both of these contrasting
attitudes. We differ, however, in what we spontaneously *pre-*

fer, extraversion or introversion, when we are exercising our various "functions," which we will now describe. Nevertheless, whatever our preferences, we are capable of *developing* our capacity for both extraversion and introversion, in response to the call of God addressed to us through the demands of life. This distinction of ability, preference, and development should be kept in mind throughout this book.

Perceiving/Judging

Leaving, for the moment, extraversion and introversion, we move on to speak of another set of endowments and preferences. These have to do with what Jung calls "functions" of the ego. "Perceiving" and "judging" are the generic terms for the functions, and they refer, respectively, to a behavior that is *receptive,* and a behavior that is *responsive.* When we exercise perceiving (P), we let the world come to us; we listen, we observe, are shaped by reality, accommodate ourselves to it; in some broad sense, at least, we are contemplative. When we exercise judging (J), on the other hand, we are the ones who are doing the shaping, at least in the formation of judgments and the making of decisions.

Sensing/Intuiting

But, as we have said, perceiving (P) and judging (J) are generic terms. Each of them, Jung noted, has two specific and sharply contrasting forms. Perceiving is exercised either as "sensing" (S) or as "intuiting" (N). And judging is exercised either as "thinking" (T) or as "feeling" (F). Let us examine these pairs in turn, but briefly, as each of the four functions will have a chapter all its own.

Sensing perception is characterized by attending, with the help of the external and internal senses, to the particular, the concrete, the here-and-now reality which is touching us, coming to us. *Intuiting* perception, on the contrary, is not interested in the particular. Rather, with influence from the unconscious and with help from the imagination, its interest is in exploring possibilities, what *might* be, the future, or the essence of things. Someone has cleverly expressed the contrast between these two forms of perceiving by noting that the combination of letters N O W H E R E can be read in two ways, as NOW/HERE or as NO/WHERE. The first way is an S reading, the second an N reading. When one recalls that the literal meaning of the politically significant term *Utopia*, derived from the Greek, is "nowhere," this little play is a useful device for expressing the difference between a down-to-earth perception of the actual, and an imaginative perception of the possible.

Thinking/Feeling

A similar contrast exists between two specific forms of judging. Sometimes our response to what we have perceived is characterized by a good deal of logic, a concern for *objective truth,* an accent on authority, justice, and structure in the shaping of life. This happens when we exercise our *thinking* (T) function. When, on the other hand, our response to reality stems more from concern for *persons,* beginning with ourselves, and from that cherishing of personal *values* which we have imbibed from our various heritages, we are exercising the feeling (F) function. It is important not to identify thinking in the present context with intelligence or intellectualism, or feeling with affect or emotion, although it is perhaps more closely linked with emotion than are the other functions, since it expresses emotions more freely.

This brief delineation of the contrasting attitudes (E/I), the functions generically considered (P/J), and the functions viewed specifically (S/N and T/F) puts us in possession of the basic ingredients of our developmental typology. Readers previously exposed to the MBTI will readily recall the basic code,

Attitude:	E --------- I
Perceiving Function	S --------- N
Judging Function	T --------- F
Generic Functions	J --------- P

and the sixteen distinct types which are exhibited, with their composite profiles, on the basis of the responses given by individuals to the questionnaire. Those readers who are not familiar with the MBTI will gradually, through this and the following chapters, gain greater comprehension of the key categories and an ability to grasp their own preferences and development.

Five Bases for the Developmental Typology

It will make for clarity in grasping the developmental typology we shall be laying out if it is seen to rest on five bases.

1. All of us are *endowed* with the two attitudes (E and I) and all four functions (S and N, and T and F). Each one of us is capable of sensing, intuiting, thinking and feeling, and we are capable of exercising each of these four behaviors in both introverted and extraverted ways.

2. But we do differ among ourselves in our *preferences* with respect to both attitudes and functions. The MBTI is a good instrument for exhibiting various combinations of preferences, with resulting "profiles" to the number of sixteen.

3. And we *also* differ among ourselves with respect to the *sequence of stages of development* of all our behaviors, preferred or not. This kind of difference is what our developmental typology will describe in some detail very shortly.

4. While the various preferences seem to be innate, the kinds of environment we experience at various stages of human development and the way in which we deal with those environments will greatly affect the *quality* and pace of development of particular behaviors and of our personality as a whole.

5. In order to become whole we need to develop all four functions, even those which are not our preferences, so that we may be free to choose the kind of behavior, e.g., thinking or feeling, called for in particular situations. As we make our way now through a description of human development, it will be helpful for the reader to keep these assumptions in mind.

Sketch of the Developmental Typology

Each of us enters upon the human journey with an original endowment, psychic as well as physical, a certain identity which is present even in the womb. It appears to us that prior to the emergence of a distinct ego the infant and the small child is given by God through the spontaneous movements of the psychic organism a "get acquainted" period, so to speak. Up to the age of six—designated by the Christian pastoral tradition as the beginning of the use of reason—it would seem that each child is given the opportunity to gain, through undifferentiated experience, a basic familiarity with all four functions.

Look at a typical three-year-old, for example. He or she will be at one moment staring off into space, in a dreaming exercise of intuition. A few minutes later the intense scrutiny of the workings of a toy tractor will signify that the sensing function is at play. Or one moment we may witness a struggling effort (the thinking function), to defend one's proprietary rights from the encroachment of a sibling and a little later an obvious effort to please the company (the feeling function). This period of childhood is a time for random and tentative dabbling in the expression and development of the four functions. A good part of the charm of being with children of preschool age consists in witnessing the rapidity and variety of the growth that is taking place.

Then, at six, the child's particular personality begins to develop and show itself more clearly. More specifically, there is the spontaneous emergence of one of the four functions as the one which throughout life will be dominant in the personality—sensing, intuiting, thinking, or feeling. And this preference, in the first stage of development between six and twelve, will be accompanied by a preference of attitude in the exercise of the preferred function. The exercise of whichever of the four functions is being preferred will take place in a flow of psychic energy toward the subject or toward the object, that is, inward or outward.

For example, consider a brother and sister now in adult

life. Testing with the MBTI, combined with reflection and reminiscence, can reveal that the dominant function for each is, let us say, feeling. Both will have spontaneously cultivated F in the period between six and twelve. But personal history may disclose that the sister was demonstrative, expressive, extraverted in the exercise of her feeling; you generally knew how she felt about life. Her brother, on the contrary, directed the flow of his dominant F inward. In her case even casual observers were able to pick up over a period of time this primary trait of her personality, whereas, in her brother's case, only his parents, and then gradually, would appreciate how deeply feeling their son was. We have chosen F as an example, but the same is true for the emergence of any one of the four functions in childhood. Not only the specific perceiving (S or N) or judging (T or F) function but also the direction of the flow of its energy begins to establish and to manifest the type of development we are witnessing. At this point some readers might like to see if they are able to identify both the first function they developed and the extraverted or introverted attitude in which this function found expression through its energy flow in childhood.

Puberty: The First "Gear Shift"

At the age of twelve, the time of puberty which many religious traditions and sociological views have recognized as significant and apt for ritual "passage," the child crossing the threshold into adolescence will, so to speak, shift gears. The automotive image is an apt one, and we might add that the psychic gear shift is more automatic than deliberate. There seems to take place spontaneously a certain disengagement from previous expression of the dominant function, and an inclination to exercise a second function, called the "auxiliary."

Evidence suggests that though the functions and the attitudes will be different for different sequences of development, the switch will always have two important characteristics. First, when a perceiving function—S or N—has been the one

preferred for development during childhood, the period of
adolescence will witness a preference for a judging (T or F)
function as auxiliary; the reverse sequence will obtain, of
course, when a judging function has been preferred in childhood. Our assertion of this first characteristic is based on observation, but it is also what we might expect theoretically, in the
light of the balancing mechanisms built into our humanity. As
we have seen, we all need both to receive from life (P) and to
contribute to it (J). It seems to make sense to suggest that the
two growth periods of childhood (6 to 12) and adolescence (12
to 20) provide an alternating rhythm of P/J or J/P. Obviously,
no human being at any stage is exclusively receptive or exclusively responsive; psychically, we need both to inhale and to
exhale for sheer survival and for health. But there is question
here of a *preference* of one over the other which makes possible its distinctive exercise and development at a particular
stage of growth.

Second, it is characteristic of the switch at puberty that
the *attitude* (E or I) in which the auxiliary function will be
exercised in adolescence will be the *opposite* of the attitude in
which the dominant function was exercised in childhood. An
example: Mary's primary function is S, a perceiving function.
She developed it in childhood, and, let us say, in an introverted
way. If T is her auxiliary function, this means that in her
adolescence she developed her thinking in an extroverted
way. Or: John's primary function is F, favored by him in an
introverted exercise before puberty; if his auxiliary is N, he will
have developed it in adolescence in an extraverted way. And
so on. Adolescence balances off childhood as regards both E/I
and P/J, in a variety of sequences depending on the spontaneous preferences of individuals.

Young Adulthood

At twenty, in the passage from adolescence to young
adulthood, another gear switching experience occurs, and the
young person begins a notable development of a third function. Here too, because the original choices of functions and

attitudes at age six vary with the individual, a continuing diversity will obtain. But, like the passage into adolescence, this passage from adolescence has two characteristics. First, the function preferred to development during early adulthood will be the opposite of the function developed in adolescence. For example, if N has been developed in adolescence, S will be the function now "chosen" for cultivation. If it was T in adolescence, now it will be F. Thus the years from twelve to thirty-five are for the development of either the two perceiving or the two judging functions. Second, the alternating pattern of attitudes will be continued; at twenty there will be a switch of energy direction from outward to inward, or vice versa. Jonathan, after developing introverted feeling in adolescence, switches to extraverted thinking in young adulthood. Julia, who as a teenager favored extraverted intuiting, exercises in her twenties and early thirties introverted sensing. Once again, though we are dealing here with no more than a plausible hypothesis based on a good deal of experience, it makes sense to us to suggest that God has built into our psychic organism a dynamism of checks and balances always intent on growth toward fullness and wholeness.

Midlife: The Critical Turn

Finally, at thirty-five, the most interesting and frequently most difficult transition takes place. One finally comes to the stage when the call of God inscribed in the processes of the psyche bids us to allow the least preferred of all the functions, the one in sharpest tension with the dominant one, to find its place in our conscious investment in life. If, for example, from childhood on, extraverted feeling has been the hinge or pivot of our development, now we will be asked, from within ourselves, to give introverted thinking an unprecedented place in the way we deal with life. Note that here too, at the third switching point, the pattern of alternation of both functions and attitudes is followed. We will have more to say, in each of the following chapters, about the emergence of this so called inferior function. This is one of the points on which Jungian psychology and the Christian Gospel of death and resurrection have something to say to each other.

The Golden Years

But what, we have often been asked, happens after fifty, when the cycle of development of all four facets of the personality has been completed? Especially given the increase of longevity in our culture, are we not appearing to squelch the challenge to keep growing just as people are entering what should be a rich and fruitful stage of life? By no means. At fifty we enter a new period of differentiated development, in which all four of the functions will be exercised on the basis of the four earlier stages of development. Might this not suggest a more positive view of "second childhood" than is generally entertained? Both young children and senior citizens range through the varieties of human behavior; the difference is in the realm of consciousness and freedom of choice. The young child moves indiscriminately from one immature function to another. The adult who has developed all four functions deliberately selects the appropriate one—now, for example, expressing compassion, now strongly insisting on justice. Have we not all met septuagenarians, for example, whose childlikeness—a very different quality from childishness—is a reminder of Jesus' saying, "Unless you change and become like children . . ." (Mt 18:3)?

Influence of Environment

This would be a good point at which to go back to the five bases for our developmental typology. What we have been saying will have clarified the first three, but let us add a few words about the fourth, which affirms the role of environment in shaping the quality of human development in each of the four stages. Our God-given endowments do not grow in a vacuum, but only in interaction with favorable or unfavorable influences from other persons and from society. These influences do not *determine* the quality of our journey from image

to likeness, for we are endowed with consciousness and freedom. But they do profoundly affect the character and quality
of our struggle to become more like God. We meet again,
therefore, Thoreau's model of solitude, friendship and society,
which we mentioned earlier. As we come to speak of Gospel
perspectives on human growth, we shall see how the mystery
of sin and grace is experienced in this meeting of persons with
other persons and with society. For now let us just observe
that, in reviewing the path of one's development through the
four stages, it is important to attend to what has actually
happened, for growth or for retardation or even harm, in our
human encounters at each stage. We shall be suggesting some
exercises to facilitate this valuable retrieval of the history of
our growth.

A Developmental Code

Finally, before returning to some further Gospel perspectives, let us invite the reader's attention to Appendix B, which
contains a complete listing and code of the sixteen types of
development inherent in the present typology. The juxtaposi-
tion of this code with that of the MBTI will enable readers
familiar with the latter to see both the correspondences and
the differences of the two approaches. In brief, the MBTI code
exhibits the variety of preferences with respect to both attitudes and functions, and it enables one to identify dominant,
auxiliary, and inferior functions. Our developmental code in
addition points to the chronological sequence in which each of
the functions is developed from age six to age fifty, with the
alternating pattern of extraverted and introverted attitudes.

III. SOME GOSPEL PERSPECTIVES

Before concluding this chapter by offering some exercises,
we would like to move back to the Gospel for a few further
perspectives on human growth. Now that we have begun to
lay out a behavioral model of development, some more specif-

ic interweavings of Jungian and Christian themes are called for.

First, a classic theological axiom has it that grace does not violate nature but builds on it. The Gospel, the good news about God's Word made flesh in *our* humanity, fits our human experience. And, though God is free and each one of us is unique, there are patterns of human development, inherent aspects of God's image in us, to which God's grace accommodates itself. The better we know and accept those patterns, the better we can freely respond to God's grace.

Second, we can already note some striking *convergences* between the Jungian and the Christian understanding of the human. Both are sensitive to the enormous pool of human energies waiting to be disclosed and set free if humanity is to prosper. Both see the emergence of consciousness and the enlargement of self-knowledge and self-direction as key for this work of revelation and liberation. Both conceive of human destiny in terms of wholeness and make room for the counterbalancing of forces in tension in the process of development. Both make much of the struggle of good and evil, light and darkness. We will have occasion to point out other affinities between these two approaches to human development, as well as some points of tension.

Third, a more specific correlation may here be noted, between the generic contrast of perceiving and judging functions, on the one hand, and what the Christian tradition has offered in the classic contrast of contemplation and action. Later, in speaking of prayer in relation to the four functions, we will elaborate on this affinity. For now let us just recall that, inasmuch as the perceiving function has to do with being receptive, open to the touch of reality both within ourselves and from without, it resembles the contemplative posture whose highest instance is the *pati divina* (receptivity to the divine) of religious contemplation. And, inasmuch as the judging function has to do with the shaping of life's reality through judgment and decision, it more or less corresponds to what the Christian tradition has placed under the term "action."

A fourth observation has to do not so much with what is

Jungian in our behavioral models as with the model of solitude, friendship and society. We have already noted the importance, in taking hold of one's own personal development through the four distinct stages, of situating that development in the context of helping and hindering environments, interpersonal or societal in character. Here we wish to add that the Gospel language of sin and grace, when interpreted with the help of Thoreau's model, provides a distinctively theological and spiritual approach to the way in which our growth has been enhanced or impeded from within ourselves, from our relationships with other persons, and from sinful and graced climates of life in society and culture. Even at this introductory stage, we hope that readers, from both behavioral and Christian perspectives, will keep blending in Thoreau's triad. This will, in spite of its challenge, make for greater wholeness in our grasp of the journey from God-image to Godlikeness.

EXERCISES

1. Spend a little time with Genesis 1:26–27 and/or Psalm 8, with a view to evoking gratitude and wonder for the gift of being created according to God's image and called to develop toward Godlikeness.

2. See yourself as a traveler or pilgrim, making the journey from God-image to Godlikeness. Let the desire to pursue the journey assert itself.

3. Spend some time with each of the functions and attitudes described in this chapter, considering each to be a personal gift of God to you. Give thanks to God, and express your willingness to take responsibility for these gifts.

4. Review the principal models of this chapter, and check out (a) the clarity of your grasp of each; (b) the degree to which each model corresponds to your personal experience.

5. More specifically, see to what extent your own personal history verifies the typology described in this chapter. In this reflection, attend to (a) the sequence of development of the four functions; (b) the alternation of extraverted and introverted attitudes in successive periods; (c) the occurrence of "gear

shifts" or crises in your development. If you have taken the MBTI, compare your profile as given in the MBTI code and as corresponding to the developmental typology of this book.

6. Making use of a Scripture passage such as Psalm 131 or Acts 17:27–28, let God's loving presence to you grow in your awareness. Then, either imaginatively or in simple awareness, direct your attention to your own unique self, as created and loved by God and endowed with rich gifts. After a while, as you are drawn, let your attention move to some persons who are especially dear to you, and to the relationships which unite you with them. Finally, situate yourself and these relationships in the larger world of time and space, human systems and structures, the social and cultural life of the "global village." Let the sense of connectedness come home to you. Be aware that all of it, and each part of it, is in God, and God in it.

7. Building on the previous exercise, try to be in touch with the way in which God reveals himself in solitude, friendship and society. And with the help of some Scripture passage such as Ephesians 6:10–20 or Revelation 12, see how the struggle of sin and grace is taking place within today's society.

8. Making use of Psalm 25:1–2 or some other verse evoking God's presence, become aware of your own natural breathing as symbolic of the natural rhythm of perceiving/judging and contemplating/acting. Let the desire for wholeness and freedom in the life of contemplating the world and in turn shaping it grow in you.

NOTE

1. D. Bonhoeffer, *The Cost of Discipleship* (London: SCM Press, 1948).

CHAPTER 2
A Gift To Be Simple

Sensing/Simplicity

A statement of Simone Weil, the remarkable French mystic whose life and writings have touched many people deeply since her death during World War II, will serve to keynote our consideration of the sensing function:

> The key to a Christian conception of studies is the realization that prayer consists of attention. It is the orientation of all the attention of which the soul is capable toward God. . . . Happy then are those who pass their adolescence and youth in developing this power of attention.[1]

Learning to pay attention may not be the whole of the educational process, or the complete goal of life itself. And, from the perspective of this book, paying attention is characteristic of *both* forms of perceiving, intuiting no less than sensing. But there is a sense in which everything, including intuiting, must begin with sensing, that is, paying attention with the help of the senses, exterior and interior. From a more theoretical point of view Bernard Lonergan chimes in with Simone Weil in the first of his four conversion maxims: *Be attentive.*[2] As we shall see, the Gospel says the same thing. Paying attention in the sensing mode is one of the four pillars of development, the first of the four wellsprings from which the river of life flows.

This chapter will address the development throughout life of this aspect of God's image in each of us, in our relationships, and in the kind of world we build for ourselves.

First, with the help of the developmental typology outlined in the first chapter, it will describe *the sensing function,* with attention to its distinctive traits and to some of the characteristic traits of those who prefer it and have developed it early and well.

Second, with the help of the Judaeo-Christian Scriptures and of tradition it will indicate those facets of *the Gospel* which seem to have a special affinity or congruence with this function. *Simplicity* is the virtue which gives symbolic expression to this dimension of our faith.

Third, it will offer some observations about the *development* of this sensing/simplicity aspect of God's image, and it will propose some exercises for individuals and groups. We cannot say too often that the best way to develop facility in any virtue or behavior is to exercise it with the help of models.

We hope that this chapter, with its exercises, will bring our readers, especially those for whom sensing is not a preferred function or who have experienced difficulty in its development, a greater share in the grace of simplicity, as well as an enlarged capacity to *enjoy* the life of the senses, exterior and interior. To see, to hear, to touch, to taste, to smell, and to observe carefully what goes on inside oneself, one's thoughts, images, feelings—these are precious gifts of God committed to our responsible stewardship. Even within the Christian tradition the body and its senses have often been despised or distrusted, as dangers to or distractions from the life of the Spirit. Such views miss the fact that when we exercise our sensing life contemplatively and in freedom, it is God, the divinely simple One, whom we ultimately see, hear, touch, taste, and smell, as Augustine so eloquently described in his *Confessions.*[3] The more we are able to practice a sensing simplicity in all the situations of life, the greater does our likeness to God become.

I. THE SENSING FUNCTION

Let us say by way of preface that, since our focus in this book is on the Jungian functions and not on their specific manifestation in all sixteen types represented by the MBTI, there will be a certain abstract character to our treatment of each function. As we have already suggested, no one really *is* a senser—or intuiter or thinker or feeler—even though some people prefer the exercise of sensing to the exercise of the other three functions. And quite apart from individual histories which bring major differences between individuals of the same MBTI type, one's preferences in the matter of extraversion and introversion, as well as one's favoring of feeling or thinking, will affect the concrete working of sensing in daily life. We will advert to a few of the resulting differences and offer a few scenarios in order to bring our description of this and the other functions somewhat closer to real life. But, for purposes of correlation with the Gospel, our primary interest is each of the functions, and in this chapter the sensing function.

The Function Described

We have already seen in Chapter 1 that the sensing function is a perceiving function, that is, part of the human endowment for letting reality touch us, come to us. In contrast to its opposite, the intuiting function, its focus is the factual, not the theoretical; the concrete, not the abstract; the practical, not the ideal; details, not the essence or the overall picture.

All of these characteristics derive from the fact that this aspect of our humanity, as its name indicates, works through the five senses, which deal with particular objects of sight, hearing, touch, taste, and smell. But note that the sensing function is a function of the psyche, not of the bodily senses as such, though it works in and through them. This insistence on the psychic character of the sensing function should help us withstand the temptation to consider sensing as less deeply human or spiritual than the other three functions, and so less endowed as a trysting place with God. Note too that, like the other functions, sensing can be directed toward *inner* reality when it is being exercised in an introverted manner.

Present Tense

From the viewpoint of the human experience of *time,* this function is attentive to the present moment—*today* is the most important day of the week. NOW/HERE, rather than NO/WHERE, is the time and the place where it engages its distinctive energies.

What a beautiful gift of God is this sensing function! It is an endowment of *every* human being—it comes with our humanity, so to speak. Without it we would not be human, created according to God's image. Psychically, it provides energy for our lives in the form of stimulation. It is when the world of sight, sound, touch, taste, and smell impinges on our consciousness through the five senses that the human drama in whatever context begins to unfold.

Our sensing serves each of the other functions and is indispensable for their distinctive contributions. Without data from the sensing function, for example, what would the structuring mind (T) have for arranging logically? And the remembrances through which our feeling function (F) energizes us need normally to be sparked by something sensible—the strains of a favorite melody, the sight of a child, or the touch of a friendly hand. Even the intuitive function (N), which is in direct tension with sensing, needs a particular starting point; without at least some tenuous fibre the web of intuition cannot be woven. The sensing function also provides enormous energies for the psyche because it is where the powerful forces of pleasure and pain take their rise. In short, the sensing function is a wellspring from which flows a distinctive stream of human energy. To cultivate this side of our personality, our relationships, our world, is to provide for human life an indispensable humanizing force.

Each of us has experienced the tingling power of sensing in our life's journey—the sparkle of leaves on an autumn afternoon, the soothing sensation of being given a back-rub, the singing of the violins in a favorite concerto, or just the simple awareness of one's inner quiet, or of the chattering of the stream of consciousness as words, melodies, feelings, bubble up from the unconscious—just standing there, just being there, paying attention to something particular. In a word: sensing.

Sensing Models

Though we all have had experience of our own sensing, there are some people in whom sensing gifts appear in a more manifest way. These are in general persons who naturally prefer this mode of perceiving over the intuitive mode, and even more those for whom sensing is the dominant function, the central point of reference, so to speak, in the personality. These last have developed their sensing first, in the childhood experience between the ages of six and twelve. Where sensing is an auxiliary function supporting either thinking or feeling, its development has taken place in adolescence, between twelve and twenty.

It is important, let us say again, not to reduce the uniqueness of individuals to stereotypes. After practically every characterization of this book the reader must understand some such qualification as "for the most part," or "generally speaking," or "other things being equal." In the present case keep in mind that it makes a difference whether a person's preference for sensing as a dominant function is extraverted or introverted. In the latter case it will be more difficult for outsiders to be aware that this is the dominant preference, as it will be most characteristically exercised by attending to what is inside the person. What will strike others about an introverted sensing type is more often the extraverted judging auxiliary functions, T or S. In extraverted sensing types, on the contrary, the preference for attending to the concrete will be more immediately manifest, precisely because it is extraverted. Also, beyond the way in which they appear to others, these types, though they share the dominant preference for S, will have other notable differences. For example, introverted sensing types can be the hardest and most persevering workers, whereas the lazy gaze at life is often present in extraverted sensing types.

It will make a difference, too, whether the dominant

senser supports the sensing preference with a thinking or feeling auxiliary preference. An extraverted thinking senser ESTP=STFN/*EIEI* and an introverted feeling senser ISFJ=SFTN/*IEIE* are likely to differ greatly in their behavior, especially in what appears for others to see, even though sensing is the dominant preference for each. Finally, recall that preference is not development and that the environments in which preferences have been developed, and the quality of one's dealing with those environments, will often mean that two people of identical type will have very significant differences in their perceptions of and responses to life.

The next few pages represent an effort to situate sensing more concretely within the total personality, with attention to: the relationships of the dominant function with the auxiliary, third, and inferior functions; the various developmental patterns which can obtain as people move through the stages of development from six to fifty; and the alternation of extraversion and introversion in the successive emergence of functions. Finally, because modeling has such a strong influence on growth, we will be describing how a relationship of two persons of contrasting types will change in the course of development. In this way we hope to remind readers that no function exists in isolation from other elements in the total personality, and that the intrapersonal and interpersonal aspects of our humanity and its development are closely connected.

A Scenario

Greg, twenty-eight, a priest and popular high school teacher of mathematics, is seen by his friends, other teachers, and students as one of the most down-to-earth realists they have ever known. Students know better than to try to deceive him, for it surely will be noticed. They are impressed by the ease with which he can remember not only complicated theorems and scriptural quotations, but batting averages and football statistics. He can be firm if necessary, but as he is good-natured, adaptable, and aware of everything that goes on in and out of the classroom, this knowledge gives him an influence over situations that forestalls many mishaps. When things do go wrong his immediate reaction puts him back in control. In sports his ability to respond instantly brings success on the field.

His best friend, Joe, twenty-six, a fellow priest and teacher, seems to be directly opposite and although they have been friends for about eight years Greg still cannot understand why. To his logical mind the relationship makes no sense, but he knows that it exists and is meaningful to him. Joe's awareness of the world about him leaves much to be desired. Greg once observed that Joe could get lost in a phone booth, but he has most certainly been lost in their native town. He cannot remember the names of many of the students he has taught in the last several years—Greg remembers them all—and seems not to be particularly interested in doing so. Joe's teasing comment on this limitation is that every time he remembers the name of a student he forgets the name of a relative. Yet there is something about Joe that makes being with him like being in another world—a bigger world in which Greg can forget the immediacy of a school problem and find himself encouraged to dream about the world of the future. Actually, Greg still resists being carried away from his "real world," but he recognizes some advantages and feels that perhaps someday it will be easier.

Joe has always had problems with discipline and feels that, having watched Greg over the past years, he is getting a better grasp of how to handle a class. But he knows that it will take him a long time to develop the kind of practical control that Greg maintains. Joe prefers a non-disciplinary style. Greg has observed Joe's compassion and through their relationship he believes that he himself is better able now to express his feelings, but this ability developed only because his first attempt, the struggle to manifest his grief at the loss of his father, was comfortably received by Joe. Greg was made to feel acceptable behaving in a way which, in the past, he would have judged to be weak and unstable.

Greg is finding, too, that Joe is increasingly acknowledging the advantages of being attentive to the more practical side of life. Joe now is able to start a conversation at the beginning of a topic, whereas his previous practice was to start in the middle, with a vagueness that left Greg frustrated and sometimes irritated.

Greg prefers to function as an ESTP. His dominant sensing makes him present to here and now practicalities. His shadow side is his intuition, which is Joe's (ENFP) dominant function. While neither will be pressed to develop his shadow side (the other's dominant function) until the period from thirty-five to fifty, they are beginning to recognize at least the possible value of such development. What they are presently experiencing, however, is the development of their respective third functions. In this they help each other, each modeling the behavior in which the other is growing. Greg's thinking function, his auxiliary, has been making way since the age of twenty for the development of his feeling which Joe has fostered. Joe, on the other hand, by learning from Greg, is developing his third function, his thinking, and is becoming more assertive. After they have reached thirty-five both will feel a greater need to develop their respective inferior functions. In that period of life, too, they can be helpful to each other, as each will be trying to develop the function which is the dominant preference of the other.

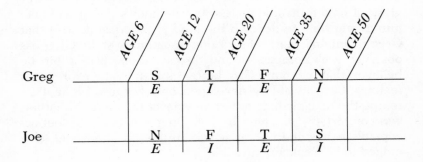

II. THE GOSPEL OF SIMPLICITY

Leonard Bernstein's *Mass* includes a lovely melody which many readers will recall, whose lyrics tell us that "God is the simplest one of all." Thomistic philosophers and theologians, who take the term in ontological as well as moral senses, will be quick to assent and will offer sometimes extremely complex arguments in support of the divine simplicity. Yes, God is an eternal and omnipresent NOW/HERE, an infinity of presence, the model of attentiveness, as Psalm 139 so eloquently proclaims: "Lord, you know me. . . ." The divine gaze is ever upon us, and it is experienced by us as mercy or judgment according to our willingness to accept that gaze. God's "eye is on the sparrow," and, writes Gerard Manley Hopkins, "See; not a hair is, not an eyelash, not the least lash lost; every hair/Is, hair of the head, numbered."[4] "You have placed your hand upon me" says Psalm 139, and continues, "such knowledge is too wonderful for me" (vv. 5f). Simplicity is a concept that defies any positive definition. Apart from the concept of being, there is perhaps no concept which takes us more deeply into the utter unnameability of God. Here, in the context of our typology, it is the moral and infinitely personal or transpersonal kind of simplicity that we are attempting to contemplate. We are viewing God not so much as the One who is continually bringing us into existence and shaping our lives but as the One who is always taking us lovingly to the divine Self, the One who is totally receptive of us. Sensing is, after all, a perceiving function, and its ultimate model is the infinitely simple, attentive, receptive God.

In the Image of the Simple God

We know this divine simplicity, sensibility, receptivity, of course, only through our acquaintance with its image in ourselves. First we want to contemplate this aspect of the human potential in its initial constitution, prior to its disfigurement by sin. From this point of view, the human call is a call to be

simple, humble, obedient, attentive, present, contemplative.
Though most of these terms will be recurring when we come
to speak of Jesus and of the Christian vocation, let us speak
briefly here of each of them, as expressive of this dimension of
God's image in us.

Simple: like God's own simplicity, it is difficult to describe
this facet of God's image positively. The best we can do here is
to offer an image from Psalm 131: "Enough for me to keep my
soul tranquil and quiet/like a child in its mother's arms, /as
content as a child that has been weaned" (v. 2).

Humble: the etymology of this term (*humus,* earth,
ground) indicates its affinity with the sensing function. We are
capable, by this gift, of being down to earth, with our feet on
the ground. The same root, by the way (*hum-*), yields some
other terms which have a kinship with sensing: hue, hum,
humor, humidity.

Obedient: the inner core of this posture is *listening.* Our
English is derived from the Latin *obaudire,* "to listen to." God
created human beings with a marvelous built-in antenna, capable of picking up the divine presence and will in every finite
reality which touches us. Though we commonly use the term
"obedience" to indicate the *execution* of someone else's wish
or will, there is a prior moment of heeding, attending, listening, which is the key to obedience. A model and master of
Christian obedience is the great monastic founder, St. Benedict, whose famous *Rule* begins: "*Listen,* my son, to your
master's precepts, and *incline the ear* of your heart. *Receive*
willingly and carry out effectively your loving father's advice,
that by the labor of *obedience* you may return to him from
whom you had departed by the sloth of disobedience." While
obedience goes beyond perceiving, this golden sentence clearly shows that perceiving is where it begins. In any of life's
contexts, when we do listen and incline the ear of our hearts,
we are imitating the Great Listener, the One whom no sound
escapes.

Attentive: the image here of stretching (*ad-tendere* is the
Latin term) brings out the quality of alertness or sharpness of

perception, which this aspect of the divine image in us possesses. One of the services that animals render us is that they exhibit, across a wide spectrum of fascinating and often amusing behavior, this capacity of human beings to be attentive. The early bird gets the worm—or the fish, or the bug—because of this poised readiness. Each of us has been given this gift for cultivation and enjoyment. The Gospel never tires of telling human beings to stay awake, remain alert, if they are not to miss the Lord's coming.

Present: this term is especially rich for designating the sensing aspect of God's image. Etymologically, it is derived from the Latin *esse* meaning "to be," plus the prefix *prae,* which expresses priority of both time and space. One is present, not absent, therefore here, not there. And one is present in the present, in this moment—*now,* not last night or tomorrow morning. "*Now* is the favorable time; *this* is the day of salvation" (2 Cor 6:2). So present and presence are apt terms for conveying the quality of being NOW/HERE. Sensing, then, is the function by which we meet or encounter both God and every creature in their self-presentation to us. This capacity for encounter, for mutual self-presentation, is a Godlike quality, a special imaging of God's infinite presence.

Contemplative: the aspect of this term which is here most pertinent is its connotation of *receptivity.* To contemplate is to gaze in such a way that the reality gazed upon enters into one and, in a sense, becomes one. Contemplative knowledge, unlike some other forms, is not interested in rearranging what it perceives, but in just holding it in a certain stillness. This capacity, too, is part of our rich endowment by the creative God who has made us in the divine image.

Each of these terms says something to us of our human potential, graciously granted in the original gift of creation. Why does our experience appear to deny it, or at least to claim that it has not been realized in our lives with the richness which these terms suggest? A good part of the answer lies in what Christians call original sin. It is time to attend to this bad news.

Sensibility Blunted

This is not the place to discourse on what is behind the dogma and the story of original sin, a pillar of Christian doctrine without which the good news of redemption would be meaningless. Let it suffice to say that we Christians believe in the reality and influence of a radical and pervasive moral evil which cannot be simply identified with our particular sins or even with our state of personal sinfulness. Though it has been basically overcome by the cross and resurrection of Jesus Christ, and though each Christian begins to share this victory from the moment of baptism, this root of all that dehumanizes remains in its effects and touches every aspect of our lives—our personhood, our relationships, and the world we create. Though we live in the era of redeeming grace, and though the second Adam has undone the fault of the first Adam, that grace coexists along with radical sinfulness as long as we are engaged in life's combat. Moreover, the grace which is ours is intelligible only with respect to the sin which it is in process of conquering. Before we examine how the grace of Christ has healed the sensing aspect of God's image in humanity, it is valuable to see just what it is that needs to be healed.

As in the contemplation of the original gift, so here a wide variety of models is available. We will leave most of them to the reader to explore. We choose just one, and begin by saying that, prior to the healing touch of Christ Jesus and the Spirit, our sensing life has been *blunted*. A dulling, a numbing, of that part of us which God intended to be the gate and the window by which reality presents itself to us, evoking intense pleasure—this is what sin has wrought in the area of human sensibility. Simplicity has departed. It is not so much that life has become complex—human nature is admirably equipped for dealing with complexity—as that complicity and duplicity have invaded the domain of perception.

God intended us to have so much pleasure through the life of the senses. Sin enormously reduces our capacity for genuine pleasure. It may well be that hedonism, so often deplored by

religious and moral people, is only a cloaked despair of pleasure.

So it is with the other aspects of sensing which we have
described through several key terms. Radical sinfulness makes
it harder for us just to stand still, with our feet on the ground,
listening to whatever life may have to say to us. Our capacity
for simple attentiveness is diminished. Our psychic life becomes like a radio where the sound is always fading away just
at the important moment, or where static keeps breaking in to
frustrate our grasp for meaning. A certain restlessness, especially through the disordered working of imagination and feeling, often deprives us of the capacity to be present to what we
are doing, to our own inner states, to other people, to God's
presence. The contemplative gaze comes only momentarily
and with great difficulty.

This presentation of what original sin has done to our
sensing gift accents the element of *deficiency*. But are there
not also sins of *excess* related to this and the other functions?
We have no wish to deny the value of the classic model of
virtue as consisting in a golden mean between too much and
too little. But, from a behavioral point of view, it may be better
to view what might appear as excessive in the development of
a function as being due to a failure to develop its opposite—in
this case, intuiting. Strictly speaking, one cannot develop sensing, or any of the four functions, too much. We are called, in
fact, to develop each of them without limit throughout our
lives. It is the lack of balance between contrasting functions,
due to our unwillingness to let the less preferred side of God's
image in us emerge, which can make it appear that we are
sinning by excess. In the present instance, for example, a
certain immobility and "locked in" posture assumed by a dominant S in the name of practicality can be largely due to the
fact that the person does not yet have a developed capacity for
imagining alternatives—a gift contained in N. There may also
be a question, when either sensing or intuiting perception
appears excessive, of not giving sufficient place to the auxiliary
judging function, whether T or F. The apparent excess of an

extraverted senser who spends a great deal of time just in contemplating nature while others are getting the work done may be due to the failure to let the judging side of the personality have its proportionate weight.

Insensible Relationships

It is well to consider the blunting and numbing of presence and attentiveness not only in ourselves as individuals but in our relationships and in our capacity for communion and community. What healing would take place in troubled families, for example, if the members quieted down long enough to look at each other, listen to each other! Often it is neurotic chatter, used as a security blanket, which overloads the circuit of interpersonal communication and makes meaningful messages all but impossible. Sometimes, too, the habit of interrupting others can become so ingrained in a person or group as to become an expectation. Conversation then becomes a competitive endeavor. At the other extreme, people in groups can secede from the healthy and enjoyable paying of attention to one another. When extraverted sensing has not been sufficiently developed, and when the price or risk is judged to be too high, disengagement from sensory communication becomes a compulsive way out of what has come to be experienced as an intolerable burden. We are also capable of finding one another dull, because we have not grown in our ability to pay attention to the rich details, the fascinating nuances, which make each person's behavior unique and worthy of our interest. An habitual attitude of social boredom is really a sin against this dimension of God's image present in human persons and relationships.

Societal Numbness

When things like this happen in families and other groups, our eyes, ears, and hands, given to mediate intimacy and communion, remain unused, underdeveloped, or are diverted to sterile pursuits. This happens not because people are malicious or not desirous of meaningful relationships—on the contrary. But, along with interior and relational blunting of sense and sensibility, we need to look to influences from society and culture as contributing to this diminishment of a truly human life. Our culture is often characterized as sensate. Science and technology, making prodigal use of the empirical aspects of reality, have called forth an almost unlimited expenditure of sensory energy. And some of their key products—audio and visual media, varieties of products for consumption by sight, hearing, touch, taste, smell—have materially intensified the sense life of human beings. As we so commonly say, our senses are constantly being bombarded within today's culture. Yet one might argue that the overall result, far from being a heightening of sensibility, has been just the opposite—a blunting, numbing, dissipating, and blandifying impact on the quality of our sense life. One does not have to be hypercritical to be alarmed at the assault on taste, refinement, sensibility, the power of paying attention, which our ostensibly sensate culture is conducting with alarming results. That millions have recourse to alcohol and drugs, which eventually dull the power of perception, is entirely congruous with what is happening to us from our culture.

The preceding paragraphs may appear to some readers to be unduly pessimistic. Let it be remembered that they are describing our human situation only as the life of sensing has been touched by sin. Our actual experience of this aspect of God's image has certainly been more positive than what we have just recorded. The experience of sin is always simultaneous with the experience of grace, for we are always living, however inconsistently, the life of the restored image of God. We need, however, to bracket for a moment this graced dimension of our sensing life, so that we may more fully appreciate the gift that has been given in Christ Jesus.

Jesus as Model of Sensing/Simplicity

It is especially in the Gospel according to Mark that we can appropriately study the theme of this chapter. The Second Gospel is the briefest of the four. Its terseness squares very well with the sensing disposition and with simplicity. Mark wastes no words; for the most part he is content to set forth the facts. The traditional association of Ezekiel's winged lion with this Gospel—as outside the great Church of St. Mark in Venice—is fitting. Some of us might think of the lion as a royal character—hence a better symbol of Matthew's Gospel—but the "king of the jungle" is actually a rather contemplative character, content to take everything in, once the basic needs are satisfied. In any case, we will seek to illustrate Jesus' own exemplification of the sensing function mostly from the Second Gospel.

There is first of all his *example.* He gives evidence of being simple, down to earth, in touch with what is happening within himself and in his surroundings. He is a carpenter and the son of a carpenter. All the Gospels show him using his sight, hearing and touch in the faithful fulfillment of his ministry. What a *gaze* he must have had! He sees Simon and Andrew, James and John, fishing on the lake, and calls them (Mk 1:16–20); similarly he notices Levi (Matthew) and calls him (2:13–14). He looks keenly at the rich young man (10:27). Whereas it is a merciful gaze that he casts upon the great crowd, who were as sheep without a shepherd (6:34), he glares angrily at his carping critics (3:5). In Luke's account, the very sight of his beloved Jerusalem brings him to tears, an excellent scene for indicating how feeling often takes its initial stimulus from the senses (Lk 19:41).

His *ears* are likewise attuned to listening, particularly to the anguished cries of the poor. Many of his miracles take place consequent upon a dialogue, in which he both listens and speaks, searching out and encouraging the faith of those who come to him. Such was the case of the irrepressible Syro-Phoenician woman (Mk 7:24–30), the blind man of Jericho

(10:46–52), and the father of the epileptic boy (9:14–29). He heard people's pleas and then encouraged them to talk as he carefully listened in the process of bestowing on them the gift of health.

The sense of *touch* is also part of Jesus' ministry of healing. He takes Simon's mother-in-law by the hand and helps her up (1:31). He stretches out his hand and heals the leper with a touch (1:41). In the case of the woman with a hemorrhage it is she who takes the initiative and is healed by touching his cloak (5:27). From that miracle he goes and brings back to life the daughter of Jairus by simply taking her hand and saying, "Little girl, I tell you to get up" (5:41). Never were the human senses so graciously employed as when Jesus of Nazareth moved among people in a healing way. He paid attention to what people needed, a primary characteristic of sensing types, especially when sensing is extraverted. Everywhere we get the impression in the Gospels that he dealt with people one by one, making himself fully present to them as if he had nothing else to do.

Jesus also preached what he practiced. Though his parables illustrate primarily his remarkable imagination, they are also rich in detail, something which could only come from his ability to see things in their particularity. The farmer sowing seed, the woman using yeast in making bread, a withered fig tree, the planting of a vineyard, the little ritual of people dropping coins into a box at the temple—none of these common events escape him, but each one becomes a point of departure for his proclamation of the kingdom.

All the evangelists show Jesus calling his disciples to an attitude of alert readiness (Mk 13:33–37). Drawing on a familiar social relationship in his culture, he instilled in his followers the mentality befitting faithful, obedient servants (Mt 24:45–51; Lk 12:42–46).

If one looks for a name or title of Jesus which sums up this dimension of his way of imaging God in his earthly life, none seems as appropriate as the title of *servant*. This biblical term is, of course, far too rich to be confined to the characteristics which we have attributed to the sensing function, but it does feature those characteristics. The four "servant songs" of Isaiah (42:1–9; 49:1–6; 50:4–11; 52:13—53:12) form the principal Old Testament background for this Christological theme in the New Testament (Mt 3:17; 8:17; Lk 4:17–21; Acts 3:13; 8:32–33). Although it had to give way to the title of "Son of God," especially as this later became the bearer of the Church's faith in the divinity of Christ, it fittingly expresses Jesus' own self-image during his earthly life, and it corresponds to one of the ways in which his first followers interpreted that life. Today, when the attraction for this title has been revived in the Church, it is important to note that it designates first of all a relationship *to God*. "Servant leadership" has become a popular term to designate the attitude desired in bearers of authority toward members of the community in which authority is being exercised. This corresponds, of course, to Jesus' own directive about leadership in the Church (Mk 10:41–45). Such an attitude, however, needs to be rooted in a posture of humble, attentive obedience toward God. It was Jesus' constant and contemplative attentiveness to what his Father was saying and asking which enabled him to pay compassionate attention to the needs of those whom God had entrusted to his care.

The title of servant is particularly appropriate for understanding the sensing function because of the presentation of the *suffering* servant in Isaiah 52:13—53:12 and in its New Testament echoes. Nothing so roots a person in the present moment, and nothing brings humility so intensely, as suffering. It is worth noting that the Latin root *pati* and the term of Scholastic philosophy, *passio,* stand both for the general idea of receptivity and for its specification in the notion of suffering. In his passion, and particularly on the cross, Jesus becomes pure contemplativity, receiving into himself the totality of the human condition, especially as a sinful condition. Paul boldly uses the terms "sin" and "curse" to describe what this mysterious judgment on our radical evil has made of God's own Son (2 Cor 5:21; Gal 3:13). In speaking of Jesus' ministry we have alluded to his use of the sense of sight, hearing and touch. On the cross these three senses are afflicted. But, above all, it is his soul which knows the smell and the taste of the human condition in its negative and repulsive aspects. His saving action—or better, his saving receptivity—is simply to take that condition in its totality into himself, in complete obedience to his Father. That is why we are redeemed by the cross of Jesus Christ. His persevering simultaneous presence to God and to the plight of his sisters and brothers has energized humanity and the world with boundless resources of presence.

Besides Jesus himself, the other New Testament figure who stands out as servant is his mother Mary. It was with the title of servant that she designated herself and her role at the moment of her supreme honor (Lk 1:38, 48). What we have already seen about the sensing function and about its Gospel correlatives—simplicity, servanthood, contemplation, obedience, and the like—can help the reader familiar with the four Gospels, particularly Luke and John, to fill in the details of Mary's servanthood.

Before leaving the New Testament for the subsequent Christian tradition, let us take a brief look at how the early Church elaborated in other writings the themes we have just studied in the life and ministry of Jesus. Actually, the Gospel passages we have made use of to draw the portrait of Jesus himself also provide us with the way in which his disciples after Pentecost appreciated him as servant. But two particular themes are worth mentioning.

Alert Expectation

The first theme is that of alert expectation of the coming of the Lord. Reflecting on the admonitions of Jesus which we have already seen, the Church after Pentecost developed an eschatology calling for alertness, watchfulness, paying attention. Letters like those to the Thessalonians, for example, or the First and Second Letters of Peter contain passages which evoke attitudes congruous with the aspect of God's image that we are reflecting on here.

Lowliness Exalted

The other theme worth mentioning is the exaltation of the lowly, and the reversal of accepted human standards of power and honor. The first three beatitudes (Mt 5:3–5), Mary's Magnificat (Lk 1:51–53), and the teaching of Jesus elsewhere (e.g., Lk 16:19–31; 19:9–14) proclaim this reversal. The Old Testament had prepared the way for this revolutionary proclamation of good news for the poor. In the psalms and prophets, but also in the historical books, we often come upon God's choice of the lowly, the poor, the weak, and his rejection of those whom wealth and power have led to the oppression of the poor. David is the youngest and most insignificant son of his father Jesse, but he is the one chosen (1 Sam 16:1–13). Hannah, mother of Samuel, had for years to suffer the taunts of her husband's other wife because Hannah was sterile; but soon she would, at the miraculous birth of Samuel, sing the song from which Mary's Magnificat would be partly derived (1 Sam 1—2). In similar fashion the psalmist calls God's servants to praise him because he "raises the poor from the dust" and "enthrones the barren woman in her house" (Ps 113:7, 9). Isaiah uses the same image in proclaiming the coming exaltation of Jerusalem: "Shout for joy, you barren women who bore no children! Break into cries of joy and gladness, you who were never in labor! For the sons of the forsaken one are more in number than the sons of the wedded wife, says Yahweh" (54:1).

Other books of the New Testament echo this refrain of God's choice of the poor and lowly. The Letter of James makes it the basis of calling Christians to respect the dignity of the poor (Jas 2:1–9). But it is Paul who is particularly eloquent in this regard. Who among you, he asks the Corinthians, was nobly born? God has chosen the nobodies (literally, the "nonentities"), so as to put to shame those who pretend to be wise and powerful (1 Cor 1:26–31). This election of the lowly, simple, humble (terms more or less equivalent in Scripture) should obviously not be construed as if God favored one type of personality over another. But it is especially in those who represent humble, simple obedience to God and the attentive carrying out of what is given them to do that we see exemplified this characteristic of God's reversal of human evaluations.

Simplicity in Christian Tradition

In considering how Christian tradition has honored the Gospel message of simplicity, we will limit our observations to the heritage of prayer and spirituality. Attentiveness to the *presence of God* has been prominent from the beginning in all schools of spirituality; theologians, especially in speaking of God's presence in essence, presence, and power, have tried to provide an intellectual grounding for the practice. Among the *forms and stages of prayer,* the "prayer of simple regard" has become classic. Its name indicates how it is practiced. Without any effort of the discursive mind, imagination, or emotions, the person praying simply presents himself or herself before God, and in quiet faith gazes imagelessly toward the One who gazes in the fullness of presence. Psalm 123 captures admirably the spirit of this kind of prayer:

> I lift my eyes to you,
>   to you who have your throne in heaven,
> eyes like the eyes of slaves
>   fixed on their master's hand;
> like the eyes of a slave girl
>   fixed on the hand of her mistress,
> so our eyes are fixed on Yahweh our God,
>   for him to take pity on us.   (Ps 123:1–2)

More broadly, the spiritual tradition has encouraged devout Christians to live fully in the present. Many are the clergy and religious for whom the phrase *age quod agis* (do what you are doing) and "the sacrament of the present moment" (a term prominent, for example, in the spiritual classic of J. de Caussade, *Abandonment to Divine Providence*) sum up a very important theme in their spiritual formation. One of the great obstacles to spiritual progress is anxiety, which draws a person away from the NOW/HERE to scrupulosity and vain regrets over past misdeeds or worry over future trials. One of the values of the exercise of simple awareness in prayer is that it deprives useless anxiety of the neurotic remembrances and anticipations, usually laden with emotion, which feed it.

In a special way, the contemplative and monastic orders and congregations in the Church are meant to be, as it were, reception centers on behalf of the whole Church. High on the mountain, in some broad valley, or even in the midst of bustling cities, these men and women represent all of us in paying attention to God with simplicity, listening to the divine Word as it seeks continually a dwelling place on earth. At the same time they listen to the creation, in nature and in human affairs. Who has not been amazed at the way in which cloistered nuns and monks keep up with current events? Something similar might be said, in religious communities of priests and brothers and in some traditions of women religious in which lay or extern sisters were distinguished from others, of the special way in which these lowly (humanly speaking) members so frequently embodied the simple attentiveness characteristic of God's servants. What is important here is that such special vocations not be regarded as substituting for the call of other Christians to pay attention to God, but on the contrary evoke in them, by way of example or model, a desire to grow in this aspect of the human vocation. The same is true with regard to those saints whose embodiment of simplicity and humility is notable. We have already mentioned St. Benedict. Francis, the little man of Assisi, has drawn millions to virtue by his simplicity. For many today Dorothy Day, who wrote eloquently of "the long loneliness" and the simple perseverance needed by those who live with the poor, is an outstanding witness to the qualities we are describing here.

Real Presence

The celebration of the Eucharist, and with it the adoration of the abiding real presence of Christ in the tabernacle, has this simple attentiveness to the sacramental presence of the risen Savior at its heart. Many other Christians and even non-Christians have been struck by the focused reverence of Catholics when they assist at Mass. It is a receptivity which has its hazards, as does every devotional posture. Sometimes it deteriorated to the point of the congregation becoming, as Pope Pius X put it, "mute inglorious spectators"; hence the liturgical pendulum swung in the present century so as to foster more active and vocal participation in the Eucharistic action. But even today, especially as some of the insensitivities of earlier periods of liturgical change have come to consciousness, we experience such moments of utter stillness, moments when it is not necessary or appropriate to say anything, but just to listen, look, and adore.

We will see in the course of this book that living liturgical worship, especially in the celebration of the Eucharist, calls for the exercise of all four functions in both extraverted and introverted attitudes. Right now we wish to call attention to the importance of the sensing function, and the postures and expressions which are congruous with it, in liturgical and paraliturgical celebration. It is important that all of the five senses be drawn into the experience of worship, at least on peak occasions. Concretely this will mean flowers and incense, as the other four senses are necessarily engaged whenever the Eucharist is fittingly celebrated—the sense of taste, we may say, when the consecrated bread really tastes like bread, and when all drink from the chalice. A good celebration will also leave some moments, especially after Communion, when each participant can be free, with gaze directed inward or outward, to be in a posture of simple regard, silently aware of the gift that has been bestowed. In this way real presence moves beyond being a technical theological phrase and becomes a lived and shared experience. When authentic liturgical celebrations occur, this experience of simple presence beyond words takes on an interpersonal character, too. There can be an awareness of one another, even in a large crowd, which nourishes and energizes all, even though it cannot be expressed in words.

III. DEVELOPING SENSING/SIMPLICITY

After all that has been said, we here wish to provide readers with some more specific and practical guidance toward the developing of their sensing/simplicity, one of the four facets of God's image in them. Here is a basic statement whose parts we will elaborate in this final section of the chapter: development toward Godlikeness in the dimension of sensing/simplicity will take place: (a) through exercise with the help of models; (b) in the midst of life's occupations and in special times and places; (c) on the basis of each one's developmental type and personal history; (d) in solitude/friendship/society.

Exercise with the Help of Models

Here we repeat, in the context of dealing with the sensing function, the simple but key point which we have already made in general. Growth in virtue takes place through the practice of virtue. Practice makes perfect. Especially where the sensing function is the last to be developed, as it is in those whose preferred function is intuiting, there will be both difficulty in such exercise and also a reluctance to believe in the possibility of development. We will return to this later. Here we wish simply to encourage all, whatever may be the place of sensing in their personalities, to reflect on how consciously and deliberately they exercise it. Such practice, to be effective, needs to combine working in the ordinary contexts of life, especially at work and in social relationships, with special times and places apart, as during retreats or days of recollection. Were we in paradise, the latter would not be necessary or perhaps even helpful; we would be in possession of ourselves, in consciousness and freedom, to a degree which is not now true of us, sinners in a sinful world. All of us need times and spaces of disengagement; with the help of environments which we ourselves shape, we can exercise ourselves in the different facets of Godlikeness. What is important about such times and spaces apart is that they reflect and in turn feed back into the daily situations in which we struggle to be like God in the face of the pressures and distractions which beset us.

Models

For many people living in the present, paying attention, disengaging from apprehension about the future and grievances from the past, constitute unfamiliar behavior, and so they will do well to provide themselves with *models.* Such models can be conceptual, like the various frameworks which we provide in this book. Even more helpful are persons who exhibit with some degree of excellence the sensing/simplicity behavior. They can be people we live and work with, and though there are trials and tensions involved in being with people of opposite inclinations, we are blessed in having around us some persons from whom we can learn how to be simple. In addition, history and even fiction offer us an abundance of such models. Among the saints, we have already mentioned Benedict and Francis of Assisi. When the latter was told to rebuild God's Church lying in ruins, he took the message quite literally and started putting stone upon stone. Another beautiful model is Thérèse of Lisieux; her "little way," learned at such a price, has in it so much of quiet, simple attentiveness to God. St. John Vianney, the Curé of Ars, might be another congenial companion on the road of simplicity. The Bible offers us numerous examples—the small stature of Zacchaeus might make him appealing to some—and most of all Jesus and Mary themselves. Each of us might do well to gather our own companions on the road of simplicity.

The Importance of Type and History

A practical effort to grow in the virtue of simplicity through the exercise of the sensing function will be most powerfully aided by attention to one's developmental type and to the historical path of one's growth thus far. Concretely this means knowing which period of life is marked by the emergence of the sensing function, and whether it was then exercised in extraverted or introverted fashion. It makes quite a difference whether, for example, sensing is my dominant function and was exercised in an extraverted way in childhood, or my inferior function, calling for special exercise in an introverted way *now*, as I enter the period after my thirty-fifth birthday. I will also be conscious of how my other three functions appear in the developmental typology, and in what attitudes.

With this knowledge of how and where sensing is situated in my personality as it has developed through my life, I also pay careful attention to the concrete history of my life, particularly to the factors, external and internal, which helped or hindered my growth in this aspect of God's image. A person developing extraverted sensing in adolescence, for example, will have been very differently affected by having to live in an ugly slum tenement, as compared with a pleasant rural scene whose natural beauty provided a feast for the senses. Readers familiar with the "intensive journal" of Ira Progoff might wish to have recourse to several of the parts of that journaling process as a help in retrieving this personal history. For example, one might engage in a journal dialogue with one's sensing function, as a way of appreciating the gift that it is and of allowing it to make its contribution to continuing growth of the whole personality.

Suggestions for Individual Growth

The following suggestions will be made within the framework of Thoreau's model of solitude, friendship and society. Individuals who desire to develop their sensing/simplicity will be helped in general by any and every kind of spontaneous or deliberate exercise of the life of the senses. This requires, above all, a conscious slowing down of the pace of life, at least at the time of such exercises. We refer here to the *inner* pace, the unconscious or half-conscious assumption which is the particular temptation of dominant intuiters that what is really important is what lies beyond the horizon, what awaits us around the next bend of the road. A wide variety of simple techniques can foster this disengagement. For example, I deliberately pause in moving from one occupation to another, or even in the midst of the same occupation—perhaps taking ten slow breaths before quietly resuming work. Such moments can be the occasion for exercising one or more of the five senses—listening for thirty seconds to the sounds around us, or, if there is no sound, to the silence; or looking out the window and counting the different kinds of objects my eyes fall on; or just being aware of the way my feet touch the floor or my buttocks and back are in contact with the chair. Similarly, for a few moments I can be quietly attentive to my inner state and by my attentiveness slow down any anxious chatter or turbulence which may be racing about.

It would be well for those who are highly intuitive to look at how much leisure they enjoy, and whether they really enjoy it and take pleasure in it. In moments of leisure, there seems to be something of a natural inclination to switch from one's more developed function, especially if it is being exercised extensively in work or profession, to the opposite function. It is important for us to endorse this spontaneous movement of nature seeking balance, and not turn moments of leisure into a continuation of the same behaviors, often tinged with neurosis, which drive us in our work. Highly intuitive types might do well to develop some sensing hobbies which call for little imagination and much attention to detail—for example, making a rug by following strictly the instructions and patterns given, or cooking one dish while being exact with measurements, timing, and so forth. Incidentally, while driving in heavy traffic is not normally an exercise of leisure, it does offer a stimulus to develop sensing, by putting a high price on distractions.

Sensing Prayer

So far as prayer in solitude is concerned, we will be helped in developing sensing/simplicity by those forms of prayer which are focused on something particular, within or without, which take place minus the exercise of imagination, reasoning, or heavy emotion, and which draw us to be fully present to present reality.

There are many forms and approaches to prayer with these characteristics. One broad category is vocal prayer, here considered as part of prayer in solitude. Some people do not profit as much by vocal prayer as they might because of the misconception that when one prays vocally one needs to be attending to the meaning of the words. Such is not the case. With such familiar vocal prayers as the Our Father, the Hail Mary, the Glory Be to the Father, and with combinations of vocal prayers such as the rosary, the character and fruit of the prayer involves an attentiveness of a different kind. We already know the meaning of the words, from long familiarity, and that meaning nourishes us even when we do not attend to it. What vocal prayer does is engage our internal and sometimes our external senses in a quieting and focusing way so that we are brought to a posture of simple, quiet attentiveness, not to the words but to the presence of God mediated through the words.

Besides vocal prayer there are many other sensing exercises of faith which help us to grow in simplicity, attentiveness, and presence. Listening to sounds, gazing on the things of nature or at a crucifix, tabernacle, religious picture, or statue, and experiencing the sense of touch throughout the body are some examples. And sometimes it is given us just to stand or sit in a silent emptiness which, by its focused character, differs from the stillness which, we shall see, lies within the scope of intuitive contemplation.

Some may ask, "But is this prayer?" Even if it were not prayer it would be a helpful way of disposing ourselves for prayer. But when it is an exercise situated within a life of faith and for the purpose of deepening faith, we believe that it is prayer, and very good prayer at that. The awareness of God's presence may not be spectacular or even fully overt. But ultimately prayer is exercised wherever faith is exercised, and for committed Christians this can take place without any explicit naming of God and without any devout movement of the emotions. In God, Paul told the Athenians (Acts 17:28), we live and move and have our being. The circulatory system of our body works without noise; the dance of the molecules in the universe is silent. Similarly, in sensing prayer, the currents of divine life can course through our whole person within an exercise of sensing that is no less real for being simple.

Crucifixion and the "Mystical" Function

As we have indicated, all can profit from the suggestions which this chapter makes regarding the development of sensing/simplicity. But those who can profit most are those who need it most, namely those for whom sensing is the inferior function, and so, in our typology, the last to be developed. So we add here a word on how a call will often come to those who favor intuiting over sensing to enter into a special experience of mystical letting go in their growth toward Godlikeness.

Recall what we said in Chapter 1 about the "gear shift" moments of development, at twelve, twenty, and thirty-five. Each of these moments can be experienced as crisis moments of considerable pain but also of rich potential. For the adolescent moving into adulthood whose dominant function is either T or F and whose auxiliary is N—for example, an ENTJ×TNSF/ *EIEI* type, or an INFP = FNST/*IEIE* type—age twenty is the point at which the call will be to let go of one's auxiliary N so as to let the third function, S, emerge. Depending on one's personal history, i.e., the positive and negative environments of the first twenty years and how one has dealt with them, this time of passage can be excruciating and dangerous, but also enriching. It can also have important interpersonal ramifications, for example when one or both partners in a teenage marriage now, at twenty, have to relate in intimacy while leading, in a sense, no longer from strength but from weakness, that is, from the unfamiliar sensing function which is now claiming its due in the total personality.

But such a transition is generally less crucifying than that which takes place at thirty-five. For then one is letting go not of one's auxiliary function but of the dominant function, and what is being encouraged to emerge is the weakest, the least

developed, of the functions. Such is the case, for example, in an
ENFP=NFTS/*EIEI* type, or in an INTJ=NTFS/*IEIE* type. It is
legitimate, even helpful, to speak of such mid-life crisis points
in the rich language of the New Testament expressing the
central Gospel paradox of life through death. "Unless a wheat
grain falls on the ground and dies, it remains a single grain; but
if it dies, it yields a rich harvest" (Jn 12:24). "Because of Christ,
I have come to consider all these advantages that I had as
disadvantages. . . . For him I have accepted the loss of everything, and I look on everything as so much rubbish if only I can
have Christ . . ." (Phil 3:7f). Especially when "the Christ" is
considered as symbol of the Self, the correlation of the two
languages can give powerful specification to the basic message
of the Gospel. Many other biblical metaphors admit of similar
accommodation: poverty and riches, lowliness and exaltation,
weakness and power, social disparagement and honor, and so
forth.

The behavioral counterpart of the strength and light
which comes in the paschal experience of death and resurrection is the deepening of consciousness and freedom which
takes place when we permit our shadow side—in this case the
inferior function—to exercise itself more consciously. Because
such exercise is an unwonted experience, it will be marked by
flaws, tensions, ambiguities. An inferior function newly born
into consciousness is as awkward as a newly foaled colt or filly.
Our temptation is often to fall back into the patterns of previous behavior, the comforting womb where we feel more at
home. When we yield to such temptation, we deprive ourselves of the fullness which God has promised in our very
constitution according to the divine image.

It is not given to everyone in equal measure to experience
such a conversion, which is at once psychological and spiritual.
Because it is a work of grace, it is not something that we can
produce through our own unaided efforts. But we can and
should dispose ourselves to receive it in the measure that God
chooses to bestow it. There is a profound truth in the observation that the inferior function is the mystical function, that is,
the facet of our personality through which we most intimately

encounter God. The knowledge of both God and of ourselves seems to require that we be somehow broken, evicted from our secure strongholds. One value of a Jungian model of such a crucifixion is that it helps us to distinguish between sacrifice and suicide. It situates a certain willingness to die within the movement of an unceasing will to live. Our God is not a god of the dead, but is always calling us to the fullness of life.

In later chapters we will recall this important feature of development for the benefit of dominant sensers, thinkers, feelers. In the context of the present chapter we are asserting a call to dominant intuiters, especially in their mid-thirties, to appreciate the rich possibilities which await them if they will, at this critical juncture, let go of dependency on their imaginations and learn to live simply with themselves, other people, the world, and God. Now and here, at thirty-five, they need to hear the song, " 'Tis a gift to be simple."

Relating with Simplicity

The interpersonal life is a second area where growth in sensing/simplicity is part of our development toward Godlikeness. Here too the simple axiom obtains: it is through spontaneous and deliberate practice that we grow together in Christian simplicity, in learning to pay attention to God's presence in the concreteness of daily living. Our ability to do so will be helped if we make it clear to one another, in all simplicity, that this is what we *want* to do. There is in fact a good deal of this kind of "conspiracy"—literally, "breathing together"—taking place within small communities today. The phrase, "simple life style," embodies for many this yearning of friends, families, and communities to get back into simple communion with one another through a shared contest with the earth. Although such yearnings can be easily sidetracked into faddism regarding ecology, diet, clothing, exercise, and the like, this stirring of the Spirit deserves endorsement. After people have shared their dreams of life—an exercise of the intuiting function, we shall see—it is important that they come to the point of beginning to embody those dreams in a simple, down-to-earth way, and with respect for the pragmatic constraints that affect everything human.

The range of exercise is broad. Communities need to take seriously the realities of time and space. A family, for example, which does not share a meal together in leisure at least a few days a week will find it more difficult to resist cultural pressures toward dispersion and anxiety. Practical ways of sharing leisure need to be developed and reflected on together, so that the diversity of needs within each group may be honored while seeking some communality of experience.

Ordinary conversation is a very central area to be looked at as a source of growth. What is the climate of conversation and dialogue and discussion within a community? When someone—when anyone—in a group speaks, do people really listen? And are people willing to live with what they hear, being more disposed to agree than to disagree, and also foregoing the necessity of expressing agreement or disagreement as soon as something is said? Noticing individual and common needs is another way of exercising attentiveness in the common life. It is not a healthy thing when the responsibility for looking after the practical side of things is half-consciously left to those who are naturally inclined toward it. The more freedom and readiness there are in members of whatever behavioral type to meet the daily needs of a community, the less will a sense of burden and resentment cloud the atmosphere.

While each member in a family, community or ministry team is called to participate in those aspects of the life of the whole group which relate more immediately to sensing, those who are gifted along intuitive lines have both a special burden and a special opportunity. Much will depend on whether the predominant flow of power and energy in the group is with the sensing or intuiting side, and on how the introversion/extraversion balances and tensions are operating. Where the members with sensing preferences are a minority, a special effort may be called for on the part of the majority to see that the practical dimensions of life together do not suffer from an excess or misuse of innovative gifts. It is fair to say that the prophetic image has been strong in post-Vatican II communities, and openness to change is felt to be a hallmark of discipleship. Servanthood does receive a good deal of homage, too, especially in what is expected of the bearers of authority. But its exercise in day by day attention to duty and to the needs of others can easily be overlooked. Growth in communion calls for all to participate in giving and receiving. In this chapter we wish to call attention to the yielding of assumptions which must be sought by intuitive types if they are themselves to grow and also to help the community develop the sensing aspect of discipleship. This is the interpersonal dimension of the call to crucifixion of which we have already spoken. Dominant intuiters at the point of the "midlife crisis" may very well experience this letting go as a key point of their mystical encounter with God.

Praying Together

Prayer together is a difficult area of community life, largely because tastes and inclinations vary so widely. Ideally, the times of common prayer in a small community will have a variety which respects the attractions of the different personality types. If each member makes a special effort to engage willingly in those forms of prayer which correspond least to his or her personal preference, prayer in common can deepen the bonds of faith and love. In what we are here considering, intuitive types need to ask whether they themselves may not benefit from trying to develop a liking for vocal prayer in common. Initially they may find themselves bored with the sameness of the prayer. But if they enter it willingly, they may discover that this is just the kind of prayer they need at this stage of their lives. They can become more tranquil and simple, and they may find themselves actually energized for their favorite intuitive pursuits. "Try it, you'll like it" is not a bad directive for tasting a different wine in prayer, communal as well as individual.

Societal Simplicity

In dealing with what original sin has done to the sensing aspect of God's image, we have already adverted to the blunting and numbing impact of the technological culture on our capacity to find God and one another in a healthy sensate life. We are dealing here with a pastoral challenge to the whole Church and to all engaged in ministry. Obviously we cannot prescribe a total strategy, but some reflections and examples may indicate a method of relating our effort to grow in sensing/simplicity to the Church's pastoral coping with the surrounding technological society.

We can, first of all, help one another to come to an awareness of what happens to us in different situations of engagement with society and culture, whether in the context of home, school, work, leisure, shopping, traveling, spending money, etc. A fundamental axiom is that whatever we do, especially with the earth and its products, changes us for better or worse, in greater or lesser degree, and in every aspect of our being, physiological, psychological, spiritual, social, etc. Take, for example, a family which in the last three or four years has found itself coming together to eat at home less frequently; quick meals at "fast food" restaurants have become more characteristic. Such an experience deserves reflection. What fruitful conversations might not be had within a parish or Cursillo or Marriage Encounter group, just in the sharing of particulars of this and similar changes in the habits of families? The key question is always, "What is happening to people—to us—from such societal influences?" From there it is an easy step to move to an evaluation of the change, from many perspectives, but particularly from those which have more immediately to do with the developing of God's image in individuals and groups, and in society as a whole.

Out of such forms of sharing can emerge, at all levels of the life of the Church, from episcopal conferences to the Lenten resolutions of individuals, particular responses of Christian freedom. The numbing of human sensibility, whose tendency is to reduce people to compulsive consumers and customers, is neither trivial nor inevitable, if we take the Gospel of human dignity seriously. Withstanding it is integral to the Church's effort to promote justice in the world, for the numbing effect tends to be pervasive. The cry of the poor for bread and justice will, by and large, be more sensitively heard by those whose own taste buds are alive to the difference between good and bad bread.

Many other examples might be given of how the Church in ministry can help people come to an awareness of the importance of the senses and of the daily routines which we take for granted, but which are meant to be places of encounter with God. Caring for one's health and helping others to care for theirs is another major area. So are the employment of leisure, the area of work and profession, the use of money, etc.

It is not enough to remind people of the bad news which they already know, however dimly. If we are not simply to intensify their frustration, Church ministry must also be able to offer practical alternatives, realistic versions of a simple life style. Here is where sensing and intuiting functions, usually in tension, can become partners. Those gifted with imagination can lead the way in suggesting alternatives, while those with gifts of practicality can give such dreams viability. There are some monastic communities, for example, which have a tradition of hospitality, or of quality in the providing of some of the basic foods and drinks (Benedictine and Chartreuse are not names invented on Madison Avenue). Are there not traditional and new ways in which good bread—fast becoming an exotic food in our culture—might be provided for more people than at present? And in various educational ministries it should be possible to cultivate taste and sensibility in every aspect of life. In a word, Christian ministry today needs to alert people to the numbing impact of the surrounding culture on human sensibility, and to provide some practical models for the daily cultivation of growth in the sensing image of God.

EXERCISES

A. *For the individual:*
1. First we recommend the little book of Anthony de Mello, S.J., *Sadhana.* A whole section of the book, pp. 9–56, is devoted to exercises of awareness. This corresponds to what we have described as sensing prayer. Some of the following suggestions are drawn from this book.
2. In some setting which your experience has shown to be conducive to prayer, sit in a relaxed alertness, with body erect and feet flat on the floor. Breathe naturally. Beginning at the soles of the feet, and slowly moving upward, be attentive to your sense of touch as it is exercised throughout the body—the feel of your feet in your socks or shoes, the press of your clothing, etc. After covering the whole body, feel free to move back to a particular spot or part of the body. If you find yourself drawn to thoughts, emotions, images, simply be aware of that fact, accept that it has begun to happen, and quietly return to your simple exercise of body awareness. Continue for ten or twenty minutes, as you feel drawn.

It can happen in this sensing exercise that, at a certain point, a "flip" will spontaneously take place into an experience of wholeness which is more characteristic of intuiting than of sensing. This phenomenon corresponds to a psychological technique for developing the intuiting function by overloading the sensing function.
3. Similarly disposed through choice of environment and through a relaxed alertness, let your gaze fall quietly and successively on the objects within range, whether indoors or outdoors. Be attentive to form, color, motion—for example, the swaying of a tree, or the movements of birds, squirrels, leaves. If you are drawn to remain with one particular object, be content with that. If thoughts, especially anxious ones, emotions or images intrude, deal with them as described above.
4. Similarly disposed, listen for any and all sounds which occur where you are, in a posture of alert receptivity and

interest in particular sounds, variations, blends, etc. Sounds such as approaching or receding footsteps, the purring or rumbling of motors, people coughing or laughing, a train whistle in the distance and the growing noise of the train as it comes near are some examples. Be content to do nothing but listen. If sounds cease—a rare happening in our world—listen to the silence, waiting for the emergence of the next sound.

5. Similarly disposed, pay attention to what is going on inside of your body and your psyche. Your breathing and possibly your heartbeat or pulse can be your entry. Then move to awareness of the stream of your own inner consciousness. Are there words—or even a song, its words and melody—which spontaneously bubble up without your summoning them? Let them flow in you, watching or listening to them as they disappear and are replaced by other material. Without any great effort, see if this exercise of interior attention actually slows and reduces the flow of inner chatter. Eventually, you may be listening to an inner silence, where the bubbles are smaller and fewer. Accept stillness if it is given. If it is not, be content to attend to what is given. Continue for ten or twenty minutes, as you feel drawn.

6. All of the preceding exercises, though they do not make explicit mention of God or call for a devotional posture, can be exercises of faith and prayer, and usually are when they are part of a whole life of faith. It is also possible, after one has practiced one or other of them, to let the sense of God's presence in them quietly emerge, without reflection, image, or emotion, but in simple advertence. Thus Anthony de Mello speaks of an exercise in which God is sensed as "sounding" through external sounds. The same basic awareness of God's presence can be had in exercises of sight, touch, and attentiveness to the inner flow of consciousness.

7. Similarly disposed as in preceding exercises, let the words of some familiar vocal prayers, for example, Our Father, Hail Mary, Hail Holy Queen, etc., flow spontaneously in you. You may either repeat the same prayer indefinitely, or move from one to another. You may wish to recite some decades of

the rosary in this fashion. If you are familiar with common parts of the Mass—offertory prayers, Eucharistic Prayer—these can be chosen for this kind of exercise.

8. If you have some familiar verses, even passages, of Scripture stored inside you, try letting this treasury flow spontaneously within you. Simply dispose yourself as above, and see what emerges, e.g., for me to live is Christ . . . that Christ may dwell in your hearts through faith . . . I live in faith in the Son of God . . . Jesus, Son of David . . . etc.

B. *For groups:*

1. Some evening, try this little shared experience involving the five senses. Choose a symbol or gesture for each external sense, e.g., the lighting of a candle; the tinkling of a bell or strumming of a guitar; the kissing of a crucifix taken into the hand and reverently passed from one to the other; the use of incense; the passing and sipping of a small glass of wine. For each of the senses the prayer could begin with a brief Scripture verse appropriate to the sense, followed by a period of silence, then the gesture involving that sense, followed by more silence. A spontaneous prayer by one person asking God, e.g., to continue the work of healing and developing that sense, could conclude each section of the exercise.

2. Engage in the recitation of an hour of the Divine Office in common. Before starting be sure to take a little time to attend to the practical details, e.g., who will read the Scripture passage, how the psalms will be recited, etc.

SCRIPTURE REFERENCES

1. Psalms:

8: A contemplation of God's image (vv. 5f are an echo of Genesis 1:26–28), especially in the aspect of stewardship. A sense of humility in v. 4.

19: A contemplation of nature and of the law as reflecting the beauty of God to the one who wishes to be servant.

113: A call to the servant to praise God, especially for the exaltation of the lowly.

119: This interminable psalm reflects the attitude of the servant, never tiring of contemplating God's law and observing it.

123: The eyes of the servant are on the Lord.

131: The contented, unambitious child as model.

134: A simple night blessing.

2. Isaiah 42:1-9; 49:1-6; 50:4-11; 52:13—53:12: the four servant songs.

3. The Gospel according to Mark, especially: 1:29-31, 40-45; 2:13-14; 15-17; 4:30-32; 5:21-43; 9:33-37; 10:35-45; 12:41-44.

4. Passages from the other Gospels, as mentioned in the text of this chapter. Note that all of the Gospels can be read for the passages which show Jesus exercising his sense of sight, hearing, and touch.

5. Acts 2:42-47; 4:32-35—the simple life of the first community.

6. Paul 1 Corinthians 1:17-34 (God's choice of the little ones); Ephesians 5—6 (the daily warfare); Philippians 2:1-18 (the humble, obedient life in imitation of Jesus).

NOTES

1. S. Weil, "Reflections on the Right Use of School Studies with a View to the Love of God," in *The Simone Weil Reader*, ed. G. Panichas (New York: David McKay, 1977), pp. 44-52.

2. Bernard Lonergan, *Method in Theology* (New York: Seabury, 1972), p. 20.

3. Book 10, Chapter 6.

4. "The Leaden Echo and the Golden Echo," *Poems and Prose*, ed. W. H. Gardner (Middlesex: Penguin, 1953), p. 54.

CHAPTER 3
The Truth That Makes Us Free

Thinking/Justice

Two brave men, saints of the Church, have been brought more fully into our consciousness through the skill of modern playwrights. One was the twelfth century archbishop of Canterbury, Thomas à Becket, celebrated in T.S. Eliot's *Murder in the Cathedral.* The other was the lord chancellor of England, Thomas More, whose life and death are dramatized in Robert Bolt's *A Man for All Seasons.* Both gave their lives in confrontation with royal power and in the name of a deeper allegiance.

In both cases the issue was one of truth, conscience, right, law, justice, fidelity to the divinely sanctioned order of a still theocratic society. Both plays breathe the spirit of these values, and while tenderness is not absent, especially in More's relationship with his family, it is the stern, objective demand of conscience as mediating God's law which is central.

Those who are familiar with Bolt's eloquent play will recall the scene where Norfolk pleads with Thomas, in the name of fellowship, to yield to the king as he himself has done. More replies, "And when we stand before God, and you are sent to Paradise for doing according to your conscience, and I am damned for not doing according to mine, will you come with me, for fellowship?"[1] Readers of Eliot's play will recall, too, the oft quoted line spoken by the archbishop: "The last temptation is the greatest treason/To do the right thing for the wrong reason."[2]

Doing what is right and doing it for the right reason, keeping one's oath to God at any price, are manifestations of our humanity at its noblest. They are also expressions of the thinking aspect of God's image which we will now examine. The same potential for heroic fidelity is in all of us as was in these two saints. By God's grace each of us is capable of standing for what is right, asserting the truth in the face of opposition, acting justly.

We will follow the same general pattern as in the preceding chapter. First we will describe what is characteristic of *the thinking function,* and of those for whom it is a preferred way of dealing with life. Second, we will sample some of the affinities which exist between *Gospel themes* and this aspect of God's image as described in our developmental typology. *Justice* will be the virtue and attitude which we choose to highlight in this comparison. Third, we will offer some observations and some exercises which aim to promote the *development* of thinking/justice, particularly in individuals and groups for whom this behavior is not a strong preference.

As readers gain more familiarity with the approach and method of our journey from image to likeness, it will be possible for us to leave to them more of the task of developing ideas and strategies. At the same time we will be introducing some new perspectives, which can be applied to all four of the functions. In this way we would encourage readers to keep referring back to the previous descriptions and reflections, in the interest of an ever fuller grasp of our human and Christian calling.

I. THE THINKING FUNCTION

Let us recall that we are dealing here with one of the *judging* functions, that is, with one of two distinctive ways of *responding* to what we have perceived, whether in the outer world or within the psyche. Thinking (T), like its opposite, feeling (F), is designated by Jung as a *rational* function, because it operates according to the laws of reason. What he has in mind is thinking that is reflective and consciously directed according to norms of reason and through the exercise of will.

What differentiates thinking from feeling is that the former operates by a linear *logic*, the latter by making subjective *values* normative. Thinking relies on *principles* of objective *truth*, and it seeks to articulate that truth with clarity and precision in the *word* both mental and spoken. It esteems right *order*, and pursues that order purposefully through precise distinctions in speech and correct procedures and structures in the organization of life. The virtue which corresponds to this ordering function, then, is the virtue of *justice*, which gives to every person, group, reality, what is due or appropriate.

When in the next chapter we describe the feeling function, we will see more clearly the contrast of the two judging functions. For now, here are some particular characteristics of this aspect of God's image in us, which will help us to recognize its operation. Thinking is firm, tough-minded, logical, cold or at least cool, unwavering, assertive, critical, wary, questioning, adversarial, distant, impersonal, and forbearing. It is characterized more by concern than by sympathy, by respect rather than by endorsement, and by authenticity rather than by reinforcement of persons. Those who prefer the function of thinking over feeling may have strong emotions, but usually find it difficult to express them freely. They are ready to pardon others once the others have acknowledged their need of pardon; but they find it difficult to ask others for forgiveness unless it is clear that they themselves have violated some norm. Even then the emotional aspect of apologizing is not easy for them. The hurt feelings of another are not for them a sufficient basis for seeking pardon.

Even with these bare descriptive terms, readers will be able to recognize the kind of behavior we are trying to clarify. In ourselves or in others, we come across it every day. For example, just let your imagination play with this commonplace street scene in any of our large cities. A police officer moves methodically down a line of illegally parked cars, impersonally filling out the summons for each, leaving it in the windshield and moving on. Should one of the offenders happen to return and begin to remonstrate, more often than not we witness a contrast of behavior: the car owner becomes emotional, pleading, irate, or cajoling, while the public official firmly explains that the violation has taken place, the summons has been written, and effective excuses should be saved for the magistrate. Or we could consider a business manager preparing a hard line budget which will entail the firing of some employees; or a lawyer drawing up a brief and working over the logical sequence of the arguments to be presented; or a college math teacher adorning the blackboard with symbols, and almost chanting to the class the rationale for the operation.

When we are concerned about our adherence to rules, when there is question of coolly asking who has authority for an important decision, when an individual or group looks for the exact word to express a belief or prescribe a code, the thinking side of our natures is coming into play. Truth, authority, and the word are important correlatives of the thinking function.

It is hardly necessary to tell readers that thinking can be exercised on the world outside or on inner reality. Getting one's principles or convictions in order, and planning the critique of a new film, are introverted exercises of thinking. A group of professional football coaches reworking the team's long list of standard plays, and a food chain executive discussing a marketing plan for a new product with the sales managers, are examples of the extraverted exercise of thinking.

The reader already knows, too, that when thinking is the dominant function, it will be supported and balanced by a perceiving function, either sensing or intuiting, as auxiliary. The *attitude*, either introversion or extraversion, of this auxiliary will be opposite to the attitude of the dominant thinking function. Since human beings never act with only a single function or attitude at work, these contingencies make a real difference for our behavior. An extraverted intuitive thinker, for example ENTJ=TNSF/*EIEI*, will be inclined to deal with a situation calling for both perception and judgment very differently from an introverted sensing thinker ISTP=TSNF/*IEIE*. The former would be at ease in directing groups, and developing plans with them, with the help of considerable inner creativity, and with concern that closure be reached without undue delay. The latter would by preference do the planning in solitude, aided by a practical grasp of details, and with less anxiety in group discussion that the plan, however good, be quickly adopted and implemented.

As our purpose here is to delineate the thinking function, not to analyze all thinking types, we will not linger with such differences as we have just described. Instead, let us take a moment to appreciate more fully what a gift we all possess in this aspect of God's image. In some Church circles, especially where people are reacting against institutionalism and authoritarianism, the qualities of the thinking function are less likely to be celebrated. Our observation of those drawn to Church ministry would also seem to suggest that it is a decided minority of both men and women in religious communities who prefer thinking over feeling. Yet we all need to take responsibility for the development of this gift within ourselves, as well as in the groups to which we belong and in the Church and society as a whole. When rational logic, truth, order, justice, and authority are not held in honor and appropriately exercised, life inevitably becomes less human. Where a clear, strong, and spontaneously assertive adherence to sound principles does not engage members of any group or society, human beings are in danger of becoming a prey to primitive, dark, and irrational forces. The absolutizing potential of our thinking side should not let us fall into the trap of disprizing or neglecting it. God, who will judge us on our use of our talents, will hold us responsible for the way in which we reflect this aspect of divine truth.

The distinctive contribution of the thinking function to the totality of human living has to do with its role in the complex energy system which enables individuals, groups, and the world at large to shape history. Human beings are made in such a way that they can derive enormous energies from creating different kinds of order. Just think of the satisfaction we have when the crime rate in our town has been reduced because of our own vigilance and that of the police. Or think of the delight that comes from appreciating a symphony or ballet which primarily depends for its effect on the ordering of casual or conflicting patterns. Civic reformers are often people who draw immense energy from straightening out situations of corruption or waste which have offended their need for order.

But what is unique about this function from the viewpoint of human energy is that it conserves and protects the contributions of the other three functions. Without a basic order in the life of an individual, group or society, the energies flowing from the exercise of sensing, intuiting, and feeling will be wasted. For example, the intense emotions generated by a return to roots in an ethnic group or religious community will go down the drain unless the group knows how to channel such a life-giving flow into the right processes and structures.

From the viewpoint of our human insertion in time, the thinking function as an ordering agent relates with a certain simultaneity to all three dimensions, present, past, and future. We have already seen how the sensing function enables us to draw vital energies from the present moment. In the following chapter we shall see that our gift of remembering through the feeling function, by rendering the past present, is a distinct source of energy. Most amazing of all, as our fifth chapter will describe, is the fact that the future, which does not yet exist in actuality, nevertheless becomes a real source of energy through the power of intuition in the form of dreaming imagination. Every human being thus spontaneously finds the wherewithal to deal with life by drawing vigor from all three sources. But for this to happen in a healthy way there is one basic requisite—order. It is the thinking function which provides that order. By setting limits, by channeling, by providing structures, it makes the surging waters of life available for life's purposes.

As is the case with all the functions, thinking serves solitude, friendship, and society. Individuals need a minimum, at least, of discipline and coherence if their life is not to be chaotic. Human relationships of all kinds depend on the propriety, the etiquette, which enables persons and groups to accommodate to one another—for example, a daily ritual of departure for work on which partners can more or less rely. And as we move beyond personal relationships to the imper-

sonal world, we experience the need of rationalizing, routiniz-
ing, for example through traffic laws and signals, regular hours
of opening and closing banks and post offices, and the like.

But the societal dimensions of the thinking function relate
to deeper concerns than these. There is good reason to characterize our Western society and culture, as it has emerged
through the scientific, industrial, and technological revolu-
tions, as dominated by thinking. Carl Jung, himself a thinking
personality, was deeply concerned with what extraverted
thinking as a cultural force might do to humanity if we did not
quickly find ways to let the compensating elements present in
the unconscious assert themselves. Nor has Jung been alone in
viewing technology as both promise and threat. And it is not
strange that in dealing with the technological society the
Church has had recourse to the theological idea and the religious ideal of justice. The right use of thinking, besides nourishing us for our personal and interpersonal lives, has a special
contribution to make to bringing the technological society into
the service of justice.

A final observation and illustration before turning to Gospel aspects of thinking has to do with the application of our
developmental typology to this function. It is not only in dominant thinkers or even in those for whom thinking is auxiliary
that we can observe its workings. It is present in all of us, and
according to our developmental type it will emerge at one of
the four stages of life. Where it is an auxiliary function, for
example, adolescence is the period for such emergence; early
adulthood is the period for thinking as the third function to
emerge. But what offers more difficulty, and therefore what
will engage our special attention later in this chapter, is the
emergence around the age of thirty-five of the thinking function in those for whom it is the least preferred function,
directly in tension with the dominant feeling function. It is our
view that often the famous "mid-life crisis" is constituted or
compounded by the challenge—which is also an opportunity—
contained in the call to let go of the dominant feeling function
so that thinking can make its contribution. This is a kind of
death experience to which dominant feelers are called. They

are being asked to lead from weakness, so to speak, and to take the risks inherent in thinking behavior. Because this is their undeveloped side, they will do it badly at first, and it may never come to be a fully comfortable manner of acting. But growth is always possible.

At the opposite pole from the dominant feeler seeking at thirty-five to develop thinking is the dominant thinker, the one who in childhood made thinking behavior the primary preference. Such persons generally are excellent models for the rest of us, who come later to develop this facet of our personality. The following case history will serve to resume what we have been saying in this chapter. But we warn the reader that we are offering only an example of one of the four types of dominant thinkers, and that, even within that particular type, individuals will be very different from one another because of the way in which their choices and their environments have affected their total development.

A Scenario

Edna, a forty-year-old hospital administrator, has always searched for the reasons behind things and statements. As a child she unfailingly asked the "why" of every instruction and prohibition. Her parents wisely came to see that this behavior was not prompted by defiance or petulance, but simply by her need to understand. Early in her life her mother became seriously ill and was hospitalized. Edna felt this intensely, but was unable to express either her personal pain at the separation or the compassion she felt for her mother. She was, however, tireless in her efforts to manage the house and care for her younger brothers and sisters who turned to her for strength. Even her father relied on her to talk with some of their creditors about the time frame for payments. She astonished them by her precision and by the assurance with which she conducted herself as she explained logically the present state of affairs and the family's plans for settling accounts.

About the age of twenty, Edna began to think of the future she might choose. She found herself dreaming of a career where she could have some impact on the medical world. This was such a departure from her former concentration on the here and now that her friends were puzzled, and sometimes had to break into her reverie to get her back into the flow of conversation. Her desire to correct some of the disorganization she had found in hospitals, especially the one where her mother had been discomforted by inefficiency, led Edna to choose a career in hospital administration. In this role she eventually made her way to important positions, and succeeded in putting her institution on a sound financial base and in improving its management and patient care. Her care to gather all the facts and figures necessary led also to the establishment of a unit in preventive medicine. This aspect of health care had always appealed to her more than corrective medicine; she did not see the sense of ministering to people with illnesses without putting as much or more energy into prevention through sound management.

A great success as an administrator, Edna nevertheless carried the secret disappointment of knowing that even her closest associates felt she was a cold person. One friend cited the example of the time she had approached Edna in tears, feeling devastated by a physician's harsh reprimand. Edna's response was to advise her friend to stop crying so that Edna might have the information necessary to prevent a repetition of such incidents. Her friend stormed out, saying sarcastically, "You're all heart!" Edna wondered what the reason was for such an outburst.

The past several years, Edna has found herself developing a new dimension of her personality, which she both appreciates and fears. On several occasions she has been strangely touched by a thoughtful or warm gesture; where she used to distrust physical closeness with friends she now experiences a feeling of joy. What makes her still somewhat fearful is the realization that her recent decisions seem to be based more on feelings of the moment than on deliberation. She has found herself liking some things and people for no special reason— she just likes them. She has also discovered, to her embarrassment, that she has become susceptible to a kind of sentimentality. On one recent occasion she was close to tears as she thought of the fact that her daughter would soon be going off to college. As she has gradually become more adept in the use of her feelings, they surface when she calls them forth; and when they come spontaneously she finds them more mature and manageable. At her son's wedding reception, for example, she found herself moved to tears without embarrassment, quickly drying them when she had to handle the problem of the young couple's lost airline tickets.

From all this it is clear that Edna prefers dealing with life as an ESTJ=TSNF/*EIEI*. Her extraverted thinking makes it easy for her to manage things, while her introverted feeling, especially during the period when she was developing her other functions, remained inside, hurting but unexpressed. Her auxiliary function, sensing, enabled her to amass much information which helped her to implement her managerial tasks; but as she approached adulthood this facility gave way to her third function, intuition, which tended to draw her into exploring future possibilities. This did not eradicate her sensing gift but rather enriched it as she learned to integrate these two functions. Her shadow side, feeling, waited for its moment to come forth into the limelight until Edna was about thirty-five. It then manifested itself immaturely at first, but gradually became more contributory to her inner peace, her relationships with others, and her professional achievements. Edna's journey to this stage may be reviewed with the help of the following schema:

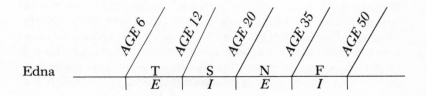

II. THE GOSPEL OF JUSTICE

As with the sensing function and simplicity, so here we are led by an aspect of God's image in human beings to understand, within the dark cloud of mystery, an aspect of God. One place to begin is with a key term in biblical, credal, and liturgical history, which unfortunately has become almost casual for most believers: God is *almighty* (Latin: *omnipotens;* Greek: *pantokrator*), the God of power and might, as our translation of the Holy, Holy, Holy now has it. God is a *thinking* God; otherwise human beings made according to God's image could not be endowed with the function and gift of thinking. Readers might want to test the completeness of their understanding of God by reacting to our attribution to God of qualities which belong to our thinking side. God truly is firm, tough-minded, logical, cold or at least cool, unwavering, assertive, critical, wary, questioning, adversarial, distant, impersonal, and tolerant. Yes, God is more than these words convey, and some of the terms carry connotations which seem out of place when applied to the divine. But basically God is all of these, and, importantly, a *just* God.

The God of Justice

The Old Testament, in both Hebrew and Septuagint forms, contains many divine names and titles which correspond to this aspect of God's image in us. We cannot spend time now reflecting on them, but mentioning some of them will bring out how prominent this aspect of God's nature is in the Bible. *Yahweh, Adonai,* and *El Shaddai* are three of the most important names. *Yahweh* is most likely a form of the Hebrew verb *to be.* While the exact meaning of the central passage, Exodus 3:14, is not completely clear, most of the plausible interpretations come out with an accent on God being transcendent, beyond all definition, exercising the full power of being, in contrast to the false gods who eventually are seen as non-entities. The name thus conveys the firm and strong detachment characteristic of the thinking function.

Adonai is Hebrew for *lord,* and draws upon this social relationship to accent the power and authority of God. *El Shaddai* is the name identifying God in the appearance to Abram (Gen 17:1). It probably means *mountain god.* The strength, endurance, and impassivity of the mountain makes such a title appropriate, and the term became the equivalent of "almighty God."

In addition to these three names, other names and titles worth recalling are creator, where God is conceived as the architect who designs and builds and governs an ordered world; ruler; king; lawmaker; judge; warrior. God is also described as the rock and the fortress. And while divine wisdom, as we find it portrayed in the psalms, Job and wisdom literature, correlates especially with the intuiting function, some of its qualities reflect also thinking characteristics.

The God Who Speaks

God is also the God who speaks. We have already said that the word—speech—is associated with thinking. In the Judaeo-Christian tradition, in contrast to some other religions, God is a God who speaks the word, not a silent God. From the majestic refrain of the opening chapter of Genesis, "Then God said . . ." to what is in some respects the definitive verse of the whole Bible, "And the Word was made flesh and dwelt among us . . ." (Jn 1:14), salvation history is a story of God speaking and humans responding, of God revealing the meaning of human existence. Closely associated with God's word is the theme of *the law* as mediation of God's word and will. Psalms 1, 19, and 119 are examples of reverence for that law which is really God in person as the norm of human life. The important themes of *wisdom* and *prophecy,* while they cannot be as easily contained within the scope of the thinking function, do relate to it inasmuch as they both draw upon the word. The wisdom literature, especially Proverbs, Wisdom and a number of the psalms, speaks of both human and divine wisdom in a way that prefigures the coming to earth of divine wisdom in the person of Jesus of Nazareth. And the characteristic trait of the prophets is that they speak not their own word but the word that has been given them to speak by God. "Thus says the Lord . . ."

What is never—or hardly ever—called into question in the Old Testament is that this divine wisdom is benevolent, this divine law is just. God is the just ruler, judge, covenant partner with Israel. While the meaning of the term "justice" in the Bible differs notably from the philosophical concept which we have inherited from the Greeks—for one thing it is not as sharply opposed to love and mercy as is usual for us today—the justice of God certainly contains the note of fairness, of rendering to humans according to their deeds, and of being faithful to the pledged word of covenant.

Only once in the entire Old Testament is a serious question raised about the justice of God—in the Book of Job. By the time this tense, dramatic dialogue of Job with his friends and with God is completed, God's justice is all the more strongly vindicated, together with the incapacity of limited humans to fathom its mystery. Something of the thinking God's zest for argument is conveyed when God confronts Job: "Then from the heart of the tempest Yahweh gave Job his answer. He said: 'Who is this obscuring my designs with his empty-headed words? Brace yourself like a fighter; now it is my turn to ask questions and yours to inform me'" (38:1–2). In the final resolution of the drama, Job's struggle with his maker turns out to be a conversion experience and at the same time an experience of enlightenment as he acknowledges both the transcendence and the power of God. The language of his surrender is rich in thinking qualities:

> I know that you are all powerful:
>> what you conceive you can perform.
> I am the man who obscured your designs
>> with my empty-headed words.
> I have been holding forth on matters I cannot understand,
>> on marvels beyond me and my knowledge.
> I knew you then only by hearsay:
>> but now, having seen you with my own eyes,
> I retract all I have said
>> and in dust and ashes I repent.   (Jb 42:2–6)

The Thinking Image of God

It is this God, firm, true, assertive, detached, just, that humans are called to image forth in their lives. No one becomes whole without somehow making the journey from image to likeness in the human qualities described in our typology, which we have just seen to be divine qualities too. That such is the human call is expressed in a variety of ways in Scripture. Let us look at a few of these ways.

Implicit in the whole first account of creation (Gen 1:1–2:4a) is the belief that humans are called to imitate the God who fashioned order out of the primordial chaos. In Genesis 1:28 this belief is explicitated with respect to the relationships of human beings with other creatures of earth. We have been given the charge of exercising dominion—a better term is *stewardship*—over the animal kingdom. The second creation account expresses the same truth in the symbolic charge of naming the cattle, the birds, and the wild beasts (Gen 2:19f). To name is to distinguish, to make it clear that this is not that; this is the role of the thinking function. The passage also implies that it is through human prudence that God's providence over the creation is exercised. Our obedience to God lives in our exercise of responsibility in the world. God's thinking rule does not substitute for ours but on the contrary calls it forth.

This same vocation of imaging the thinking God is expressed in many other ways in the Old Testament. We choose to mention here the themes of *fidelity, justice* and *wisdom* as honored ideals. Since covenant was so central to the political and economic life of this tribal people, it is natural to expect an accent on thinking qualities such as fidelity and justice. Those who are worthy of honor are those who keep their pledged word, pay their just debts, observe due order in all their dealings. One of the facets of wisdom that is cherished is the gift, especially esteemed in rulers, of providing order and justice in society. Most of the pertinent passages in the patriarchal society of the Old Testament are about males, and the models held up for imitation are the male patriarchs, judges, and kings. But there is one classic passage (Prv 31:10–31), a portrait of a perfect wife, which offers a feminine model of thinking behavior. Everything in this household is perfectly managed. Servants are warmly clothed, land is bought at a good price, the poor are cared for, and the husband and sons of this wise and provident woman are justly proud of her. What is especially worthy of note in this passage is the place that *work* holds in thinking behavior. One of the marks of the thinking function is that it is interested in getting jobs done with efficiency and order.

We may say, then, that the injunction to be holy as God is holy, as seen in Chapter 1 of this book, contains within itself the commandment to mirror forth in human behavior the truth, justice, and ordering wisdom of God. Human beings image God in their behavior by showing forth such qualities as these.

Sin as Disorder

As was the case in our reflection on sensing/simplicity, so here our appreciation of the restoration of God's image can be enhanced by a realization of what sin—our radical sinfulness—has done to this thinking aspect of our humanity. The Bible is rich in descriptions of this particular disfigurement. Here let us attend to such key themes as disorder, untruth, lawlessness, and injustice.

One of the principal images of the disorder which sin brings is the story of the attempt to build the tower of Babel. What is significant here is that the sin of rebellion against the divine order has its punishment in the confusion of speech of humanity, the deforming of the human capacity to image God by speaking a clear and truthful word. The passage, Genesis 11:1–9, is obviously not a scientific attempt to explain the multiplicity of human languages, which in itself represents a beautiful variety in God's many-splendored creation. Nor is the point that the effort to build a tower or a human city with the name or identity which would go with it is contrary to God's law. The sin, similar to that of the first parents, was in the ambitioning of an absolute autonomy in creating a human order. The punishment, really inherent in the sin itself, was disordered speech—"Yahweh confused the language of the whole earth" (v. 9)—and the consequent alienation of peoples—"Yahweh scattered them over the whole face of the earth" (*ibid.*). In a contemporary reading, the story speaks of a profound disordering of our human capacity to communicate with one another.

The tower of Babel story is situated in those chapters of Genesis which describe the history of humanity consequent upon the fall and prior to God's calling of Abraham, Isaac, and Jacob. In these chapters, especially in those immediately following the sin of Adam and Eve, we read of the disorder they have brought upon us. The very cornerstone of human life, marital and familial love, loses its original strength. Woman will give birth in pain and will be lorded over by man (Gen 3:16). Relationships between humans and the earth are troubled—"accursed is the soil because of you" (3:17). The labor of making a living from the earth is now toilsome and associated with death (3:17–19). The story of Cain and Abel symbolizes the extension of the reign of disunity to the relationships of brothers (4:1–16).

The Genesis account of original sin also speaks of the symbolic enmity between the serpent and human beings, that is, the woman and her offspring. From this beginning Jewish and Christian tradition will develop a whole theology of the disordering of cosmic life by sin. Human beings, meant to be God's stewards over the creation, now become subjected to what the New Testament will call variously principalities and powers, rulers of the world of darkness, Satan, the prince of this world, and so on. Beneath the imagery of such expressions is the assertion of disorder, emptiness, subjection, and injustice.

The prophets of Israel, in their denunciation of injustice, portray for us in vivid language what happens when religion and morality are invaded by disorder. Especially striking is the linkage of idolatry and empty ritual with human oppression. Though the prophets do not speculate on the connection, it is

clear that in their view justice toward the neighbor is insepara-
ble from true worship, e.g., Isaiah 1:10–20; Amos 5:21–27;
Micah 6:1–8. Today a good many Christians tend to shy away
from those biblical passages where God relates to the chosen
people as a God who is just and who asks justice of those
created according to God's image. But such passages can be
particularly helpful for those whose current need is to develop
the thinking side of their personality.

Among the New Testament portrayals of sin as injustice,
untruth, and disorder, we wish to call the attention of readers
to material in both John and Paul. The Fourth Gospel and the
First Letter of John pay special attention to themes of power,
justice, truth, and their opposites, e.g., John 8:31–59; 12:20–50;
1 John 2:3–11. The Pauline corpus often alludes to the degrad-
ing subjection to cosmic powers which has come about
through sin, e.g., Romans 8:20–25; 1 Corinthians 2:8; Ephesians 3:10. The classic depiction of degradation in terms of
untruth, injustice, and subjection is the Letter to the Romans,
e.g., 1:18—3:20; 5:12–21; 7:14–25.

Honest exposure to such passages as these can be a search-
light on the disorder, injustice, and untruth which afflict us in
our inner life, our relationships, our world. Such an exercise
need not be masochistic; rather, it can dispose us to hear and
more deeply appreciate the good news of Christ Jesus, who has
become our truth and our justice (see 1 Cor 1:30).

Jesus the Just One

For our contemplative gazing on Jesus as model for developing this side of our personality, the Gospel according to
Matthew is especially appropriate. It is a particularly well
ordered and structured Gospel. It begins with the two chapters of the infancy narrative and ends with three chapters
describing the passion and resurrection. Its central portion,
devoted to the public life of Jesus, is clearly divided into five
books, each of which contains a narrative section leading to a
discourse of Jesus. Matthew's theme, too, is a thinking theme,
the kingdom of heaven. He wrote for Jews for whom juridical

reality loomed large, and who would want clear evidence that Jesus and his life really did contain the messianic qualities described in the law and the prophets. This Gospel, it has been said, "is the great charter of the new order which, in Christ, completes God's plan."[3]

Especially in the Sermon on the Mount (chapters 5–7) Jesus presents himself in Matthew as the new Moses. In fact, the new law itself is embodied in his very person. He has come with a juridical purpose, to bring the law and the prophets to their completion (5:17). At the same time he goes beyond the old law, promulgating one which is more exigent because more interior. "You have heard that it was said . . . but I say to you . . ." (5:20–48). He taught, Matthew says, "with authority, and not like their own scribes." That is why "his teaching made a deep impression on the people" (7:28f).

It is because he embodies the new law within his own conduct that we are able to contemplate his exercise of truth, assertiveness, authority, justice, and a certain logic which is not without touches of wit.

This thinking behavior appears especially in situations of conflict, when his enemies are bent on entrapment. The coin of tribute scene (22:15–22) finds him taking his critics beyond the particular legal question of taxation to the basic norm of justice: both God and every human institution are to receive their respective due, without confusion. Christians down the ages and in our own day, faced with tyranny and oppression, have been challenged to imitate the cool assertiveness of their one Lord (see Acts 4:19; 5:29).

Even in his occasional outbursts of anger, as when he clears the temple of hucksters, Jesus makes an appropriate response—assertive but not aggressive—to a situation of intolerable disorder. God's holy dwelling place must not be profaned by greed (21:12f). His anger with Peter, to whom he has just promised a unique share in his own power, comes because the impulsive disciple is calling into question *the* imperative in Jesus' code of conduct: "The way you think is not God's way!" (16:23). But undoubtedly the most terrible instance of his wrath was his passionate denunciation of the scribes and Pharisees in Chapter 23 of Matthew. Here the source of the anger is probably the same as that which we observed in the prophets, the linkage between dishonor to God and oppression of human beings. This is what the hypocritical regulations of his adversaries were doing, and Jesus vented the full force of his diatribe against it.

Perhaps the most delightful instance of Jesus' exercise of thinking comes in the account in the Fourth Gospel of the woman taken in adultery (Jn 8:1–11). Confronted with compassionless legalism, he makes no plea for mercy toward her but instead enters into a legal tactic. "All right, if the law calls for her to be stoned, let the law be carried out—*but* . . ." And, with the authority which he consciously owns, he adds one more regulation, admirable in its sense of proportion. The one who is without sin is the one empowered to begin the legal execution. So he transforms a situation of near tragedy into one of an ironic justice. The only one who is qualified to punish is not interested in punishing. And he completes this dramatic epiphany of the divine logic by saying to the woman who stands legally innocent: "Don't sin again." The scene, we may say, shows Jesus in a remarkable alliance of his imagination (N) and his passion for true justice (T), both of which are drawn into the service of his compassionate heart (F).

Jesus preached what he practiced: a respect for *truth* ("All you need say is 'Yes' if you mean yes, 'No' if you mean no"—Mt 5:37), *justice* ("forgive us our debts as we have forgiven those who are in debt to us"—Mt 6:12), and *order* ("what then will a man gain if he wins the whole world and ruins his life?"—Mt 16:25).

He taught his disciples to be assertive, too. "Don't be afraid" was his constant admonition to them, e.g., Matthew 10:17–33. Nor do the evangelists record that he ever discouraged his followers from seeking power. His only concern was that they understand where true power lay and what were the conditions for gaining it. The scene with the sons of Zebedee and their ambitious mother is illuminating in this regard. It is through humble service that greatness comes (Mt 20:20–28). And only those willing to become as little children will achieve greatness in the kingdom, which has its own kind of logic (Mt 18:1–4).

But the most dramatic setting forth of the theme of justice, power, and truth is the scene of the Last Judgment (Mt 25:31–46). Here the Son of Man is depicted not as the tender and merciful shepherd but as the impartial king and judge dealing out to good and wicked alike their just due. It is the supreme moment of truth for humanity. The power and will to separate, to distinguish, to discriminate, is a striking characteristic of the thinking function, and it is depicted here in stark, unambiguous terms. The doctrine of hell as eternal punishment remains unfathomable for us, and it is only through the gift of faith that we can assent to it. But appreciating the thinking side of God and of the divine image in us can help us to understand the place of hell in the economy of salvation. Ultimately this difficult doctrine pays tribute to our human dignity and freedom. We are capable, by God's grace, of such virtue that eternal intimacy with God is its congruous fruition. And we are capable of resisting God's love with such malice that an eternal refusal of love is the logical outcome.

Mary and Joseph

The two human beings who especially modeled truth and justice for Jesus in his human development were, of course, Mary and Joseph. Mary appears in the Gospels both as one who is already well versed in thinking attitudes and as one who, as the first of the disciples, needs to learn the strange ways of divine justice. At Nazareth she appears cool and assertive in dealing with the message of the angel (Lk 1:34, 38), and her Magnificat reveals her as ecstatic in her celebration of the ways of God's power (Lk 1:51–53). At the finding of Jesus in the temple, she is conscious of her authority as mother, but at the same time she must hear from her son that there is a greater authority than hers (Lk 2:48–51). This divine pedagogy continued in Jesus' public life, at Cana (Lk 2:1–11), in the scene where Jesus refuses to leave the circle of his new family of disciples to come out at the bidding of his mother and other relatives (Mk 3:31–35), and in the moment of separation on Calvary (Jn 19:25–27).

As for Joseph, Mary's husband, the Church's devotion as it developed down the ages has attended to the statement that he was a just man (Mt 1:19), and Matthew's Gospel portrays him as faithfully carrying out the role assigned him by God.

Let us briefly indicate some ways in which the rest of the New Testament enlarges on what we find in the Gospels about themes of truth, justice, and power. Whereas Jesus himself does not seem to have attributed to himself titles of power and majesty, the community of his disciples, once enlightened by the gift of the Spirit, came to appreciate more deeply who he really was, and named him accordingly, for example as lord, king, and ruler. Most readers will be familiar with the Christological hymn of Philippians 2:6–11, where his transition from being suffering servant to being the Lord acclaimed by the whole of creation is so powerfully set forth. Elsewhere the Pauline literature celebrates the victory of God and of the Christ over the principalities and powers, e.g., 1 Corinthians 15; Ephesians 1:15–23; 2:11–22; Colossians 2:14–15. And the entire Book of Revelation is a dramatic portrait of the cosmic power struggle between God and Satan, culminating in the wedding banquet of the Lamb and his bride, the Church, in the heavenly Jerusalem. Particularly striking is the portrayal of Christ as king in Revelation 1:9–20, followed by his stern and authoritative message to the seven churches (Rev 2—3). In these and similar passages readers will find the qualities of strength, authority, truth, assertiveness, justice, and order, which we have seen to belong to the thinking function.

Because the title of Christ the King complements the titles which we correlate with the other functions—servant (S), priest (F), and prophet (N)—we offer it as an appropriate symbolic representation of the thinking function in its fullness. It holds before us our primary model for developing this side of our humanity. Along with the passages just mentioned and others in Revelation, as well as the scene of his passion where he responds to Pilate's question whether he is a king (Jn 18:33–

37), Psalm 72 portrays him as the king who is both just and compassionate.

Thinking Aspects of Christian Tradition

When we turn from the New Testament to tradition, we find a rich variety of ways in which the thinking side of our humanity takes Christian form. We shall begin with the individual, and then move into a discussion of communal and societal embodiments of this aspect of God's image in us.

First of all, we find that the spiritual tradition has made much of *method, discipline,* and *order* in helping Christian individuals grow in holiness. We seem today to have passed through a period when many people felt the need to get away from method in prayer for the sake of spontaneity. Excessive insistence on method, they felt, had put intimacy with God into a straitjacket. But today the pendulum seems to be swinging back. Sometimes under the influence of non-Christian techniques of meditation and sometimes by a return to traditional Christian forms, there is a new awareness that body, mind, and spirit need to be properly *disposed*—or *composed*—if we are to meet God perseveringly in prayer. A methodical attentiveness to the physical environment of prayer, to posture, to the quieting of the mind through techniques, and also to the importance of making a good reflective transition at the end of prayer—all of this is part of a heritage which we seem to be rediscovering. Such concerns represent an expression of the thinking function, often together with the sensing function, within the life of prayer.

The examination of conscience, especially the particular examen, which focuses on a single virtue, vice, attitude, or practice, is another instance of traditional attentiveness to order in the life of the spirit. Christians, too, have long been encouraged to draw up a *personal rule of life* adapted to their own needs and desires. *Regularity* has been prized, in daily prayer, weekly or monthly confession, visits to a spiritual director, and the like. That such frameworks of practice run the risk of substituting for the Spirit goes without saying, at least for thinking types who may be tempted to make a fetish of order. But for feeling types regularity may represent a special call from God, who is a God of freedom but no champion of chaos. God may visit us without notice, to be sure, but we are required to deal with God as with a respected friend. By creating an orderly context for prayer we manifest the good will and desire which God will bless.

Order in the Common Life

This same attention to order and structure has traditionally found communal expression too. We think here of the *rules and customs* of religious communities, third orders, and other associations, especially those created by the great founders, Basil, Benedict, Augustine, Ignatius, and Teresa, among others. The saints, beyond all other Christians, have appreciated that rules and structures are no subsitute for love. But they also realized that, especially as charismatic origins gave way to inevitable routinization, the initial vision needed to be embodied in word, covenant, discipline, and organization, if it were not to fade.

Canon Law and the Institutional Church

Beyond specific ways of life, the Church as a whole also needed law and other juridical structures and processes to promote the common good and safeguard the rights of individuals and groups. As we shall see in our final chapter, justice is not outside of love but is one of the forms that love takes. We may and must be critical of ecclesiastical law, traditional or newly enacted, when it does not reflect the spirit of the Gospel or when it oppresses something deep within our humanity. But the sinfulness that makes its way into law and into the exercise of authority should not trap us into the folly of believing that we Christians can do without law and structure in relating to one another. The Christian attitude toward Church law is prefigured in the attitude of the psalmists in Psalms 1,

19, and 119. For them the law of the Lord is not viewed as a restriction of freedom but as its enhancement. "Having sought your precepts, I shall walk in all freedom" (Ps 119:45). Good law frees us from fear of transgression by providing us with guidance for following God's will. "Your word is a lamp to my feet, a light on my path" (Ps 119:105). It is true, as St. Thomas Aquinas has said (*Summa Theologica* I-II, q. 106, a. 1), that the principal law of the new covenant is the interior grace of the Holy Spirit written in our hearts, and that all merely human and external regulations have been radically relativized by the gift of the Spirit. Nevertheless, the law of the Church shares in the quality of sacramentality which belongs to the Church as a whole. It is, and is meant to be, a sign of the paschal mystery. Far from making Christians submissive in the pejorative sense which we shall shortly explain, such reverence for ecclesiastical law should evoke our assertiveness, and sometimes even our anger, when we meet laws or other exercises of authority which are unworthy of the body of Christ and which obscure its beauty.

The Institutional Church

Closely linked with issues of Church law is the broader question of the institutional and hierarchical character of the Church. Today, as often in the past, the tension between the charismatic and institutional aspects of the Church's life comes in for a great deal of debate. Without getting involved in the intricacies of that discussion, we wish only to note a link with the relationships of the thinking and feeling functions. Recognition of the important role of the former will dispose us to esteem the institutional features of the Church's life. The institution, as compared with the group, manifests to a high degree those qualities which we have associated with thinking. It tends to be cool, distant, impersonal, impartial, and so forth. Without oversimplifying, we may say that the tension between feeling and thinking in the growth of human beings largely corresponds to and interacts with the tension between charismatic and institutional features in the life of the Church. The feeling function, we shall see, is the function of intimacy, and it is within small groups of friends or members of the same family or basic community that the warmth of intimacy is experienced. But the Church, as the body of Christ in history, is not a small group or even a conglomeration of small groups. In its worldwide, perennial character it is a public and societal institution which must be rugged, assertive, objective, even at times impersonal. It is a mistake to expect intimacy from any human institution. All we can reasonably ask is that it respect our need for intimacy, which will be satisfied not by the institution but by life in the group. If Christians need to be energized in their faith by interpersonal exchange with others in face-to-face relationship, they also need to be able, with the very warmth they receive from such intimacy, to go forth into the larger Church and to stand in solidarity with the millions of other members of the Church whom they will never meet in this life. As we said in speaking of Church law, such an acceptance of the institutional character of the Church does not imply submissiveness to the evils of institutionalism. It is, in fact, by developing thinking behavior that Christians energized by the intimacy of small groups will be able to provide for the Church fitting structures and institutions.

Mission for Justice

This positive appreciation of the role of structures and institutions takes on even greater importance when we reflect on the Church's mission and ministry for justice in today's world. What is it that distinguishes that mission today from other eras? It is primarily that, along with the traditional works of mercy, the work of justice is now seen as included in Jesus' command to evangelize the nations. But together with this insistence on justice as well as mercy goes the realization, gained largely from the insights of sociology and other anthropological disciplines, that persons and their relationships are greatly affected by the kind of social environments they build for themselves or permit others to impose on them. Even more, structures and institutions are now seen to be constitutive of the human reality, no less than individual persons and their relationships. When people act and interact over a period of time, within family or parish, in the world of work or education or health or leisure, the creation of such frameworks is inevitable. The Christian concern is that they be vehicles of grace, not instruments of sin, that they serve to make us more human, not less human. They will enhance or disfigure God's image in us, and will themselves visibly embody Godlikeness or unlikeness.

But while all four of the functions are capable of embodiment in structures and institutions, there is a special affinity with the thinking function present in this aspect of life, as we have noted in speaking of the institutional Church. This affinity contributes to making justice the appropriate virtue to correlate with the thinking function. A good part of education for justice today, then, needs to consist in the development of the thinking function in individuals, in their relationships and group processes, and in the way they organize themselves for action in the world. The transformation of social structures thus becomes organically or artistically one with the conversion of persons and of personal relationships through the Gospel.

Liturgical Celebration

Counterpointing the Church's engagement in mission and ministry is its life of corporate worship. In the sacramental liturgy in general and the celebration of the Eucharist in particular we find yet one more area where it is important to draw upon the gift of thinking. We speak commonly of the sacramental system, and the term is appropriate. Previously we observed that *the word* relates especially to the thinking function. What is characteristic of the sacramental word is that it is embodied in ritual gesture, frequently together with the employ of earthly material—water, bread and wine, oil. The sacramental rite both expresses and confers *meaning* in key human experiences: birth, marriage, reconciliation, sickness, and the like. A well ordered celebration of the Eucharist or

any sacrament will permit past, future, and present to energize the celebration, by way of *anamnesis, maranatha* (Come,
Lord), and real presence. Particularly in the Mass the Christian
community hears and speaks a word about all three dimensions of time, as time is revelatory of eternity.

This linkage of the thinking function with liturgy and
worship as sacred structure can be pastorally enlightening. It
will caution us against the mistake in celebration of identifying
spontaneity with formlessness. A reverent celebrant of the
paschal mystery calls for a certain sense of sacred etiquette
and propriety. Otherwise our sacramental language will be
inherently contradictory. We will be proclaiming the new
order of creation even while yielding to the chaos which that
order has overcome. And we will be permitting the precious
energies which flow from remembrance, attentiveness, and
dreaming imagination to be dissipated and lost.

The Theological Exercise of Thinking

A final *locus* for communal thinking in the Church is
theology, which is faith exercising itself reflectively through
the word (*theo-logos*). However open a theology may be in its
journeying within the dark caverns of faith, eventually it has to
come to light, and to say "Yea, yea" and "Nay, nay." There is
an Amen, a firmness in faith, which theology is called to serve
(2 Cor 1:17-20). There is a difference between the stammering
articulation of meaning which is the best we humans can do in
speaking of God, and nonsensical babblings. Theology has to
draw on human reason and logic to enunciate, to distinguish,
to set limits, to define, and to establish cognitive structures for
the practice of Christian living.

Though all kinds of sound theology do this, not all do so in
the same fashion or to the same extent. One could probably
construct a typology of the historical forms of theology based
on the four functions (and perhaps also on introversion and
extraversion). We will not attempt that here. But we do want
to point to one great example of a theology strongly character-

ized by thinking in the Jungian sense. It is represented by Thomas Aquinas, and more generally by the medieval summas, disputed questions, scriptural commentaries, and the like. Readers seeking examples of the thinking function in a theological expression might want to study carefully a single question of Aquinas' *Summa Theologica,* or make an outline of the entire work, starting with the definitions and distinctions given by the Angelic Doctor at key points. Or they might wish to analyze the structure of his beautiful anthem, *O sacrum convivium* (O sacred banquet), which he composed for the office of Corpus Christi. They will find in it a limpid and calm, rational yet poetic, statement of the Church's faith regarding the Eucharist as a banquet relating us to past, present, and future. The riches of Christian doctrine which we owe to theologians like Aquinas are one further reminder of the importance of the thinking function for the whole life of the Church.

III. THE DEVELOPMENT OF THINKING

If the preceding pages have been effective in portraying the importance of the thinking function for the development of God's image, the question now becomes: How can I grow in the habitual exercise of this gift? Let us repeat what we have said in speaking of the development of sensing. All of us are capable of and responsible for developing this side of our humanity. But according to the typology we are following in this book, the primary period for such development will vary according to different personalities. Thinking will have its day, so to speak, in childhood, in adolescence, in young adulthood, or in later adulthood. Our remarks here will be directed especially to the last of these, that is, to those for whom thinking is the *least* preferred function, and in tension with their most preferred feeling. Somewhere about the age of thirty-five, such persons will experience what is perhaps the greatest challenge of their lives as far as growth is concerned. They will be asked to let go of their strength—the feeling function, to be described in the next chapter—in order to let their "shadow side" emerge and grow stronger. What can they do to assist the process?

Developing Assertiveness

The first and perhaps the most helpful thing they can do is to practice *assertiveness.* Helped by models, that is, by living or historical or fictitious persons who excel in it, and also by reflections like the present one, they are called to an asceticism of thinking behavior. But before we speak about the ladder of assertiveness, let us say a word about the twin obstacles to the ascent, namely immature and disordered fear and anger. Some people, especially those with a preference for feeling behavior, carry with them through life an excessive burden of anger and fear. The anger may be born of habitual submissiveness, which invariably produces resentment toward those who have imposed on us, as well as anger directed against ourselves for submitting. The fear develops from an excessive concern about our acceptance by others. One strategy which is *not* appropriate is to suppress or otherwise seek simply to get rid of these emotions. For one thing, fear and anger are gifts of God, given so that we may deal assertively with the threat of different kinds of evil. Fear is, as it were, our defensive platoon, to be employed when evil attacks. Anger enables us to take the offensive against evil. Both fear and anger are necessary ingredients of *courage.* Who has ever been courageous who was not first afraid? And who has ever had the stamina to carry the fight to the enemy without drawing on what the Scholastics called the "irascible appetite," that contentious and combative side of our humanity. Courage in turn is at the heart of *hope* which, unlike mere optimism, keeps its prow pointed toward the future in the face of contrary pressures from present reality. The strategy then must rather be one of letting the fear and anger be healed, liberated and transformed in the process of our becoming assertive. When that happens, then our very fear and anger become for us fresh sources of power and energy.

One does not become assertive overnight. There are stages in the ascent to assertiveness, as the following chart indicates. The two sets of arrows stand for what happens, respectively, to me and to another as I practice assertiveness interpersonally.

Assertiveness	↑	↑
Aggressiveness	↑	↓
Hostility	↓	↓
Submissiveness	↓	↑

Often the dominant feeler begins from a posture of *submissiveness,* that is, letting oneself be put down by others. Fear is working so strongly that one takes shelter in a cringing attitude. Take a minor but extreme example. I have just spent some hours making my room or my apartment as neat and beautiful as possible, and feel wonderful about the result. A friend drops in and casually deposits his dripping umbrella on my new rug. In my mood of submissiveness I don't utter a word but remain as pleasant as I can be, while inwardly I am churning. The thoughtless friend's arrow goes up and mine goes down.

Now submissiveness is *never* a better option. The best that can be said for it is that it may be the place from which I patiently have to start my climb toward assertiveness. The next rung up, therefore, is preferable, although it may not seem so—*hostility,* here in the sense of a devious retaliation which aims at hurting the other without running the risk of exposing myself. At this stage fear is less paralyzing—I do something—but my anger is not yet strong enough for assertive or even aggressive response. In the example given a hostile reaction might be that I still say nothing about the dripping umbrella on my clean rug but observe, "Haven't you put on some weight?" or I show little interest in what my guest is saying to the point of causing him discomfort. Hostility turns both arrows down—the other person is conscious of having been dealt a low blow without knowing why; and I am

conscious of having dealt it. Not a very mature form of thinking behavior, this is still better than submissiveness.

The third rung of the ladder is *aggressiveness*. Here fear
has diminished and anger has grown to the point where I
break loose into a somewhat violent reaction. I might say "Get
your damn umbrella off my clean rug" in such a way that my
visitor is ashamed, while I at least am happy about having had
the courage to speak up. Aggressiveness is an example of
overkill. A feeling person finds it so hard to confront someone
that it requires a "revving up" that frequently goes beyond
control. Still not the ideal response, this behavior is better than
being either submissive or hostile.

The truly assertive response, which often has to draw
upon imagination—and so here N can come to the aid of an
emerging T—makes both persons feel good. It is not only a
firm and free dealing with a difficult situation on my part, but
it invites the other person too to be assertive, thus evoking
genuine sorrow rather than compulsive guilt feelings. In our
scenario, for example, as I took the person's raincoat I might
say, "I'd appreciate it if you would leave your umbrella in the
vestibule, so that it won't drip on the new rug." Basically, both
of us can feel better, and the apology which my words elicit
from my friend will probably take its cue from my own freedom.

The point of assertiveness is not to have one's wishes
carried out more frequently but to express what I want to do
and to say, in a way which respects my own dignity and that of
others. Whether I choose to be silent or to speak in a given
instance, it will be on the basis of truth and right, not from
craven fear or disordered anger. Jesus before Pilate, choosing
first to be silent and then to speak, is our model (Jn 19:8–11).
Such behavior is close to that commended by the philosophy of
non-violent resistance to evil, as espoused by people like Gandhi, Martin Luther King, and Archbishop Helder Camara.
With such models, and with persevering practice, we need not
fear that charity will suffer in our human relationships. It is the
truly free and assertive person who is most able to yield a point
when the common good or the needs of the weak call for it.

While the principal *locus* of assertiveness is interpersonal relationships, its origins are in inner self-esteem and it has major fruits in societal life. Each of us can be cowed by forces within ourselves, feelings of fear, guilt, inferiority. We can also, in dealing with them, stop at the equivalent of hostile or aggressive reactions, which fall short of fully honoring God's image. If such is our temptation, we need through alertness and constant practice to deal assertively with the adversary within ourselves. Societally, it is clear that social customs can build submissiveness, hostility, and aggressiveness into the assumptions from which people in different groupings operate. Think of the culturally induced submissiveness of black people in the United States and in South Africa, and of comparable racial or ethnic attitudes elsewhere; or the structures, subtle or blatant, which have told women that they are inferior. Assertiveness, then, is a thinking behavior which needs to be exercised consistently in all three dimensions of life.

Power Through the Word

Another way in which we may develop thinking behavior is through the conscious cultivation of both oral and written speech. The word, we have seen, brings truth, clarity, and order to life. In this it contrasts with emotion, which tends to have a fluid, even amorphous character. A person developing thinking would do well to build the habit of precise objective thought and speech, to get acquainted with the definitions of things, and even to take pleasure in the nuances of meaning and connotations to be found in synonyms or similar words. Scrabble and crossword puzzles might be especially suitable forms of recreation for those who need to develop their thinking.

Dominant feelers can also develop their thinking side by cultivating a relationship with someone who embodies this function in a notable way. In this way the dominant feeler can freely express opinions and criticisms about the thinking friend without the latter taking it personally as a feeling friend might do. Who that person is to be is often not left to our choice. We may be married to him or her. Feeling parents may even find themselves having to relate to thinking children, and if the trial on both sides can be great, so can the opportunity. Or we may, with little choice, belong to the same religious community or else work side by side with a dominant thinker. But it is also possible to choose a qualified man or woman with thinking characteristics as a spiritual director or as a study partner. In any case, with the insights and incentives gained from the present chapter, such an association can provide a favorable environment for growth. There will be pain of course, both the pain of having to deal with the other's contrasting way of dealing with life, and the humiliating pain of tolerating my own faltering steps in a behavior in which I am not at my best. But the reward is great—the precious pearl of wholeness in growth toward Godlikeness.

Justice Ministries

An excellent context for growth is involvement in a project or ministry whose success requires thinking as a primary quality. We have in mind here especially efforts to promote justice in the world or in the Church by effecting change in structures, policy, organization, and the like. Such endeavors call for hard-nosed and hard-headed gifts, coolness in conflict situations, tolerance of others, hard work without comforting results, mastery of complexity, and the like. Today the mission of justice appears to attract a good many feeling types. This might appear strange until we notice that this call often comes about mid-life, when thinking is spontaneously looking to assert itself in the lives of such personalities. If what we have said about assertiveness is sound, we would expect that initially the efforts of feeling types to wrestle with intractable structures will not be very adept, and will even court a certain violence of disposition. Some who have been previously unquestioning and submissive with respect to the structures of the Church or of civil society will rather suddenly become harsh zealots. But, with cool perseverance and by relativizing the feeling expectations which they brought initially to the ministry of promoting justice, such persons can both grow personally and contribute to the development of society. In any case, some dominant feelers whose ministry has been mostly compassionate service of needs may feel the call about mid-life to change to a more administrative or organizational type of work, or at least to balance their high-feeling ministry with some apostolic or leisure activities which require them to stretch their thinking capacity.

Experience of the Cross

Whether in the process of changing ministry or in some other way, dominant feelers will typically be invited in a distinctive way into the mystery of the cross about mid-life. What we said in the preceding chapter about crucifixion and the "mystical" function has a special application here. Dominant feelers come to their middle thirties with the ingrained assumption that the heart, intimacy, the cherishing of values, are what life is all about. They will ordinarily have developed habits and skills enabling them to deal with life, particularly with relationships, from this inner core of their strength. But now all this may begin to be called into question, not only by life outside of themselves, which refuses to be reduced to an affair of the heart, but by a secret voice from within, a side of their own personality to which they would rather not listen. But what we said in the preceding chapter about dominant intuiters developing sensing is to be said here about dominant feelers developing thinking. The wholeness and holiness which they seek can be found only in the mystery of the cross, in the letting go of strength and acceptance of weakness. They are being called to a mystical experience of God by taking the risk of cultivating their shadow side. The exercise of thinking in the various forms which we have described is the peculiar form of foolishness, littleness, and powerlessness, to which Christ calls them. It puts the dominant feelers in touch with how much their good behavior has been motivated by the effort to please. Growth in assertiveness will bring a purer intention and less dependence on whether people are pleased or not. Thus our willingness to be weak, that is, to let go of our preferred feeling so that our undeveloped thinking may have a chance to grow, will bring a new and clearly God-given strength. The knowledge that Jesus himself embodied in quintessential fashion the qualities of this aspect of God's image will give them the courage and stamina to persevere in developing those qualities within themselves. And they will be enormously helped through the exercise of thinking prayer.

Thinking Prayer for Individuals

The life of prayer and worship is an obvious place where growth in thinking can and should happen. Here again we will follow the familiar pattern of solitude or individual prayer, friendship or group prayer, and society or liturgical prayer. In general the forms of prayer which correspond to the thinking function will be forms which employ the gifts of the rational and pragmatic mind. Reflection on doctrinal truth, on moral principles, on the order and disorder of one's life, are some examples. So also, as we have indicated, is the traditional examination of conscience, especially when it is carried out with an accent on the commandments, on one's duties, and on a few good resolutions.

Devout reading of the word of Scripture or of other classical texts is another excellent exercise of solitary thinking prayer. The movement from the objective, inspired word to one's inner, graced word can be a source of strength and constancy for those who practice it perseveringly. This kind of prayer is, as it were, a spiritual chewing of the rich fare of the table of the word, with a view to deeper savoring.

It is possible that people with a strong feeling preference may experience difficulty not only in praying in these ways, but even in believing that such exercises are prayer at all. At best they may be seen as ways of disposing or purifying us for "real prayer," which is identified with the movements of the heart. Such a view—unjust to thinking prayer—has been unwittingly fed by books on prayer in recent decades. Overreacting to the previous excessive accent on method and concept in prayer, some spiritual writing sets too sharp a contrast between head and heart in our relationship with God. But, as in our relationship with humans, meeting God in the clarity of the word or the strength of principle is just as worthy of being termed union with God as a meeting in the tender movements of the heart.

We may here recall what has been said about the value of keeping a journal. There are, of course, many genres of journal discourse, as those familiar with the "Intensive Journal" process of Ira Progoff will know. We might say that in such a journal all four functions find expression, and that the special value of the *written* medium is that each of the other functions is integrated with the thinking function, whose special province is the word. There are, too, some kinds of journal keeping, for example the recording of resolutions, of plans of life, or of one's own "first principle and foundation" which are more distinctively expressions of the thinking function and serve more directly for its development.

Some Communal Forms

When people pray together, they need to know how to accommodate themselves to the needs and the desires of one another. What an irony, to say the least, when common worship and prayer, intended to bind Christians together, have the opposite effect because of disagreement over its form. The painful accommodation that is asked of dominant feelers in this regard—especially if intuiting is their auxiliary function—is to be willing to enter fully into forms of group prayer which are fixed and structured. The divine office in common is a good example. It does not afford a group much of an opportunity to exercise warm intimacy or the expression of personal feeling. It requires a certain letting go of the first person singular as we face not toward others but with them toward the transcendent God. But whatever the difficulty in esteeming it, a steady effort to do so will reward those who need it most.

Liturgical Prayer

So far as societal prayer is concerned, we have already indicated that it is verified especially in liturgical worship. Even more than a communal recitation of the office in a small group, participation in a large-scale Eucharistic liturgy, especially when it is celebrated with ritual distance, exactness, and objectivity, makes special demands on those who have come to associate prayer and celebration too exclusively with intense and overt emotions. But the kind of celebration that takes place at St. Peter's in Rome, or in large traditional monasteries, has its own power to energize Christian faith. Even the use of Latin or some other unfamiliar language can add to the value of such public prayer. In transcending some of the familiar preferences deriving from age, sex, national and ethnic traditions, and personality, with practice we can all be helped by thinking prayer to find more deeply the transcendent majesty of God.

EXERCISES

A. *For the individual:*
1. Take the "Principle and Foundation" of *The Spiritual Exercises* of St. Ignatius Loyola. First try to appreciate its simple logic. Then ask: What scriptural passages come to mind? Reflect on them. Then apply the logic to your own life, using your own words to describe the goal of your life and the helps and hindrances which assist or hinder the attainment of the goal. Then ask in general where there is disorder in your use of the helps and subjection to the hindrances. In what ways are you not yet interiorly free? Ask God to help you to make an overall plan for growing in this freedom. Finally, make a few key resolutions touching some concrete strategies for carrying out the plan.

2. First reflect on a scriptural passage in which someone is articulating a creed or charter of life, e.g., Matthew 5:1–12; Philippians 3:1–16. Then begin to write out *a set of basic principles* by which you wish to live, e.g., "Every human being I meet is worthy of my respect." "When I come into conflict with the culture in which I live, obedience to God is paramount." Review such a personal creed periodically.

3. Draw up *a plan of life* for yourself, including in it a daily and weekly schedule of prayer, reading, provisions for work and leisure, the use of money, etc.

4. Take one of the key footnotes of the one-volume Jerusalem Bible or a major term in a theological dictionary of the Bible, e.g., covenant, light, truth. After reflecting on and relating the many texts given, draw up a short statement on the theme as you have come to find meaning in it for your life.

5. Take a psalm, major passage, or whole book of the Bible, e.g., the Letter to the Ephesians. With the help of the Jerusalem Bible footnotes or some commentary, seek a better understanding of God's word, attending to the structure of the work, cultural setting, precise meaning of terms, etc. If you are so drawn, take notes and write out your own summary, paraphrase, or reflection.

B. *For groups:*

1. With adequate preparation and careful observance of directives, including pauses, etc., recite the Divine Office or "Prayer of Christians" together over a period of time. Occasionally reflect together about the quality and fruit of such common prayer, and about how it can be improved.

2. With the help of a priest, plan and celebrate *small Eucharistic liturgies* that are marked with the characteristics which this chapter has attributed to thinking prayer and worship. Reflect on the quality and fruitfulness of these celebrations.

3. Together assist at *a larger Eucharistic celebration* or vespers in a monastery or church where the services are well conducted. Reflect on the experience.

SCRIPTURE REFERENCES

1. Psalms

1, 19, 119: All three of these psalms celebrate the beauty of God's law and of its observance.

93—100: These are mostly psalms which acclaim the divine majesty.

104: A celebration of the divinely established order of creation.

105, 106, 107: Recitals of sacred history as guided by God's providence.

2. Genesis

1—3 The original order of creation; disobedience; just punishment.

32:23–32 Jacob wrestles with God.

35:1–15 Jacob at Bethel.

3. Exodus 3:1–20: The great theophany to Moses.

4. Job: The entire book, but especially chapters 38—39, where God's majesty and wisdom are revealed to Job.

5. Proverbs 8 and Wisdom 9: celebrations of divine wisdom in its ordering of the world.

6. Isaiah: The four servant songs (42:1–9; 49:1–6; 50:4–11; 52:13—53:12), especially for the interplay between assertiveness and gentleness.

7. Revelation 1—3: Christ in his majesty and stern judgment of the churches.

NOTES

1. Robert Bolt, *A Man for All Seasons* (New York: Random House, 1960), p. 132.

2. T.S. Eliot, *Murder in the Cathedral* (New York: Harcourt, Brace, 1935), p. 44.

CHAPTER 4
With a Joyful Heart

Feeling/Gratitude

There is something about the Emmaus story (Lk 24:13–35) which gives it a special power to move the hearts of Christians in every generation. So many of its details relate to aspects of the feeling function that some readers may wish to begin this chapter with Luke's words, not ours. It is filled with touches of intimacy, remembrance, and a poignant sadness surprised by the joy of a touching reunion.

A stranger on the road breaks into the bubble of gloom in which two heartbroken disciples have enclosed themselves for solace. At first he is gentle, simply inquiring into the reason for their distress. But after they have recounted the sad, sad story, he does what thinkers often do for feelers, though he does it by entering into the feeling mood, by recalling a familiar story. Feelingly, yet with a certain rationality, he provides a context, a structure, in which their little story finds a new and joyful meaning within the larger story, which they too really know and love, but which, in the turbulence of their grief, they had forgotten. As their hearts burn with the kindling of a new vision, they press closer, not wanting to part from this wonderful stranger who has befriended them. At eventide, he lets himself be drawn and shares with them the intimate experience of a meal. They *know* him in the breaking of bread, and that revelatory moment becomes the unforgettable story they bring back to the larger community—which of course has its own story to tell: "The Lord has risen and has appeared to Simon."

This chapter, we hope, will bring grateful joy to the hearts of readers. That is what the feeling function is all about: the human heart, that inner shrine of cherished values, the temple where goodness dwells, the abiding home of the many-sided heritage which nourishes every human being and binds us together as family, nation or Church. Whatever the physiology of memory, the heart is the place for the kind of remembrance and story which draws energy from the past. It is, most importantly, the organ of intimacy and interpersonal feeling, the place where we meet and hold those whom we can call friends and dear ones. The heart was the tabernacle where Mary kept her most precious memories for pondering (Lk 2:19, 51). And, wrote Pascal, it is the heart that has reasons of which the mind knows not.

In our journey of exploration of God's image in us, we have come, then, to the feeling function, symbolized by the heart. The development of this chapter will be the same as for the preceding ones. First, we will ponder the nature and characteristics of this function and see it embodied in one or two models. Second, we will examine some of the many ways in which the Gospel expresses and nurtures this side of our humanity. Gratitude, and the special kind of joy that flowers from grateful remembrance, is the virtue we choose here to highlight. And third, we will ask how we can grow, as individuals relating to one another in the context of society and culture, in becoming more like our feeling, remembering God.

I. THE FEELING FUNCTION

Let us begin by recalling the nature of the feeling function. It is, for Jung, a *judging* function, part of the psychic apparatus by which we respond to what life offers. We may be surprised that feeling is regarded as a rational function. But in Jungian terminology this means only that it is part of our *willed response to reality*. In this sense it is just as rational as thinking, and no less necessary for sound judgment and decision. In terms of the "transcendentals" of philosophy, it is a response based on what is *good,* i.e., on *value,* whereas the response of the thinking function is based on what is *true.*

Our previous characterization of thinking makes it easier for us to describe feeling, in its contrast and tension with thinking. Here are some terms pointing to the contrast:

Thinking is	*Feeling* is
tough-minded	tender
logical	personal
cool	warm
adversarial	harmonious
argumentative	agreeable
distant	intimate
wary	trustful
questioning	believing
frank	polite
concerned	compassionate
respectful	affirming
tolerant	sympathetic
authentic	supportive
assertive of truth (verum)	valuing good (bonum)

While all four of the functions are exercised interpersonally, the sphere of personal relationships is the "home turf" of feeling. Its primary standard in all things is: How will this affect persons—myself as well as others, particularly those I really care about? When a choice is to be made, feeling keeps present the question: What will be good—even best—for those affected by the decision? What will cause the least disharmony and pain in the group?

Feeling is the interpersonal function par excellence because it carries our human capacity and yearning for *intimacy*—being close to others, sharing life with them, and especially enjoying the sharing of feeling good. It is feeling, then, which constitutes the principal bond of *the group,* beginning with *the family,* which is the primary group. Here again it contrasts with thinking, which is the primary constituent of *the organization.* It was in the family that we all first experienced being human as an exercise of intimacy, being in close touch with others. Our mother's arms, in fact her womb, began our life with the "I-thou" of intimacy.

"Being in touch," by the way, is an important term and reality for the lifelong development of feeling. Touching, together with seeing and hearing, is the principal vehicle through which intimacy grows. This is one convenient place to comment on how, in our very constitution, the distinct functions have their own intimacy. The feeling function gets its start, so to speak, in the *excitation* of the senses, which experience pleasure when satisfied and pain when not. Because life brings privation as well as satisfaction, the infant soon comes to know both *fear* and *anger,* those important human ways of dealing with privation and threat. Often the crying child is experiencing both fear and anger together. When a familiar loved one is present to calm the infant, *security* and *trust* ensue, and the path is opened to the flower of feeling—*joy.* Because feeling follows some such pattern of development as this, strikingly different from the path of thinking, we might say that it has a language of its own—gesture and touch and glance more than word. When it does borrow the word from thinking, it shapes it to its own purpose. The somewhat incoherent sobbing of an eight-year old and the joyful song of a young man or woman at the first blossoming of romantic intimacy are examples of the kind of behavior especially dear to feeling.

Feeling is the function which carries our *values,* the basis on which we discriminate between good and evil. Such a judgment has a more embodied and less detached character than the judgment of right and wrong pronounced through the thinking function. This latter function works on the basis of clearly enunciated principles, whereas our underlying value-judgments are less susceptible of cogent logical formulation. They really stem from the moral heart as it has been shaped in and through exposure to love and to the goodness of persons who embody such values. Values, then, are a matter of heritage and tradition, and for that reason are probably harder to dislodge than cognitive principles of right and wrong.

This linkage of the feeling function with values handed on through the human processes of intimacy within specific traditions is effected through *remembrance*. Dominant feelers love to remember and seem moved, often to tears, by tender or painful reminiscences. One thing they model for the rest of us—though we all have had experience of it—is the power which the past has to energize us as we try to create a better future out of present reality. We shall have later occasions to return to this connection of feeling and remembrance. The principal vehicle for the exercise of such remembrance is *story*. And the primary place where it is important that good stories be told is the place of intimacy—the family, the group, the basic community. More of this too later.

We have deliberately begun by describing the feeling *function*, not any feeling *type*, because once again we wish to insist on the fact that we are speaking of a gift bestowed on every human being, along with the call to develop it. The beauty of *each* person is connected with what we call the heart. Such expressions as "the heart of the matter" and "putting our heart into it" indicate this dimension of integral human behavior. Life would be so much poorer, however qualified we were for logical thought, pleasure in the exercise of the sense life, and freedom to explore new and exciting worlds through imagination, if we were without the impulse or capacity to share such riches with loved ones. Deep down we all feel that a life that offered everything except intimacy would in reality offer nothing worth living for. Holiness in an individual can inspire us, but it is the experience of intimacy—especially when we ourselves are within the circle of affection—which is the greatest joy that life can offer. It is this remembering joy, which gives thanks for the graciousness which has bestowed on us our capacity for intimacy and the sharing of cherished values, that represents the full flowering of the feeling function. Few lines express this as well as the opening burst of Mary's Magnificat: "My soul proclaims the greatness of the Lord, and my spirit exults in God my savior" (Lk 1:46).

Feeling Types

Those whom by a kind of shorthand we call "dominant feelers" are individuals who in childhood have spontaneously favored the kinds of behavior we have just been describing. And into adolescence and adulthood, even though they will be engaging in "gear shifts" in order to let other sides of their personality emerge, their primary preference will continue to be behavior that is concerned with persons and their welfare, and with the importance of keeping basic values present in the individual and communal decisions of life. They are "people-persons" and tend to view other persons and their actions in a subjective way. Open to and in need of intimacy, they are particularly vulnerable to praise or blame, whether it comes from others or from themselves. They are generally conscientious and willing—sometimes too willing—to accept responsibility for things going well or badly in a group. They are especially liable to feelings of guilt when there is dissension or when someone else feels offended. This sensitivity to whether people are content or not can lead them to conform to what others expect of them, at least up to the point at which their own basic values are being challenged. At this point they will protest. Their own personal suffering will often come either from being with others who are suffering without the possibility of relief, or from the tension of trying to satisfy conflicting demands, particularly from persons whom they care about or fear.

As frequently throughout this book, let us pause to recall that these statements, while generally true, must yield to the unique reality of each individual. Two dominant feelers may be very different from each other. They may have quite diverse personal histories, for example, and so the fear and anger, the joy and delight which play a great part in their lives may be handled by them in different ways. Also, it will make a difference whether the dominant feeler is supported by sensing or by intuiting as auxiliary function. Not only in such matters as job preference but in basic ways of relating to other people, the combination of dominant and auxiliary functions needs to be considered in describing the inclinations and preferences of different personalities.

Another significant basis of difference will be the introverted or extraverted character of the dominant feeling. Sometimes sparks can fly not only between dominant feelers and dominant thinkers in a group but also between two dominant feelers of opposite attitudes. The introverted feeler looks within for harmony, and may actually appear cold to outsiders, because the warmth of feeling is being directed inward. Something similar is true with respect to the introverted feeler's loyalty to values. It will generally be intensely cultivated within and may reveal itself with passion only when the threat to that loyalty has reached a certain level of seriousness, provoking an atypical emotional outburst. Such outbursts are also possible in the same circumstances for extraverted feelers. What is often expressing itself in that case is undeveloped thinking. The person whose feeling function is extraverted spontaneously likes to be an agent of social harmony, a bridge over troubled waters, and is commonly a very successful host or hostess. This extraverted feeling type generally has a good "feel" for what climates of feeling are prevalent in a group, for example at a meeting, and for what steps are needed to move climates from conflictual to consensual. *Tact*, a word derived from the Latin word for touching, and *timing*, an instinctive sense for the right moment to speak or not, are important ingredients of their leadership qualities. They will often be leaders in promoting values, especially humanitarian ones, in society.

Whatever differences may exist among dominant feelers, there remains a communality which justifies talking about them as a generic type. Our actual experience in our R/W and in counseling situations, as well as in day to day dealings with people of this type, convinces us that they are excellent models of the virtues corresponding to the feeling function. The following scenario may clarify by example the operation of the feeling function.

A Scenario

Jerry, thirty-seven, a writer and the father of four children, has always felt a deep love and affection for his wife, Joan, thirty-five, and cared for his children with warmth and compassion. Those who work with him, however, have never gotten through his reserve. They find him practical, dependable, open-minded, flexible, and dedicated to his values, but somewhat aloof. His relationship with his wife has, with the passage of years, changed in a way which has required mutual patience. As the children began to grow he was often hurt by Joan's rather confrontational questioning of some of his decisions which she thought were too easy on the children and too costly to himself; she suggested that he be more objective, sacrifice himself less, and expect more from them. At such times the gentleness that had first attracted her to him before their marriage came across to her as weakness. He in turn, who had admired her cool and collected objectivity in the face of trauma, now tended to see her behavior toward the children as being cold and unfeeling.

One of Jerry's special gifts has always been his ability to notice what needs to be taken care of, whether it be house repairs, incipient car problems, or financial savings. Joan at times has teased him, saying that he could even notice the grass growing. More seriously, she can be annoyed by his precision and his flawless memory of events which frequently are to her advantage to forget. She has had reason to be grateful for his power of observation, as on the occasion when he noticed from the yard that she was beginning to drive to church with a plant on top of the car.

Very recently, this couple has seemed almost to exchange

their behavioral preferences. A few months ago Jerry discovered that doing the monthly accounts was no longer his "thing." He found himself becoming distracted, disinterested, even inaccurate. Somewhat to the surprise of both, Joan readily accepted his proposal that she handle this chore and, more surprising still, has been enjoying it.

Jerry's approach to the children has also been changing in recent months, coming around to what Joan had wished for so often in the past. He is "laying down the law" to the children, insisting that they take more responsibility and assume some of the tasks which previously he himself had performed. But Joan is having a difficult time because her husband is employing the same behavior toward her, with a logic which she cannot fault, but with more harshness than she feels warranted. Her feelings in fact were rather hurt a few weeks ago by his immediate agreement with her suggestion that she might get a job in order to help the financial picture. Somewhat out of touch with her own emotions, she did not understand her own hurt at his ready agreement, since it was she, after all, who had made the proposal. Quite different was her reaction a year ago when Jerry hinted, in what she felt was a rather hostile manner, that with only one wage earner in the family their savings were diminishing. On that occasion she would have preferred that he come right out and suggest that she go back to work. But now that she has picked up his hint, she finds his instant cool agreement rather insensitive.

Jerry's preferences indicate that he functions as an ISFP=FSNT/*IEIE,* and Joan's reveals a behavioral pattern of ENTJ=TNSF/*EIEI.* When they first met, Jerry was attracted to Joan's ability as a dominant thinker to stand up for herself and to be her own person. Joan in turn found Jerry's dominant feeling tender and warm after she had gotten behind the sensing exterior. Having intuition as an auxiliary, Joan enjoyed planning and she soon found that Jerry's auxiliary sensing helped to keep her in touch with practicalities and to carry out what she would otherwise have left as a merely dreamed-of possibility. As they learned more about each other, Jerry came to find it hard to handle Joan's thinking and also to deal with the children according to her way of logic and objectivity. At times when his feelings moved him to tears over some personal problem, she on her side did not quite know how to cope with his emotions, believing that they made little sense and interfered with reaching a reasonable decision. Her secret wish was that he would stand up for himself and face problems more objectively.

As the couple developed their respective third functions after the age of twenty—Jerry his introverted intuiting and Joan her extraverted sensing—each was in effect turning to the auxiliary function of the other and developing it in the same attitude as the spouse. This explains the surprising ease with which the doing of the monthly accounts was transferred from Jerry to Joan, who was no less amused by his new distaste for the task than amazed at her own developing zest for it.

It was at about the age of thirty-five that Jerry began to develop his shadow side, thinking, and Joan her shadow side, feeling. More susceptible to hurt during this period of passage, and feeling strangely vulnerable and sensitive, she found his growing and still immature and at times coldly logical thinking difficult to accept. Before Jerry in his turn was adept at handling the exercise of his thinking function he began to rebel against his feelings of submission. Unable as yet to be assertive, he managed only to express hostility, his indirect way of telling Joan that in all fairness she should go back to work. Growing in his struggle against submission, he did manage to tell the children that they must stop imposing on him, but he did this in a somewhat aggressive manner. And Joan, on her side, was more susceptible to hurt in her struggle to develop her feelings. And so, as this husband grew in his ability to be assertive without hostility or aggression, his wife was growing in her ability to feel without excessive sensitivity. Together, despite their experience of suffering, they were developing both tenderness and respect for each other in their shared development toward wholeness.

While Jerry, as the dominant feeler, is the principal protagonist of the scenario, we have deliberately chosen to portray his relationship in the most intimate of life's relationships with a wife whose personality is as opposite from his as can be. Once again we see that each function, whether dominant or inferior or whatever, exists not abstractly but within a concrete personality relating to other similar and dissimilar personalitites. The following schema sums up the personality structure of this relationship.

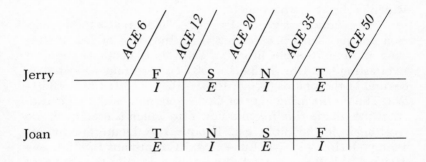

II. THE GOSPEL OF GRATEFUL JOY

What does the Gospel, whose values shape the lives of Christians, have to say about the feeling side of our humanity? In what way has God through the mission of Jesus Christ and of the Spirit come to meet our humanity in its psychic structure and processes? By now readers are more or less in a position to anticipate our approach. They may even wish to consult their own understanding of Scripture and tradition first, and then make use of the following pages to confirm, complement, or challenge what they themselves have already found. We will be following the same sequence as in the chapters on sensing and thinking.

The Goodness of God

It needs no great persuasion to convince Christians that the feeling function reflects the goodness, tenderness, mercy, and proclivity for intimacy of God. At least we do not need to be persuaded of this as an objective affirmation. There is all too much evidence, however, that even deeply dedicated Christians who spend their lives in God's service are often reluctant to accept the divine call to intimacy and to total trust in God's benevolence. It is never out of place, then, to remind ourselves that God exercises in transcendent fashion and with infinite perfection those qualities which we have subsumed under the feeling function. Let us point toward some biblical themes which orchestrate this belief.

"Yes, Yahweh is good" (Ps 100:5). So deep was this conviction among God's people that from the time of David they sang in their temple liturgy: "Yahweh is good—his love is everlasting" (1 Chr 16:34; Jer 33:11), a refrain repeated in several of the psalms (100:5; 106:1; 107:1; 118:1; 130:7; 136:1– 26). The *enduring* quality of God's goodness and love constitutes the divine *fidelity,* another term which is used over and over again in the Bible, e.g., Exodus 34:6; Deuteronomy 7:9; Psalm 89; Hosea 11:7–9; Luke 1:54; 1 Corinthians 1:9; Hebrews 10:23; 11:11. Because God's fidelity is rooted in the covenant with the chosen people, its firmness is guaranteed by the *promise* to be always with the people. It is at this point, perhaps, where the *word* of promise is appealed to, that fidelity is seen to have an affinity with both thinking and feeling functions. With the latter it shares the qualities of intimacy, commitment to personal values, goodness, and a felt love for the partner in covenant. But the pledged and irrevocable word gives to fidelity firmness, truth, and authenticity, along with a kind of binding public ratification, all of which enable it to be the solid foundation for an absolute hope and a sacred responsibility. When the people are in special need of God's help, their characteristic prayer is that God remember the promise of fidelity made once for all, as well as the mighty deeds done in times past for their ancestors, e.g., Psalms 44:1– 8; 60:6; 77:1–20; 89:49; Isaiah 63:11–19; Micah 7:18–20. God is thus revealed as one who will not forget, who is constitutionally not capable of forgetting the word pledged in covenant to this people, e.g. Isaiah 43:1–7; 49:14–17; 54:4–10; Hosea 11:7–

9. We might almost say that in the biblical view the divine essence is constituted by loving and faithful remembrance.

What is celebrated even more, perhaps, because it is even more revelatory of what God is like, is the divine mercy and *compassion*. God is always faithful; not so the people. Were God only a thinking God, that might well be the end of the affair. God would have every juridical ground, so to speak, simply to break off with this faithless people. There is, in fact, a partial tradition reflected in the Bible that God will keep the covenant only on condition that the people observe its part. Were this to be the decisive position, it would mean, we might say, that in God thinking had triumphed over feeling. But especially as the divine self-revelation comes to a peak in the incarnation, death and resurrection of God's own Son, it becomes manifest that the divine commitment to the people— now seen clearly to be the whole of humanity in all ages—is absolutely irrevocable. This does not mean that God has ceased to be a thinking God who judges justly and punishes sin. In both the Old and the New Testament it is clear that conniving with or simply condoning moral evil would be unfaithful to the very nature of God. But what happens is that the motif of justice becomes progressively integrated with the theme of mercy and compassion. Nowhere does this truth find more eloquent expression than in the climax of Paul's pondering in his Letter to the Romans of the mystery of the infidelity of Jews and Gentiles. He ends the three powerful chapters, six to nine, with an acclamation of the triumph of God's fidelity: "God has [with absolute justice] imprisoned all men in their own disobedience only to show mercy to all of mankind" (Rom 11:32). Universal compassion, unlimited mercy, Paul is saying, is the last word of all, revealing the innermost depths of the God of Jesus Christ.

Thus the chain of feeling themes is forged: goodness, fidelity, remembrance, compassion—and all within the circle of *intimacy*. The remarkable thing is that, though the covenant is made with a whole people, and eventually with all the peoples of the earth, it is from beginning to end a covenant characterized by intimacy. We humans are capable of intimacy with just a few, or with several, even though as life goes on we can enlarge the circle of those who participate in varying measure in our deeper relationships. But God's capacity for intimacy is without limit. And so we find the Bible using not only societal, thinking metaphors—ruler, judge, king—to speak of the divine relationship with the people, but also metaphors of intimacy. God is designated as a tender *shepherd*, e.g., Psalm 23; Ezekiel 34; Luke 15:4–7; John 10:14–18. Though the relationship of *father* is infrequently mentioned in the Old Testament, e.g., 2 Samuel 7:13; Psalm 89:30–33, it is at the heart of Jesus' revelation of the one whom he addresses familiarly as *Abba*, and who he assures us is our tender and compassionate father too, e.g., Matthew 5:48; 6:1. 4. 6. 9. 14. 18; John 14:7. 21. 23; 16:23. 27; 20:17; Romans 8:14–17; Galatians 4:6–7. Yahweh is also portrayed with the qualities of a loving mother of the people, particularly when there is question of expressing that mother's compassion, e.g., Isaiah 49:14–15; 66:13; Luke 13:34. God is depicted as a bridegroom who takes Israel for his bride and remains a faithful husband to her despite her repeated infidelity, e.g., Psalm 45; Song of Songs; Hosea. Elsewhere the image is of God as a beautiful woman embodying wisdom and drawing humans away from the seductions of folly, e.g., Proverbs 8:1–21; 9:1–18; Wisdom 6–9; see John 7:38–39.

In bringing to a close this reflection on God as model of feeling, we call attention to what the New Testament and Christian tradition tell us about the inner life of God. It is especially the Fourth Gospel which makes it clear that the God who has come to offer sinful humans divine intimacy has not come for the sake of assuaging any divine loneliness. On the contrary, God wants to share the eternal intimacy and communion which is the very marrow of divinity. Jesus with utter familiarity addresses himself to his *Abba* (best rendered by such endearing terms as "daddy") as he speaks of "that glory which I had with you before the world was" (Jn 17:5). Our Christian faith, as a Trinitarian faith, speaks to us of the intimate knowledge and love of Father, Son and Spirit which *is* life eternal. It is *this* God, infinite in intimacy, in whose image humans are created, and by that very fact called to intimacy with God and with one another.

The Feeling Image of God

When we turn to reflect on God's image in the feeling side of our humanity, our design is once again to marvel at how wonderfully we are made, how richly endowed for life in solitude, friendship, and society. Let us begin with the capacity of each person for intimacy and with the special beauty found in such relationships. Such a reflection will help us to see the inseparability of the three dimensions of life symbolized by Thoreau's three chairs.

Readers who have kept abreast of spiritual literature in the past few decades, especially as it has been influenced by psychology and psychiatry, will already have been exposed to the conviction that for us humans *to be* is *to be with*. Life is constitutively interpersonal, interdependent, dialogal. Studies of infant and even fetal life, for example, show conclusively that the newborn infant is vastly more dependent on parents and family than any other animal species. Other studies suggest that physical and psychic health, and even life itself, is contingent on the quality of intimacy which we enjoy. The lonely, the isolated, especially among the very young and the very old, often die, almost literally, of broken hearts.

"It is not good," God said at the beginning, "that the man should be alone" (Gen 2:18). We have already seen that some theologians interpret Genesis 1:27 as implying that God's image is primarily found in relationship, especially that of man and woman. In any case this intimate relationship constitutes the basis on which marriage, family, society, and history are built. Small wonder that it became in the Bible the primary symbol of intimacy between God and the chosen people, Christ and the Church. What we suggest right now is that readers pause to be in touch reflectively with this aspect of their own human experience. Married or not, each of us has felt the desire for intimacy, and its presence or absence in our life. We know what energies, in the form of light, joy, healing, and hope, are derived from sharing life with others in family, group, community, or common ministry. "How good, how delightful it is," we sing with the psalmist, "for all to live together like brothers and sisters" (Ps 133:1). Surely, the call to develop God's image has as one of its most beautiful aspects this potential for ever growing intimacy.

Such an endowment means, as the title of a popular book some years ago indicated, that each of us is "free to be faithful." The call to intimacy, we may say, is a call to a vowed existence. Hannah Arendt has noted, in *The Human Condition,* that the future of humanity is contingent on our being able to depend on people's fidelity to their promises.[1] Once the value of promise and fidelity is eroded in any society, that society is in deep trouble. The radical bond of trust, both interpersonal and societal, keeps us together in the face of adversity. And the more impersonal, contractual, and institutional connections of our public life depend in the long run on something deeper than merely legal obligations. They depend on the more personal commitments which bind friend to friend, neighbor to neighbor, and on the mutual recognition, even among strangers and adversaries, that ours is a common humanity. The freedom to be faithful, then, is another aspect of God's feeling image in us which is worthy of our wonder and praise.

Both intimacy and loyalty are exercised by partners who share common values deriving from a common heritage. The special gift which makes this possible is *memory.* Intimate relationships are nourished most of all by remembrance, with the aid of stories, mementos, celebrations. These energize and often heal our various relationships, as well as deepen our commitment to the covenant which binds us. We have all experienced that friends, sweethearts, lovers, spouses, spontaneously seek to know ever more about the past history of the other, and even when they know certain features they never tire of hearing the stories over and over again. Families are more closely united when they celebrate Thanksgiving or Christmas dinner or a golden wedding anniversary. Even as we move out from the inner circle of intimacy to larger associations of an ethnic, national, or religious character, we are rejuvenated each time we celebrate the particular story which binds us, whether it be St. Patrick's Day, the Fourth of July, or the Easter Vigil.

All of this can give us a fresh and positive view of the place of *tradition* in our lives. As the traditional hymn has it, we need to "tell the old, old story" again and again. "Tell the next generation" was how the Jewish people in particular phrased this key principle of an historical identity which they maintained in the face of the corrosions of time and cultural change (see Dt 4:9–10).

Out of this kind of living from the past comes a form of energy which is aptly named as *joy* and *gratitude*. We can be joyful in the experience of present beauty as well as in the anticipation of a future good; but there is a joy, perhaps more primary, associated with the feeling function, and it takes the special form of gratitude. The Latin root of this word, from which also "grace" and "graciousness" are derived, has the sense of "that which pleases." When we remember the goodness shown and shared in the past by God and by other human beings, there comes a kind of *com-placency* (being pleased with) in the best sense of that term. When persons are strongly marked with gratitude and are thankful for the blessings of life, we need have no fear for their emotional health and stability. It is clear that they are being nourished and healed from their past history in a way which carries them buoyantly into the future.

These, then, are some of the facets of God's image in us which bear a close affinity with the feeling function as Jung describes it. The more we are in touch with this complexus of gifts, the better will we be able to deal with the negativities which blemish them as a result of sin.

Hurt Feeling

Let us return to the symbol of *the heart* as a focus for reflecting on sin's damage to the feeling image of God. Hardness of heart is a frequent image in Scripture for what we do to ourselves when we sin. There are a few striking passages where Yahweh is said to harden hearts, e.g., the heart of Pharaoh (Ex 4:21; 7:3; 9:12, etc.; see Rom 9:17–18), and the heart of the people so that they do not heed the prophetic call to conversion (Is 6:9–10; Mk 4:12; Jn 12:39–40; Acts 28:26–27). What is really being conveyed through such expressions is that not even our resistance to God is capable of frustrating the design of divine mercy; as the Portuguese proverb has it, God writes straight with crooked lines.

More commonly the responsibility for being hardhearted is put directly with sinful humans, e.g., Psalm 106; Isaiah 1:4; 5:1–7; Jeremiah 2; Hosea 4–13; Luke 13:34–35; 19:41–44; John 3:19. Jesus himself meets the effects of sin on the human heart not only in his enemies but even in his friends and disciples, at least in the form of a certain paralysis or lethargy which makes them less ready to believe the good news, the Gospel of unlimited trust in God, e.g., Luke 8:25; 9:41. He comes to a people bogged down in habits of unbelief, a certain numbness and insensitivity to human values, especially in the form of the oppressive burdens which people lay on themselves and on others in the name of piety.

This sickness of the heart is expressed in Scripture as *spiritual amnesia.* "You have *forgotten* the God who made and saved you; you have forgotten his mighty deeds, his clear proofs of love and fidelity." Such is the frequent reproach of forgetfulness addressed by the divine lover to the unfaithful spouse, e.g., Jeremiah 2:13; Isaiah 1:4; Hosea 2. Psalm 106 is a striking description of sacred history which counterpoints Israel's forgetting—"they forgot the God who had saved them"—with Yahweh's faithful remembering—"for their sake he remembered his covenant." The power of grateful remembrance is also distorted by sin into traditional*ism,* through the anxiety-ridden absolutizing of religious observances, e.g. Matthew 23:13–32.

This paralysis and decay of the gift of holy remembrance cuts the people off from the values which constitute their real tradition. They are no longer free to be faithful, but are condemned to continual or recurring infidelity. Many passages in the prophetic literature depict the self-inflicted plight of such a faithless people, e.g., Lamentations 1:1–22; Joel 1:2–12. And because this aspect of God's image is that which endowed us with our capacity for intimacy, its paralysis and wounding deprive the people of affection and the blessings of friendship. The ultimate perversion of intimacy, which profanes love's gestures into a commodity for barter, is sometimes portrayed in the starkest terms by the biblical description of God's people as a shameless harlot, e.g., Jeremiah 3:1–5; Ezekiel 16 and 23; Hosea 2:1–13. When Jesus told his enraged enemies that the prostitutes would enter the kingdom before them, was he implicitly setting the institutionalized sin of Pharisaism in this traditional context, the venal adultery of Yahweh's chosen bride (see Ez 16; Hos 1—2)? Few metaphors have the power of this one for expressing the disfigurement of the beauty of intimacy through infidelity and idolatry. In Christian history too this metaphor has often been invoked to call individuals, communities, and the whole Church to repentance.

Two further aspects of the paralysis of holy remembrance are of special importance, and they are closely linked. Our capacity for *gratitude*, with the special joy that it brings, is radically crippled by sin. This can sometimes take the form of our forgetting the source of our gifts and talents, and so of a proud attribution to ourselves of whatever good we have. "What do you have that you have not received as gift?" (1 Cor 4:7). Or else it can lead us to forget that we are gifted, and so can induce a grumbling or sad-faced acquiescence in mediocrity, as in the parable of the one who buried his talents (Lk 19:11–27).

Deprived of gratitude and joy, people will more likely be without true *compunction,* and hence without *compassion.*

These attitudes are closely linked to the lack of grateful joy. Real contrition for sin always coexists with a realization of being loved and gifted. The prodigal son comes to this simultaneity of sorrow and joy, gratitude and compunction, in the arms of his merciful father. Where gratitude is lacking, it is unlikely that genuine sorrow for sin will be present. And it is also likely that those who have not freely entered into the experience of God's mercy cannot be disposed to accept compassion from others or show it to them. All of these negative attitudes—ingratitude, the lack of true joy, the absence of compunction, the hardness of heart that holds back from showing and accepting mercy—are clustered about the wounding of the heart and the spiritual amnesia which that wounding effects in God's image.

The Wound of Memory in Our Day

If the Bible is rich in resources regarding the wounding of feeling, so is our contemporary world, especially through what psychology and the social sciences tell us about the dark side of ourselves. The neurotic and psychotic afflictions which can make life an agony for people are commonly related to the unhealthy functioning of conscious or unconscious memory. How many human beings, even from infancy, are incapable of dreaming a worthwhile future because they have found no past worthy of remembrance? And we are all too familiar with the way in which, within marriage and family, memory is frequently employed to drive spouses, children, or parents from intimacy to alienation. In the larger society there are the collective myths, stereotypes, and projections which erode the very possibility of understanding between hostile ethnic, national or ideological factions. The violence of places like Northern Ireland and Central America today finds abundant kindling wood in the hateful stories that one group recounts about the other. Carl Jung was deeply sensitive to the massive damage and danger which exist when whole peoples project their unacknowledged darkness onto other peoples. He saw this happening particularly in the relations of the capitalist

West and the communist East after World War II. Few would say that we are in a less dangerous predicament today, when mounting fears and angers from such projections have at their disposal frightful weapons of mass destruction.

Thus, in our day, in the lives of individuals, within their most intimate relationships, and in a world of massive violence and confrontation, we experience the tragic plight of wounded feeling. How shall our sick, paralyzed, and violent memories be healed? For Christians the basic recourse is to the tender heart of our remembering God, manifested in Christ Jesus.

Jesus, Healer of the Heart

The Gospel according to Luke offers the most appropriate perspective on the heart of Jesus and his ministry of healing broken hearts. Joy in God and gratitude for God's gifts fill this Gospel, e.g., 2:14; 5:26; 10:17; 13:17; 18:43; 19:37; 24:51f. To a special degree, too, it is a Gospel of intimacy. The three chapters of its infancy narrative portray in very moving terms how the domestic scene was drawn into the public processes of salvation history in the tidings brought to Mary and also to Zachary and Elizabeth. Prayer is intimacy with God, and Luke's is the Gospel which speaks most frequently of Jesus praying or showing us how to pray (3:21; 5:16; 6:12; 9:18, 28–29; 11:1–13; 18:1–14; 22:41). The themes of compassion and gentleness are prominent in Luke. "Luke, in Dante's phrase, is the *'scriba mansuetudinis Christi'*, the faithful recorder of Christ's lovingkindness. He is anxious to stress his Master's love of sinners (15:1f, 7, 10); to record his acts of forgiveness (7:36–50; 15:11–32; 19:1–10; 23:34, 39–43); and to contrast his tenderness for the lowly and the poor with his severity toward the proud and toward those who abuse their wealth" (1:51–53; 6:20–26; 12:13–21; 14:7–11; 16:15, 19–31; 18:9–14).[2] Women, who represent the feeling function more than men—statistically as well as symbolically—are prominent in Luke's Gospel, e.g., 8:2–3; 13:10–17; 21:1–4; 22:27–31; 23:49, 55–56; 24:1–11. Finally, mention ought to be made of Luke's classic introduction (1:1–4), which makes explicit the narrative character of all four Gospels. "I am telling the story once again," he says to Theophilus (literally, lover of God), "so that you may know how well grounded in tradition is the teaching you have received."

The prominence given to Mary in Luke's infancy narrative prompts a first reflection on the feeling dimension of Jesus' life and ministry. Even through Luke's and Matthew's infancy accounts we know precious little of the factual details of the life of Jesus of Nazareth prior to his healing and prophetic ministry. But we do know that he was a human being, with capabilities and limitations primarily shaped, so far as his personality was concerned, by intimacy with his parents. In this he was like the rest of us. It is no mere fancy of devotion, then, to say of the "hidden life" that, in view of his call and of the kind of person he showed himself to be, it had to be rich in the quality of its intimacy. How many great and wonderful people have we ourselves met who make us wonder just how they got that way? Then we meet one or other or both of their parents, and all becomes clear. Both the richness of Jesus' capacity for intimacy and his ability to relate to people in a public and conflictual way undoubtedly owe much to the climate of intimacy set for him by Mary and Joseph at Nazareth. Modern psychology thus provides, to a great extent, confirmation of the imaginative portraits of the holy family at Nazareth painted by Christian devotion through the centuries. Luke's infancy narrative is excellent material for prayer as it evokes symbolically the beautiful intimacy of the Nazareth years.

We do in fact find Jesus in his adult life showing a rich capacity for friendship. A few are named, especially in the Fourth Gospel, as his special intimates—"the disciple whom Jesus loved" (Jn 13:22; 19:26; 21:7, 20), and Lazarus, with his sisters Martha and Mary (11:1–5, 36). He is also shown dealing fondly and familiarly with his chosen disciples, e.g., Luke 22:14–15; John 13:1–15; 21:4–23. The most moving scenes of intimacy, however, are those in which he relates to the needy and despised. He touches them, e.g., Luke 4:40; 5:13; 8:54, and lets himself be touched by them, e.g., Luke 7:36–38; 8:43–48. He even on one occasion lets himself be overcome in a little verbal joust by a woman who will not take no for an answer (Mk 7:24–30). And that very special experience of intimacy, particularly in the East—the sharing of a meal—he enjoys with the religiously and culturally marginated, notably with Levi (Matthew) and his friends (Mt 9:9–13) and with Zacchaeus (Lk 19:1–10). It was in such a context that, in Luke's description, he permitted and even encouraged a sinful woman, undoubtedly a prostitute, in an unheard of gesture of intimacy, to bathe and anoint his feet, an office which his Pharisee host had neglected (Lk 7:36–50).

And so here is someone who moves in the public scene, in the midst of great crowds, but in a warm and personal way which reveals a heart completely free for intimate love. He has his small circle of friends and disciples, but his goodness and freedom are such that every relationship, even the passing touch of strangers, finds him fully present to the needy who come to him, as well as to the hostile whose barbs and snares he knows how to withstand, though he is vulnerable to them. And toward the city, which embodies the values of the heritage which he loves so dearly, his heart goes out with a tenderness that brings him to tears as he contemplates its destruction (Lk 19:41–44). On another occasion he compares himself to a mother hen offering shelter from danger to her brood, but experiencing rejection from the people he loved so much (Lk 13:34–35).

We have already noted the connection of the feeling function with the life of the senses, with gaze and hearing and touch. As Jesus himself said, he was moved to active compassion just by looking out upon the wretched crowds "lying as sheep without a shepherd" (Mt 15:32–39). Undoubtedly the same connection existed between his hearing the cries of the afflicted and his being moved to pity, e.g., Luke 17:13; 18:38–39. And everywhere there was the touching and being touched by individuals but also by the crowds which jostled him, sometimes to the point that he and his disciples were in danger of being trampled, so that he had to take refuge in a boat offshore (Mk 3:9–10; 4:1). On another occasion the crowds pressed them so much that they could not find the space to eat

(Mk 3:20; 6:31). Wherever he went, contact with him gave to helpless, almost hopeless, people, deprived of their story, a new story which would transform their lives. The typical reaction of those whom he cured was to run off and to share the joyful news with others: "Look at what he did for me! This is what he said to me," e.g., John 4:39.

It is not only in Jesus' person to person relationships that we can study his attention to feeling. When he forms the community of his disciples and sends them forth to share in his ministry, he pays a great deal of attention to how they related to one another and to others. He sends the seventy-two in pairs, and his instruction regarding their behavior deals in part with how they are to handle such interpersonal matters as greeting others, being welcomed or not, sharing meals and lodging (Lk 10:1–2). He is also at pains to remind them that they are to treat one another with love and gentleness and humility; it is in service that they will find true greatness (Lk 9:46–48; 22:24–27).

Jesus' broader teaching contains several features worthy of note because of their connection with the feeling function. While the particular kind of stories he told speak more to the imaginative than to the feeling side, being intended to open up new possibilities of hope and conversion, many of them had a deeply feeling content, especially when they drew upon familiar and traditional memories. Thus the parables of the sower (Lk 8:4–15) and of the lamp (Lk 8:16–18), and particularly the story of the good Samaritan (Lk 10:29–37), as well as the trio of stories about the lost sheep, the lost drachma and the lost son (Lk 15), all have a remarkable power to stir the affections and to bring us back to basic values. With keen sensibility, too, Jesus knows the symbolic power present in the child, and he employs it on several occasions to dispose people's feelings for his demanding call (Lk 9:46–48; Mt 18:1–10; 19:13–15).

Of special interest is Jesus' ambivalent attitude toward tradition. He denounces, of course, the traditionalism which substitutes oppressive religious customs for the genuine heritage (Lk 11:37–44). But he also has at times to put some

distance between the old covenant and the new, as when he
sets forth his new way in the Sermon on the Mount: "You have
learnt how it was said . . . but I say this to you . . ." (Mt 5:20–48).
Nevertheless he truly loved his people and their heritage, and
he was deeply pained by the way in which it had been pervert-
ed. He spoke of the fathers with affection, and claimed them
for his witness (Jn 6:46; 8:56). He affirms the enduring validity
of the heart of the old covenant: "Do not imagine that I have
come to abolish the law or the prophets. I have come not to
abolish but to complete them" (Mt 5:17). In brief, we find him,
in the name of fidelity to tradition, bringing all the vehemence
of his passion to bear on traditionalism.

At the heart of his teaching was *compassion*. Both in
parables and in more didactic language he offers God as the
model of mercy, and he makes willingness to be merciful, even
toward one's enemies, central to the good news, e.g., Luke
6:27–35; 17:3–4; Matthew 18:23–35.

There are, then, countless passages, especially in Luke,
where the example, the strategies, and the teaching of Jesus
model for us the feeling side of God's image. But the most
powerful incentive of all is contained in what he did and said
the night before he died. In the intimacy of a meal, and with
such added touches as the humble washing of his disciples'
feet, he asked to be remembered. It was the meal of remembrance par excellence for all faithful Jews—the memorial of
Yahweh's mercy in liberating them from slavery. Any request
for remembrance coming from a loved one about to die is
deeply moving. But Jesus, giving to the limit and beyond,
leaves his loved ones the very vehicle and sign of remembrance, himself, his own body and blood, as food and drink.
Were we dealing with a merely human strategy, we would say
that this was a stroke of genius. If we want to find the center of
power and energy in Christianity it is here: the one who loved
us to the point of dying for us asked us to remember him
whenever we celebrate this meal together. Like the two disciples on the road to Emmaus, Christian hearts until the end of
time will be energized and healed by this memory.

It is largely because the Last Supper and the Eucharist

which memorializes it in union with Calvary are acts of ritual offering that we suggest that the name of Christ having a special affinity with the feeling function is that of *priest*. It is true that he neither exercised nor claimed the technical office of priest in his ministry, and also that the Letter to the Hebrews which celebrates his priesthood rather focuses on his entry into the heavenly sanctuary. But it is the heavenly offering which constitutes the core of the Church's offering in history. Ritual in general and the Eucharistic rite in particular represent the celebration of the originating "myth" by which a people, through anamnesis, continually renews itself. From this point of view the priestly people and the office which represents it is engaged in drawing energy from the nourishing roots, the heritage by which it lives. Without excluding its reference to the present and to the future, the Eucharist is the heart of the traditioning process by which the Church is constantly called to fidelity.

The Church Constituted by Remembrance

If space permitted, we might study how, throughout the New Testament, this process of remembrance was embodied in preaching and teaching, community formation, ritual celebration, and the exercise of ecclesial authority. Persecution from without and dissension within are met by recourse to the heritage. The question of continuity and discontinuity with respect to the Jewish heritage of the new community constitutes the principal source of tension, as we see it described, for example, in the stories of Peter and Paul in the Acts of the Apostles, or in Paul's Letters to the Corinthians and Galatians. And so already in the apostolic Church we find the traditioning process, the faithful handing on of the story and the teaching, as a substantive element in the life of the Christian community.

It is this role of remembrance in constituting the Church that we wish to describe more reflectively, as it designates an important societal employ of the feeling function. We are used to definitions of the Church which attend to unity of belief and doctrine, sacramental ritual, moral code, and authority and governance. All of these certainly help to comprise the identity of the Church. But we commonly tend to neglect a bond which is, in a real sense, prior and deeper, the bond of *anamnesis,* i.e., remembrance. Before the Church is a corporate teaching or ethical system or sacred institution, it is an embodied story. It is continually being recreated by the narration of what God has done for our humanity in Christ Jesus. The central symbolic expression of this is the Eucharistic prayer of the Mass, so powerful a story and remembrance that it makes the risen Lord and the mysteries of his earthly life truly present in the sacramental signs and, through them, in the body of worshiping disciples.

The Lord's "Do this in remembrance of me" extends not only to the celebration of the Eucharist but to every aspect of the Church's life. Evangelization, catechesis, ministry, and formation are all, most basically, processes of passing on the "old, old story," and of joining that great story to the particular stories of individuals, groups, and peoples.

This insertion of the feeling function and of its correlatives—memory, story, traditioning—into our understanding of every aspect of Christian life and ministry represents a powerful source for energizing and healing individuals, groups, and the whole Church. Out of such an approach in various contexts come gratitude, compunction, compassion, and all the other forms in which power flows creatively from the remembered past into the present. The restoration of God's image in the form of redemptive remembrance—that is the aspect of the good news which is here in question.

Such a view as this provides us with a positive evaluation of the importance of tradition. It often happens that people intent on salutary change in the Church and in society experience the past primarily as burden and barrier hindering creative advance. Such a view not only falls under the celebrated axiom that those who neglect history are doomed to repeat it but also misses a basic human truth, that the power to create the future lies largely in our ability to recreate the past.

Johannes Metz has given theological voice to this truth in

his elucidation of a theology of hope.[3] The power of the future, he asserts, is in *memoria passionis Christi*—the memory of human suffering which comes to a peak in the passion of Jesus Christ. Only in the suffering of the *anawim* (the poor) of all ages, retrieved through our remembrance, can we find the force powerful enough to liberate us from present oppression. But, the German theologian warns, not all remembrance is life-giving. He distinguishes "nostalgic" and "dangerous" memories. The former are recollections of "the good old days" which seek to escape the call of the future, and which lock us into present paralysis. Dangerous memories, on the other hand, are dangerous to all forms of present enslavement and the weight of a dead past. They are a threat to the human oppressions which are disclosed as radically unfaithful to the original gift. Metz's distinction rings true to anyone who reflects on what happens in periods of personal conversion or in the great liberation movements of modern times. Leaders who know how to tap into human energies will not fail to say "Remember!" The Roman Catholic Church in the past few decades has seen such an exercise of "dangerous memories" spark personal conversion and communal renewal. When Vatican II called religious communities, for example, to a process of simultaneous *renewal,* i.e., a return to the charismatic origins of each community and of the whole Church, and *adaptation,* i.e., a fitting of the expression of the original charism to the needs of today, it generated a process of creative *anamnesis* which is still powerfully at work.

III. DEVELOPING THE LIFE OF FEELING

We come again to speak of developing a specific aspect of God's image—here the gifts related to the feeling function. According to our hypothesis, development takes place through four successive stages and in sixteen diverse patterns depending on one's spontaneous choice of functions and attitudes. So we remind ourselves once again that we are very different from one another. Some of us have been exercising our feeling life with full consciousness since primary school days, and our present call, so far as this function is concerned, will be to disengage from its expression so that thinking may have a better chance to emerge. Others have, since adolescence, been employing their feeling side especially as a support for their dominant sensing or intuiting. But the group to whose growth we will be especially directing these remarks are dominant thinkers, who have made thinking their primary preference from childhood on.

How then can someone, who from the age of six has spontaneously been logical, orderly, and fair, now at mid-life and beyond reach out toward balance and wholeness by favoring feeling as one's "shadow side"? The first spontaneous effort of such types, of course, will be to ask for directions and then to plan the most strategic approach. Much more is needed. A brief response is: *Cultivate intimacy with God and with other people.* While we will also be speaking of other aspects of feeling, our remarks will center around growth in intimacy.

Some dominant thinkers may tend to be apprehensive when they hear themselves invited to engage in intimacy. There is a metaphor which may help them to understand the dynamics of intimacy: the psychic "bubble" or skin. Our bodily skin is an important part of our sensing apparatus. As we have seen, it has a good deal to do with the life of feeling. The excitation of touch is intimately joined with the arousal of the heart. But here we are speaking of our psychic "skin" or "bubble." Each of us wears, mostly in an unconscious way, an interpersonal extension or expression of ourselves, through which we "touch" others and let them "touch" us, or on the contrary exclude them from this kind of relationship. Physical and psychic skins or bubbles are closely linked. Just recall what usually happens in a crowded public elevator. We are usually silent, face the door, and avoid eye contact with others. When the door finally opens at a floor, there is a sense—sometimes almost an audible sigh—of relief at being delivered from such close contact with strangers. What is behind such a reaction?

Physical closeness has, on the one hand, sparked a psychic attraction toward personal closeness. But, particularly in our culture, we really do not want such intimacy with passing strangers. And so a certain tension results. We *choose* to exercise intimacy with people whom we know and trust and love, not with anonymous others.

The point here is that nature's God has provided us all with a wonderful organism for the free exercise of intimacy, tenderness, and affection. Both physical and psychic in character, it involves sensing as well as feeling functions. Thinkers are *not* being asked to be promiscuously intimate; in fact, the two terms are mutually exclusive. But what is being suggested is that they relativize the distance and coolness which habitually govern their relating to others. Their own growth calls for them to take the risk of sharing their "bubble" with some others, at least with members of their family or small community, or with individuals with whom an incipient relationship of mutual attraction is present.

For some dominant thinkers just the thought of this invitation brings feelings of real fear. It may also bring apprehension because of some unfortunate connotations of the words "intimate" and "intimacy" in popular usage. Genital sexuality is only one way—a beautiful and potentially holy way—in which human sexuality, our capacity for intimacy, may be expressed. Concretely, what some dominant thinkers may need to learn is to be comfortable, for example, in holding infants and even cooing to them, or hugging a senior citizen, or just feeling free to pat someone's arm or shoulder, or complimenting others on their appearance. More than likely, the first feeling gestures of someone not used to making them will be mawkish or sentimental, just as the first venture of the dominant feeler into assertive behavior may be hostile or aggressive. But practice makes perfect. A good rule of thumb is: When in doubt, take a chance. Thinkers, particularly if their thinking is introverted, might do well to cultivate a bias of leaning toward, not away from, others.

Intimate behavior will be easier for dominant thinkers to

practice in a group of dominant feelers, especially when this feeling is extraverted and exercised with sensitivity toward contrasting types. It will be a painful experience of course, but also, in a context of faith, an experience of the saving cross. The spontaneous and somewhat illogical behavior of many feelers together may give confusing messages to the logical mind of a lone thinker. When the overload of meaninglessness in such a person reaches a certain point, a kind of "flip" can take place, and for sheer relief and even survival the thinking one will have recourse to a spontaneous but immature expression of feeling. This is not an ideal situation, to be sure, but given the human condition it is one that is both understandable and a step toward wholeness. The point we are making is that the company of dominant feelers, whether freely chosen or not, may be the special grace which a dominant thinker needs, especially around the midpoint of life.

One of the keys for developing feeling is for the thinker to let go of the assumption that all speech and action, all judgments and decisions, need uniformly to be brought before the tribunal of logic, good order, and truth. Pascal's word of wisdom is worth repeating: The heart has reasons of which the logical mind knows not. A logical principle may embody a good deal of truth and fidelity, but it is not identical with the eternal truth and fidelity which is God. Persons come before principles, and before one acts on a principle it is important to consider what will be the effect of the action on personal values. Ultimately, and ironically, the thinker who clings exclusively to thinking is being irrational. The basic Gospel law of losing one's life in order to find it is verified in the lives of thinkers when they make room for the feeling side of their personality.

Besides the general strategy of exercising intimacy in the company of dominant feelers, there are some more specific strategies of growth. Enlisting the auxiliary function in support of the desired development can be a source of strength in a period when one's primary strength is being suspended in its exercise. An intuitive thinker, for example, might let imagination suggest playful forms of speech which might build more humor into a relationship. To laugh together over some absurd fantasy is not a bad way of breaking down excessive sobriety and distance. A sensing thinker might construct some strategies regarding the connection of sight, hearing, and touch with movements of the heart. Listening to music with the whole body and with the heart, and learning to exercise the senses in spontaneous feeling gestures, even and especially in the company of others, are two examples. Some families, especially through cultural or ideological influences, do not show many signs of warm affection among the members and with others. It is possible, without artificiality, for one or two members to change this. They will often find that others have been secretly open to the change, but have been too shy to inaugurate it.

Another specific and very meaningful exercise of feeling consists in asking others for forgiveness when we have hurt them. It has been said that dominant feelers find it difficult to forgive, and dominant thinkers find it difficult to ask for forgiveness. Whether or not one has failed in strict justice, hurting the feelings of another through insensitivity calls for a heartfelt "I'm sorry." Few ways of "sharing bubbles" can be as productive of growth as making amends for hurting another's feelings.

We have alluded once or twice in this chapter to the experience of the cross which dominant thinkers will commonly have about mid-life as they hear the call to develop their feeling side. Recall what we said in the chapters on sensing and thinking about the inferior function as the "mystical function." Letting it emerge, and for the sake of that emergence letting go of the dominant function, means that we are dealing with God, other humans, life itself, from our weakness, not from our strength. The dominant thinker, so accustomed to acting according to what makes logical sense and what is according to right order, needs to bear the pain of a seeming absurdity in what is being asked at this stage of life. Such a person, however, is not without supports for the trial, and prayer is one of these supports.

Intimacy in Prayer

What has traditionally been called *affective prayer* is especially needed by thinking types. Whatever engages the heart,
whatever has the pronounced character of an "I-thou" relationship and of intimate dialogue, and whatever through the
exercise of remembrance brings the one praying back to a
joyous, grateful, compunctious renewal of covenant, will serve
the development of feeling prayer. The range of forms is vast,
and readers will think of many that we do not mention here.
The dialogue of Jesus and Peter at Caesarea Philippi (Mt
16:13–20) is a model experience of mutual naming that can
move the heart. "Who do you say I am?" asks Jesus in the
intimacy of our personal prayer, meaning, "Who am I for you?
What is your most cherished way of naming me?" And we in
our turn can put the same question to him: "Lord, what is your
name for me?" And then we can listen as his heart names us
through the affection of our own heart.

A second scene of intimate dialogue between Jesus and
Peter contains a similar power. It is recorded of Peter that
after his denial of Jesus during the passion he went out and
wept bitterly, something which was psychologically as well as
spiritually healing (Lk 22:62). But that was only the beginning
of the healing which needed to take place. Luke records that
after the resurrection Jesus appeared to Simon Peter (24:34).
We are left to imagine what a tender reunion that was. But the
Fourth Gospel offers us one of the most intimate scenes of the
risen life (Jn 21:15–23). After serving breakfast to several of the
disciples on the shore of the Sea of Galilee, Jesus asks his
penitent disciple three times whether he loves him. This dialogue too can lead the dominant thinker into more feeling
relationships with the loving, forgiving Master.

Our prayer can also be a walk down memory lane with
Jesus and Mary and our patron saint and the dear ones who
have gone ahead of us to eternal life. How would I identify
persons, places, happenings which will forever be for me the
special vehicles of his love and his desire for my return of love?

When did I really begin to commit myself to spend my life in the service of God? It is such remembrances which seem to be reflected in Luke 5:1–11, 27–32, and in John 1:35–51, as well as elsewhere in the Gospels. I can also ask what are my regrets, my memories of unfaithfulness, and bring them once again to the Lord for healing.

The Jesus Prayer, when we let it repeat itself within us with an accent on the heart—it has been called the prayer of the mind in the heart—has great power for fostering intimacy. So does the method of contemplating the mysteries of the Gospel, which dates back to the time of the Desert Fathers, and which was handed on by St. Bonaventure and St. Ignatius Loyola. Various exercises of devotional life, the rosary, the stations of the cross, and the various litanies to Jesus and Mary and the saints may also be mentioned, as also the devout singing of hymns both traditional and contemporary. Sometimes a hymn of childhood recalled decades later can recreate a deeply cherished experience and bring tears to one's eyes. Where one has the leisure and situation for praying in a church, chapel, or oratory, especially where the Blessed Sacrament is reserved, this is a precious traditional way of growing in personal love of the risen Lord.

All of these are forms of solitary prayer, though some of them can be shared with others. Thinking types would do well to seize whatever opportunities there are for joining others in prayer which is devotional or otherwise affective. Faith sharing and charismatic ways of praying are two forms that come to mind. Thinkers can also be helped by celebrations of the Eucharist in larger or smaller assemblies with an accent on congregational singing and a warm, meaningful exchange of the kiss of peace.

Finally, let us mention spiritual direction as an important instance of Christian intimacy. Sometimes, especially when the relationship is sustained over a period of years, it can become one of deep friendship. In any case, the situation of spiritual direction is an exercise of Christian intimacy. The relationship of confessor and penitent can be the same, especially now that a former anonymity in the celebration of this sacrament is being transcended. What Aelred of Rivaulx wrote at the very beginning of his classic treatise on spiritual friendship finds application here: "Here we are, you and I, and I hope a third, Christ, is with us."[4]

Let that beautiful word "friend" be our final word for expressing how the feeling function is best helped to flower in gratitude and joy. Very simply, the question which the thinking person desirous of growing in feeling needs to ask is: "What role does friendship—with God and with human beings—play in my life?"

EXERCISES

A. *For the individual:*

1. Dispose yourself for prayer and then read the dialogue of Jesus and Peter in John 21:15–17. Let the words "I love you" flow freely in you like an aspiration or mantra, understanding that it is sometimes Jesus, sometimes you, and sometimes both simultaneously, who are speaking the words.

2. In a similar way, and perhaps beginning with the same passage or with Matthew 16:13–20, see what names, directly addressed to Jesus, flow from your unconscious, e.g., my brother, my friend, my teacher. Similarly, see what names he calls you by. If one name is more attractive than the others, linger with it, letting it repeat itself over and over again.

3. Over a period of days or weeks take the infancy narrative of Luke (1—3) for your daily prayer, and see if you can become part of the different scenes, listening to what is said, asking your own questions, even reverently touching, e.g., asking if you may hold the Christ Child in your arms.

4. After an appropriate hymn, e.g., "I Will Never Forget You, My People," begin recalling the persons for whose presence in your life you are most grateful and then the persons you feel you may have hurt or offended. Hold each one in the presence of the Lord, in gratitude, sorrow, intercession.

B. *For groups:*

1. If you are part of a group that prays together regularly, have the group reflect on whether there ought to be more music and song, or more personal expression of how each one is seeking and finding God, experiencing difficulty, etc.

2. Although your group may not be charismatically inclined, you may profit occasionally by attending a charismatic meeting and adapting some of the prayer forms back into your group.

3. If you have the opportunity, go as a group to a Eucharistic celebration where there is a Gospel choir, and participate. Or attend a service at a Baptist church.

SCRIPTURE REFERENCES

1. Psalms: Almost without number are the psalms which convey affection and intimacy, or which remember God's deeds for the people, e.g., 8, 16, 22, 23, 25, 27, 51, 63, 71, 84, 103, 104, 105, 106, 107, 108, 116, 123, 128, 130, 131, 136, 139.

2. The Books of Ruth and Tobit are stories full of tender affection, and the Song of Songs is a romantic celebration of human and divine intimacy.

3. Isaiah contains many passages which express the intimate affection of Yahweh for the people e.g., 41:8–16; 43:1–7; 49; 54:4–10; 61. So does Hosea, with even more passion, e.g., 2:1–3; 8:24; 11:7–9. Lamentations depicts with deep feeling the plight of Israel because of sin, and waits in hope for deliverance.

4. All four Gospels have abundant material. We make special mention of Matthew 11:25–30 (Jesus calling the poor to intimacy); 16:13–20 (his dialogue with Peter); Luke (all the passages we have mentioned in this chapter): John 1:35–51 (the call of the first disciples); 2:1–12 (Cana); 4:1–42 (the woman at the well); 10:1–18 (Jesus as good shepherd); 13—17 (the last discourse and prayer of Jesus).

5. Paul has many passages expressing Christian intimacy, e.g., Philemon (expressing his tender love and concern for the former slave, Onesimus); Philippians 2:1–11 (a very personal

call to loving humility after the example of Christ Jesus); 3:7–21 (his passionate love for Christ); Colossians 3:5–25 (exhortation to interpersonal love and tenderness).

NOTES

1. Hannah Arendt, *The Human Condition* (Garden City: Doubleday, 1959), pp. 212–223.

2. *The Jerusalem Bible*, Introduction to the Synoptic Gospels, p. 14.

3. For example in *Faith History and Society: Toward a Practical Fundamental Theology* (New York: Seabury, 1980), pp. 88–118.

4. Aelred of Rivaulx, *Spiritual Friendship* (Washington, D.C.: Consortium Press, 1974), p. 51.

CHAPTER 5
Eye Has Not Seen

Intuiting/Hope

There is a story about a group of top executives attending a lecture on management theory. The speaker, an eminent theoretician, was deadly on the platform, and droned on for an hour and a half. The elite audience sat and squirmed and groaned and barely endured—all except one. This was a highly gifted native American who had made his way into the elite circles of corporate life. He sat perfectly still, eyes shining, a gentle smile on his lips, obviously enjoying himself. One of his companions happened to notice him, and when the ordeal was over asked him what in the world was so delightful about such a boring lecture. The native American answered, as from a far away place, "It was so wonderful when the bear jumped into the water." In the first five minutes of the lecture, he had decided on an alternative use of his energies, and had through his imagination left the auditorium for a happier place.

Those gifted with a well developed intuiting function are rarely at a loss in situations of entrapment, dullness, or violence. Someone has said that violence is due to a lack of imagination, and the observation is true of individual, relational and societal forms of violence which afflict our world. And a key aspect of the redemption of God's image wrought by Christ Jesus is the liberation of human imagination so that it may dream of alternatives to sinful violence. If memory is the road to grateful joy, imagination is the secret of dreaming hope, the way into a genuine future. This is what we now want to explore. Lest our journey be too meandering—a proclivity of intuiting types—we will follow the by now familiar map:

144

first, we will describe the intuiting function and discuss intuiting types; second, we will see how the Gospel meets this side of our humanity; and third, we will offer some suggestions about developing this aspect of God's image.

I. THE INTUITING FUNCTION

Our second chapter has acquainted us with one perceiving function, *sensing,* and with its characteristics of being simple, attentive, down to earth, focused on present actuality. Intuiting is just the opposite. It needs, of course, to start with something present and actual; like a soaring bird it requires a place from which to take off. But once given a spark from sensing, intuiting disengages from the *now/here* and is carried into the *no/where* of Utopia. By the employ of imagination, Jung says, and by drawing on the unconscious, the intuiting function opens on what is *possible, not yet, future.* Details are of interest to it only as avenues to the *essences* of things. It likes to perceive on the basis of spontaneous *hunches* rather than by way of calculated measurements, and so it is aptly characterized as a kind of "sixth sense." It often prefers the *abstract* rather than the concrete; we can recall that the Latin *abstrahere* means "to withdraw from." When we are intuiting, we are, in a sense, no longer here but there, and sometimes neither here nor there—just nowhere.

Words like "beyond" and "yonder," as well as activities like floating, diving, and soaring, hint at the spirit of this elusive side of our humanity. Though we can meet God through each of the functions, intuiting represents in unique fashion the presence of the *transcendent* in the midst of life. That is why, in the game of correlating, intuiting has been placed with the transcendental *pulchrum* (the beautiful); one understanding of beauty is to see it as the point at which finitude and infinitude meet without meeting. *Horizon,* therefore, is another term which conveys the uncapturable essence of intuiting. Standing on the shore and gazing first at a limitless expanse of ocean, then at a limpid blue sky, then at the horizon is an exercise which can help us appreciate this gift.

There is an interesting difference between intuiting and thinking, which of course are not opposed to each other and can both be preferred by the same individual. With thinking it is the abstract *concept* which calls for distancing from involvement with persons; with intuiting it is the *symbol*, with another kind of abstraction, intimating what is beyond the sensible, which calls for a distance linked more to imagination than to the cognitive mind.

Two further terms help to clarify intuiting: *creativity* and *freedom*. Technically, both creativity and intelligence, at least the intelligence which is measured by standard I.Q. tests, correlate with the intuiting function, though not with each other. Whereas our sensing side serves us in part by alert perception of familiar patterns, certainly an important skill, intuition serves us in part by spontaneously rearranging, adjusting, improvising. We "see" new combinations of old forms, are gratuitously given new weddings of words and ideas (puns, metaphors, and parables all go with intuiting), and fashion the humdrum leftovers of life—culinary, intellectual, social, or whatever—into surprising fare for ourselves and others.

Freedom in this context intimates release from immobility and sameness, from fixed agendas. Like the term "creativity," freedom is an apt designation for the intuiting function. But it is important not to inflate the sense of these two words, or to canonize intuiting types and their preferred behavior. Being faithful to customary patterns is no less a service to growth than breaking out of such patterns—everything depends on what life calls for at a particular moment and on the quality of the chosen behavior, and indeed of its choosing. At a deeper level of freedom, compulsiveness in fantasizing or dreaming is an enslavement, and a quiet abiding in the "sacrament of the present moment" can be a true exercise of liberation.

A final point in this initial description of intuiting brings us back to remarking that it is a perceiving function. Because of its association with creativity we might be tempted to conceive it as a *doing* faculty, a judging function. No, it belongs to the receptive and contemplative side of our nature. Whatever achievements it may lead to, it remains a way of letting life shape us, energize us.

In summary, then, intuiting is the perceiving function which companions and contrasts with sensing, as follows:

Sensing is concerned with	*Intuiting* is concerned with
the five senses	the imagination
the actual	the possible
concrete facts	abstract ideas
things	symbols
details	essences
the present	the future
now/here	no/where
immanence	transcendence
finitude	infinitude
unum (the one)	*pulchrum* (the beautiful)[1]
acceptance	creativity

A Common Gift

Once again it is the communality of this aspect of God's image in us that we wish to accent before looking at it briefly in those who prefer it as a primary behavior. For each one of us it is a fourth source of energy for the struggle of life, one that interacts with sensing, thinking, and feeling, as we shall see in the final chapter. In the spontaneous living of each day, intuiting provides buoyancy, resiliency, and hope. Like circus clowns we are all continually being confronted by obstacles, disappointments, our own failures. Because of the gift of intuiting, we do not lose hope. There is always some recourse for us clowns. Much gratitude to God is due for this precious gift of dreaming, imagining, improvising, hoping against hope. It can be a profitable exercise to recall some of the times when we have employed this gift for meeting the challenges of life, for serving a common effort, for growing in maturity. It might be good to begin with some of the ordinary examples that we tend to take for granted. What was it that made me, after six years, decide to rearrange the furniture in my office so that I now, sitting at my desk, look out the window on the city? When my budget request was turned down, how did I hit on an alternative route for achieving the goals I had set my heart on? And what enabled me, in one of those ticklish family situations, to appease both wife and mother without yielding to dishonesty? Most changes in our physical, spiritual, or social routines come about because of some spontaneous spark of insight or hope.

When groups deal with thorny problems, the working of intuition often provides an appropriate solution and in the process brings fresh energy and solidarity where before routine and sterile tensions prevailed. Criticism and even persecution from the outside can be a blessing for a small community or ministerial team; they force us to employ our collective imagination in order to meet the threat. Where the gift of intuition is at work in a group, there will be less likelihood of hidden or overt violence, and the road to assertiveness, which we explained in our chapter on thinking, will be less rocky.

Of course when we think of intuition, imagination, and creativity, we are more inclined to think of the geniuses whose visions and dreams have made the world more human: scientists, technologists, architects, humanitarian dreamers, patriotic visionaries—and prophets, as we shall see. All of these gifted persons have enriched humanity by their dreams and, most of all, by the contagiousness of their dreaming. It has been truly said that the *dream* must come before the *project,* that is, creative imagination must be permitted to play in freedom with new possibilities before common sense and critical reason give realistic embodiment to whatever is practical in the vision. A premature practicality deprives us of the wherewithal to be practical. The play of the mind in fantasy and dream is, in the long run, one of the most practical things we can do with our energies. As individuals and groups and in the larger society, we need to do it more and better, given the present threat of catastrophe in the world. And there are indications that God, working in the processes of human history, is offering more resources to meet the need. Whether in hope we call the age that is beginning by the name of Aquarius or the Holy Spirit or any other, there are signs that society is reaching for the resources of intuition in order to energize its struggle for survival and development.

Intuiting Types

Being aware of how intuiting is part of the life of all of us helps keep us from stereotyping, criticizing, or exalting those for whom it is a primary behavior. Still, our understanding of it can be helped by observing the several types of people and also the sequential development of those who have this as their dominant function. There are four intuitive types in whom this gift will have developed in childhood in either extraverted or introverted attitude. Then either thinking or feeling—in the opposite attitude to that of the dominant intuition—will have developed as auxiliary function in adolescence. Expressed in our code, this means that we are dealing with four intuiting types:

(1) ENTP = NTFS/*EIEI*
(2) INTJ = NTFS/*IEIE*
(3) ENFP = NFTS/*EIEI*
(4) INFJ = NFTS/*IEIE*

What all four of these types have in common is a preference for and childhood development of perceiving the world with the characteristics which we have just described. The entertaining of future possibilities with the help of imagination is the primary source of energy for these people. The first two types, because of a thinking auxiliary, will combine this liking with a proclivity, when there is question of what to do with the results of intuiting, for organizing the vision or dream in an analytical, ordered way. The first type, because of the extraversion of the intuition, does the exploring best in a give-and-take with others, but would rather do the organizing apart from others. The second type is just the opposite—when such a person joins a project with others, the new dream will have already been dreamed, or will be dreamed when the group disperses, through the introverted use of intuiting. An example of the first type—not exclusive of course—could be an experienced director of photography for an epic Hollywood film; an example of the second type could be a computer analyst or economic theorist employed by the World Bank to help it keep abreast of rapidly changing international market situations.

The third and fourth types would have in common a drive to put their vision to work in the area of personal values, for humanitarian goals, for example. They would want their vision to make a difference to some significant others, whether few or many. They would differ from each other in a fashion analogous to the differences between the thinking intuiters. The third type would most commonly be energized by exploring insights with or at least in the presence of other people who showed their appreciation. At the same time this type would be governed with respect to the impact or utilization of the insights by a set of inner values concerning how people ought to relate to one another and to God. Gifted speakers and promoters with religious or humanitarian convictions will often belong to this type. The fourth type will relate vision and values in just the opposite fashion. The conjuring up of the vision will more likely happen in solitude, though the imagination may have initially been sparked by a moving interpersonal exchange. When it comes to sharing the vision itself with others, this will take place with a good deal of emotion and sensitivity to how well it is being received. An instance of this type might be, for example, an earnest advocate for social change based on some new theological or pastoral approach.

We offer one final observation before moving on to a scenario. When the first developed and therefore dominant function—here intuiting—is introverted, what outsiders see is more commonly the auxiliary function. What may impress me most about a famous architect at first meeting, for example, is the striking ability to adapt form to function with a certain economy and coolness of style. But if I am dealing with a person whose type is INTJ = NTFS/*IEIE*, it may be some time before I really come in touch with the brilliant innovative mind which is being expressed in orderly designs. Similarly, a feeling intuiter whose intuition is introverted (INFJ = NFTS/*IEIE*), especially if shy or timid, may come across as a predominantly caring and sensitive person; the governing insights may be less accessible, especially to casual acquaintances.

A Scenario

Judith, a forty-year-old educational consultant, combines her career with making a home with her husband Dan and two teenage children. Her obvious friendliness has served her well in her work, especially when she has found it necessary to identify needed changes which were painful to teachers. Her strongest though less visible characteristic is her imaginative way of finding new methods for avoiding and correcting flaws in systems—less visible because these ideas come to her after her group discussions have furnished the information and stimulus she needs. She rarely makes recommendations until she has had time to herself for reflection. Once she has pondered over problems and come up with possible solutions, she arrives quickly at presenting definite choices, leaving the implementation methods to the school officers.

During the past several years, however, Judith has found herself developing more of an interest in carrying out some of her ideas. This has helped her to be more practical in her suggestions and more attentive to the details of her clients' problems, as well as her own. She remembers more specifics but finds this a mixed blessing, because now she more often recalls nagging personal concerns. In the past she could hardly remember what she had been worrying about as her quick mind hurried on to explore new vistas.

When Judith finished college at twenty-one and took her first job, teaching emotionally disturbed children, she could look back on four student years during which she had found it difficult to say no to any request for service. She wondered during her practicum if she would ever make it through her first year as a teacher, trying as she surely would to comply with demands from family, friends, and principal. Saying no was next to impossible if yes would satisfy another's need. Once she took the job, however, she found herself beginning to question why she had given in to demands so easily, and she gradually became more inclined to want reasons before agreeing to a request.

Judith and Dan had married when she was twenty and he was twenty-three. He was attracted to her ability to see beyond his faults and present limitations to appreciate his future potential. She found delightful his ability to point out the traits he noticed in her and to remember with tenderness every detail of their shared experiences as well as birthdays and anniversaries in her family. He shared her outgoing feelings, and it was even more difficult for him than for her to deny requests which imposed unfairly on his time. While resenting and decrying these impositions on her husband when they came from others, Judith did not hesitate to add her own requests. Dan on his side appreciated her easy acceptance of his recent failures in promptness which, since he had prided himself on his punctuality, he viewed as a new quirk.

Recently some new tensions have come into their relationship. Judith, for example, became quite angry when Dan somewhat deviously pressured her to curtail her long business trips, something about which he had never before expressed concern. She was able to understand the reasonableness of his new attitude, but contended, as she would not have done in the past, that they could sustain the separations if in their time together they were careful to be more present to each other, enjoying every moment. She herself has in fact become better able to savor the present. She is also developing a new enthusiasm for sharing the beauties of nature with Dan, and finds herself more drawn to the physical side of their love-making.

Judith's basic preferences and development pattern are those of the INFJ = NFTS/*IEIE* type, and Dan comes across as manifesting the characteristics of the ESFJ = FSNT/*EIEI* type. Her dominant function, intuition, together with her auxiliary feeling, attracted her to work with disturbed children, with whom she could try creative corrective therapy. Her auxiliary extraverted feelings served her well in clothing her natural shyness and her introverted intuition, which often came across as a non-responsive attitude. This feeling suspended itself temporarily when she reached twenty, and her developing thinking helped her to systematically control her time and activities to her own advantage. It also enabled her to do a better job of handling the emotionally disturbed children without becoming excessively emotional herself. Later, as her thinking function developed, she chose the position of consultant when she realized how much more influence she could have on educational management.

At thirty-five Judith found herself developing her sensing qualities, and because they were extraverted she found more enjoyment in sharing them, especially with Dan. At the same time she picked up within herself some signals that sensing was her least developed and shadow side. She found herself becoming annoyed with little things which previously she would never even notice—a barking dog, mindless chatter, Dan's habit of tapping his fingers on the table. These were things she could handle, however, in view of the positive elements in this new-found gift of awareness of little things, sights and sounds and touches she had never appreciated.

Dan's ESFJ = SFTN/*EIEI* preferences had led him, as an outgoing and friendly child, to build up a wide circle of acquaintances to whom he related harmoniously. In high school he was an athlete who enjoyed the feel of the rushing wind as he ran. He liked to build model planes, and he apportioned the time spent in various activities in a very careful way. As he came to know Judith he found his intuition growing and felt that he could share her interest in the future, her global concerns, and her conviction that their possibilities were limitless. What he found hard to understand as they moved through their twenties was that in spite of her basic kindness Judith often became hostile or aggressive when she disagreed with him. He couldn't see why she could not just state her case. As he reached thirty-five, however, he came to understand her behavior of those years, because he found that he himself now wanted to be more assertive. Long years of acquiescence, however, had made it a real challenge to disagree simply and quietly without fearing resistance from others and his own inability to defend his own stand. His hostile pressure on Judith to stop traveling stemmed from his anticipation that she would disagree vehemently. In actuality, all she really wanted was for him to tell her what he thought and permit her to do the same. It was not long before she came to see that she actually preferred to stay at home and become more involved with their farm and house, especially by exercising her gardening and culinary skills.

Dan too has undergone significant change. Having developed his thinking function to the point of being able to say and do what he really wants without hostility or aggressiveness, he has decided with Judith's agreement to run the farm. He now finds himself able to manage well, to face controversy, and to drive a hard bargain, all of which he had never believed would be possible.

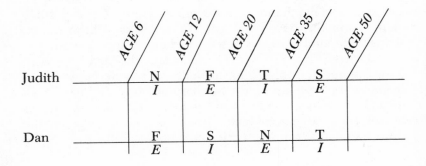

II. THE GOSPEL OF HOPE

A line from a recent hymn can serve to keynote the Gospel encounter with the intuiting function; "The dream I have today, my Lord/ is only a shadow of your dreams for me/ only a shadow of all that will be/ if I but follow you."[2] If our magnificent capacity to "dare the dream" is only a shadow of the divine dreaming, what must God be like? We have unfortunately been encouraged by much of our religious education to think of God exclusively as a tireless worker, the omnicompetent producer. But what God did on the seventh day, and what the sabbath of the Lord is, is a question rarely asked. What does the one who blessed the sabbath among all days and bid us keep it holy do within the eternal sabbath rest? We can only say that it is spent dreaming dreams. Just what that means escapes us, but we do know that it is what makes our dreams possible, and Godlike.

There are several ways in which the intuitive side of God finds expression in the Bible. Imagination—an infinity of impossible possibilities—is implicit in the assertion that God is creator, architect, potter, wise and provident shaper of history. The wisdom literature and many of the psalms have a number of passages which celebrate God's fantastic imagination, manifested both in the variety and interplay of creatures and in the divine shaping of human destiny, e.g., Psalms 8; 19:1–6; 104; 139:13–14; 147; 148; Wisdom 7:15—9:8; 10—19; Sirach 24; 42:15—51:11. In Job the speeches of Elihu and especially of Yahweh celebrate the often playful wisdom of the Creator, the range of whose creative power runs from prescribing traffic directions for constellations (38:32) to making the ostrich without common sense yet able "to make fools of horse and rider" (39:17–18). The dreams of the prophets for the liberation and prosperity of the messianic age are really resonances of the divine dreams communicated through them to the people, e.g., Isaiah 60—62. The same is true of the apocalyptic passages of both Old and New Testaments, e.g., Ezekiel 38—39; Daniel 7—12; Zechariah 9—14; Revelation. Both Jesus and Paul are implicitly extolling the dreaming imagination of God when they celebrate the marvelous way in which the process of creation/redemption is guided, e.g., Matthew 11:25–27; Romans 11:33–36; 1 Corinthians 1:17—2:9; Ephesians 1:3–14; 3:1–21.

God Imaged in Human Creativity

These are just a few hints of what is involved in a call that most of us may not have thought about. We know that we are called to be like God. But how many of us have dealt with that call as a summons to creativity, to the development throughout life of the power we have to make life new by imaging ever new possibilities? Behind this deficiency is a misconception of the Creator/creature relationship and of the obedience which it entails. Our dreaming God is not in the least interested in the wooden performance of assigned movements by slaves or marionettes. On the contrary, as the parable of the talents indicates, God expects from us imaginative enterprise (Mt 25:14–30). Recall once again the summons to stewardship inherent in our creation according to God's image and likeness (Gen 1:28). When we put what we now know about the evolutionary character of the earthly creation, including the human, together with the command of Genesis, it amounts to a commission to complete an unfinished universe by exercising our imagination in freedom. God does not continue to fashion the creation by providing us with detailed blueprints prior to our dreaming of new possibilities. The divine creativity is not diminished but on the contrary enhanced by enabling us to participate in it. Through the arts and sciences, through skills and techniques, we are meant to fashion civilizations and cultures as embodiments of both God's glory and human creativity. This is what, as a matter of fact, has happened in human history. That it has not taken place flawlessly is something that we will attend to in a moment. What is important for us to appreciate now is the key role of the *image* in the image of God. Without it the other aspects cannot function, for it is imagination which is the faculty of the future, the anchor of hope. With God, as Jesus says, all things are possible, because

God is a dreamer. And by being created according to God's image we have been called to share actively in the divine dream.

Dream Slayers

In the preceding chapters we have described the effects of our radical sinfulness on the gifts associated with the other three functions. Here we want to do something similar with intuition. In the chapter on feeling we indicated that the wounding of grateful remembrance and the wounding of dreaming hope are connected. Among the possible ways of developing our present theme we choose to concentrate on the two extremes of the wounding of imagination: first, its paralysis or numbing, and, second, its trivializing employment. We are all too familiar with both.

All of us have had some experience of being locked into a present attitude or situation that we cannot or do not want to change. Severe depression is an extreme example, a condition which leaves a person relatively hopeless because there is no effective envisioning of alternative possibilities. Every encouraging suggestion from others becomes grist for the mill of despondency. Socially, too, we have met people, individuals and groups, whose traditional routines, sometimes concerning the most trivial details, have an enslaving effect on them and often a controlling influence on others. In relation to the Jungian functions, this is what happens when sensing is inflated and intuiting is not permitted to emerge. Spiritually, it is to such a posture that the call to *metanoia* is addressed, e.g., Matthew 3:2; 4:17. *Meta* indicates a transition from one state to another, while *noia* points to the mind or heart which must undergo such a change. Paul's Letters have a number of expressions which accent that the Gospel calls us to conversion, transformation, transfiguration, and the like, e.g., Romans 12:2; Ephesians 4:23. But where sin holds sway, paralysis and numbness hinder such change. Let us note that the remarks just made about sensing and intuiting are not intended to suggest that dominant intuiters are less in need of conversion

than dominant sensers. All of us of whatever type are called to
be free with respect to our dominant preferences. Conversion
for a dominant intuiter may well consist in coming to terms
with the practicalities of life. But here we are considering the
paralysis which takes place when intuiting is stricken by our
sinfulness.

We experience the same deficiency at times in relationships, whether they be our own or belong to others whom we
are trying to help. A tacit agreement, for example, between
husband and wife, or among the members of a religious community, to leave whole areas of a relationship undiscussed and
unhealed is frequently (not always however) a sign that hope of
changing for the better has died. A veneer of civility can hide
deep alienation when people no longer invest their energies in
sounding out possibilities of rapprochement. Imagination has
ceased to be employed in the service of love.

In the larger Church and in society as a whole, this same
numbing of creativity can assume at times demonic propor-
tions and perpetuate age-old enslavements. When Pharisaism—addictive attachment to formalities and externals—and
traditionalism—addictive unwillingness to admit change—are
in the ascendency, both the powerful and the powerless lapse
into an impotent despair. Joseph's brothers, the other sons of
Jacob, were doubtless locked into such rigidity and, as later in
the case of Jesus himself, the presence of one who dared to
dream became an intolerable threat: "Here comes the man of
dreams. Come on, let us kill him" (Gen 37:19). How many
situations of tyranny have been characterized by this murder-
ous hatred toward real or suspected dreamers who might
socialize the vision of a different kind of life? The world of
today offers us abundant examples. In Russia and Czechoslova-
kia, as well as in many security states in the West, dreaming is
subversive. The greater evil is not that thousands of innocents
are imprisoned, but that society itself becomes a prison. And in
the darkest dungeon of all languishes hope, imagination, the
future.

But if the powers of darkness sometimes imprison the
imagination, they can also do the opposite in such a way as to

effect the same eventual destruction: they sometimes seduce the imagination into sterile and empty fantasy. This precious treasure, meant by God to be expended on the humanizing and divinizing of life on earth, is squandered on the trivializing of existence. Commercial television is a familiar example. Thanks to imagination, we have enjoyed the richness of mass culture and entertainment, but at what a price! When TV becomes a tool for the manipulation of aspirations, how deadly becomes its impact on the imagination as well as on the heart. From nursery school to nursing home, through escapist "drama" and games and contests and exploitative commercials, it evokes the "vanity and chasing of the wind" of which Qoheleth wrote (Ecc 1:2, 14, etc.). Add other teasings of people's dreams of the good life: gambling casinos, lotteries, off-track betting; the current fascination with computer games and calculators employed in the spirit of gadgetry; the pageantry of beauty queens and bowl games. It adds up to a whole dimension of our present culture in which imagination is pitted against itself. It is far from our purpose here to engage in a diatribe against popular entertainment and culture. But the wholesale frivolous waste of creativity dishonors God's image in us. In the long run this second effect of sinfulness on the imagination coalesces with the first. Both psychologically and spiritually meaningless fantasy can only reinforce the atrophy of creative imagination. At a time when humanity is critically in need of new visions and dreams, to acquiesce in such destruction would be a form of mass suicide. Genuine hope for our wounded humanity is something very different from a bland optimism regarding the abuse of God's gifts. The Gospel can be heard as good news only by those who are in touch with their present misery. The plight of imagination in our culture cries out for redemption.

Jesus: Prophet, Dreamer, Fool

Each time we turn to the person and ministry of Jesus as our principal model, there is a special joy of anticipation. What will we find in him that corresponds to what we have found in ourselves? And, as we encounter in him the relevant traits—in the present case intuitive traits—we are again amazed at the "fit" between human need and Gospel fulfillment. This time it is the Gospel according to John, together with the Johannine Letters and the Book of Revelation, which holds a special treasure for us. The Fourth Gospel is to a special degree the Gospel of the beyond. We are reminded of the hymn, "Look beyond the bread you eat," which captures the heart of the Eucharistic discourse of Chapter 6 and in fact of the entire Gospel. In its limpid symbolism this Gospel is pervaded with sacramentality—life and light primarily but also birth and death, water and wine, water and land, water and blood, water and Spirit, seeing and hearing and tasting and touching, and many others. It draws us through its symbolic discourse beyond the letter to the spirit and the essence of all that is real. Its "realized eschatology" renders the future already present, while remaining future. It is full of aspiration and yearning and promise, and the Spirit who stands for God the Future is particularly prominent at certain key points. How appropriately has the Christian tradition, in assigning Ezekiel's four creatures symbolically to the four Gospels, made the author of this Gospel the soaring "eagle of Patmos." Its most typical impact is to invite our spirit to soar toward that state and condition of limitless communion which Jesus describes and prays for in John's version of the Last Supper.

Through John, as well as through the Synoptics—and particularly through the parables of the latter—we can come into touch with Jesus as prophet, dreamer and fool. Here we will attend primarily to the first of these three, and we suggest that this is the title which best fits his intuitive side, as well as ours.

The Role of the Prophet

A little book by Walter Brueggemann, *The Prophetic Imagination,* can be our guide in the following broad sketch of the prophetic character of Jesus' life and ministry.[3] The theme is developed historically by situating Jesus in the tradition of prophecy in Israel, reaching back to the leadership of Moses in the confrontation with the "royal consciousness" of Pharaoh. The tradition continues in the prophets, major and minor, of the period of monarchy in the political history of God's chosen people. Our correlation of prophecy with the intuitive function is not based on any naive view of the prophet as a predicter of future events. Nor would we want to neglect the fact that the prophet must exercise all the functions; thinking, for example, enters into the role of *krisis* (judgment) as the prophet is called to denounce present evil; likewise the feeling function is involved in reminding people of the violated covenant. But the prophet's primary role is the faithful communication of God's dream on behalf of the people. Before being a speaker, the prophet is a seer, and a listener, and God speaks to him especially through his visual imagination and through impulsions to symbolic gestures. Needless to say, the prophet is called to accept God's judgment on his own sinfulness and to relinquish his own personal vision of life for the one that God communicates to him.

The prophet, says Brueggemann, typically comes upon a scene of *numbness* and of acquiescence in sinful enslavement. The first impact of the prophetic movement is to enable people to *groan, complain,* and *mourn.* Psychologically and socially as well as spiritually, the essential conditions of hope begin to exist when people perceive and audibly acknowledge their misery and need. Every groan contains a hope for deliverance. Now the prophet very often evokes this first movement of hope by stimulating the "dangerous memories" of which we spoke in the last chapter. Present attitudes, behaviors, structures are evaluated in the light of the primordial covenant—"This is not what God had in mind—it is not being faithful to your covenant—it is not your *real* story but an *un*story." Thus the summons to remember leads gradually to the call to dream, on the basis of the remembered promise of God. "You don't have to live this way—there are alternatives—listen to what God says about the future." " 'I know the plans I have in mind for you'—it is Yahweh who speaks—'plans for peace, not disaster, reserving a future full of hope for you' " (Jer 29:11). " 'Console my people, console them,' says your God. 'Speak to the heart of Jerusalem and call to her that the time of slavery is ended' " (Is 40:1–2).

With such utterances does the prophetic imagination mediate between God's vision of the future and the people's hope of deliverance from the present. What then ensues can be described in the language of psychosocial and spiritual energy. The process of liberation has begun. Brueggemann portrays how song and dance are drawn into the revitalization of the people's hope. He describes the alternating rhythm of groaning under the burden of the oppressive present and joyfully anticipating the promised future. In the great tradition of the spirituals of the black people Americans have an example of how mourning and jubilation can energize a movement toward emancipation. The same basic dynamic would seem to be at work wherever God initiates the redemptive process through a prophetic figure and movement. Let us say in passing that what with the Bible we are here describing as a societal phenomenon has its counterpart in the interpersonal and even intrapersonal dimensions of our lives. For each of us is like a people or a city, within which the master-slave relationship is verified in different ways; and each of us comes in our development to moments when the message is heard: "Tell Pharaoh to let my people go." Pharaoh here becomes a metaphor for the tyrannical rule of the psyche by the dominant function, and the people are the inferior function, whose time of emergence from a shadow existence has come.

It is against the background of this understanding of the prophetic imagination that we can appreciate Jesus' ministry from a new perspective. We see him in all four of the Gospels enabling people to complain by his own complaints, e.g., Matthew 11:16–19, 20–24; 12:38–42; 15:1–9; 16:2–4; 17:17; John 2:13–25; 5:39–47; 8:34–47. He denounces the "royal consciousness" of the leaders who are not open to the God of surprise. Above all he holds out a vision, which in the Synoptics is named as the kingdom and in the Fourth Gospel as eternal life, and he begins to embody the vision in his own behavior and in the behavior which he encourages in his disciples. Around him

there begins to form a community of those who have caught
the spark of his dream and want to dream along with him.

Parables and Symbols

Two specific teaching vehicles of this movement into the
future can be especially helpful when we read or prayerfully
reflect on the Gospels. The first is, at least in the Synoptic
accounts, Jesus' favorite mode of teaching—the parable. As
recent scholarship has made clear, Jesus' use of parables was
not just a pedagogical device for holding attention or conveying spiritual truths through sensate images. Rather, in them he
is drawing on his own remarkable imagination to evoke a
saving exercise of imagination on the part of his listeners. This
is what happens in us if we read the parables as they were
intended to be read. Caught up in a story, yet giving a perhaps
complacent assent, we suddenly find that we are being challenged to complete the story in our own life at the risk of
changing some fundamental habit or viewpoint—to recognize,
for example, that it is I who have kept going to my own little
Jericho, eyes deliberately averted from the wounded body
across the road, and leaving to some Samaritan of ill repute
responsibility for the affair, or that even after decades of a
devout life I am not yet convinced that an assortment of trivia
has kept me from the pearl of great price. It is no exaggeration
to say that Jesus spent more time disposing people to be open
to a few basic questions in life than in providing them with
specific answers to lesser questions. The parable has a good
deal in common with a *koan*, a question posed by a Zen master
to disciples not with a view to their giving the correct answer
but as material for struggle leading to enlightenment. Both
forms are designed to evoke a posture of listening to the
beyond. We mention again that intuiting is a *perceiving* function. In a way which contrasts with sensing, this use of imagination is a contemplative one. We let go in order to listen to the
music of the spheres, which is "silent music" (William John-
ston).

The second vehicle of orientation to the future is *symbol,* so prominent in the Fourth Gospel and perhaps a major reason why this Gospel is the favorite of so many who read and pray the Scriptures. For symbol, in contrast to the merely informational sign, not only points but carries beyond itself. When we have prayerfully read a Johannine passage we are typically left in an empty, joyful, aspiring mood. Readers can test this out with particular mysteries in the Gospel according to John. "Come and see," Jesus says (1:39). At Cana "he let his glory be seen, and his disciples believed in him" (2:11). Or, "look around you; look at the fields; already they are white, ready for harvest" (4:35). Countless phrases and statements like these are invitations, not to analyze the symbolic content, but to soar on eagles' wings to the yonder of faith. Symbolic imagination of this kind is not a chatty internal movie projector but a transparent opening to contemplation.

Jesus the prophet is not far from Jesus the dreamer and the fool. It is rather commonly the lot of intuitive types to be considered "out of it," not in touch with reality—a fair characterization if "reality" were ever to be reduced to present, sensate detail. The Synoptics record a scene in which Jesus' own relatives so regard him and seek to save him from himself (Mk 3:21). Herod treats him like a fool (Lk 22:8–12), and so do his mockers during his passion (Mk 15:16–20) and on Calvary (Lk 23:35–38). Especially in the hour of his abandonment, in the garden and on the cross, what were his own doubts about what he had done with his life? Did he himself feel like a fool, a dreamer who had missed life's opportunity and led others astray? Mark's account of the agony uses a strong Greek term which might be taken as hinting that Jesus was "beside himself" in fear and anguish (14:34). Later Paul will describe himself as a fool for Christ (1 Cor 4:10; see also 2 Cor 11—12), and great saints like Francis of Assisi and Ignatius of Loyola have felt called to embody the foolishness of the Gospel into their own life-style and that of their followers. The Eastern Church has one category of saint not had by the Western Church: the fool. In whatever expression, the universal Church down the centuries has been deeply influenced by this aspect of the Gospel, and convinced with Paul that it is through the foolishness of the cross that God's wisdom triumphs over perverse human wisdom (1 Cor 1:17—2:9).

From this perspective, the resurrection becomes God's surprise for his dear creation. The risen Christ is, as it were, the slain clown joyfully leaping up again to the bewilderment of his slayers, and exclaiming, "See, I'm alive—I'm still here." Only a dreaming God could have created such a scenario for the human circus, and only in proportion as we enter into this dream do we experience both the foolishness and the surprise.

The Early Church: Maranatha

Our last chapter acquainted us briefly with the extent to which the apostolic Church lived by the "dangerous memory" of the crucified and risen Lord. What is even more striking in Acts, the Letters, and the Book of Revelation is the degree to which it was, simultaneously, a community energized from a future dreamed in hope. Almost the last word of the entire Bible is the early Church's acclamation—its favorite mantra, we might say: "Come, Lord Jesus" (Rev 22:20)—a translation of the Aramaic *marana tha.* Paul, at the end of his First Letter to the Corinthians, actually uses the Aramaic, possibly in the indicative form of *maran atha*—the Lord is coming (16:22). Eschatology permeates the entire New Testament. In his Letters to the Thessalonians, for example, Paul has to deal both with the common belief that the second coming is imminent and with the consequences of this belief in people's attitudes and behavior (1 Thess 4:13–18; 2 Thess 2:1–12). A dreaming yet energetic hope vitalizes the early communities among both Jews and Gentiles, as we find these portrayed in Acts and the rest of the New Testament (Acts 1:7; 3:20; 1 Cor 1:7; 7:26–31; 15; Jas 5:7–8; 1 Pet 1:13; 4:7).

It is quite clear that this expectation of deliverance is far from inducing passivity. One striking example in Paul may be cited here. Chapter 8 of Romans is in some ways the peak lyrical moment of that dramatic Letter. Paul is celebrating the liberation that has *already* happened: "The law of the spirit of

life in Christ Jesus has set you free from the law of sin and
death" (8:1). What is more, "The Spirit of God has made his
home in you" (8:9). But then, almost in the same breath, he
indicates that the Spirit has been given in order to groan
within us, to be the inner divine principle of *our* groaning,
together with the rest of creation, for the *not yet*, the liberation which will be accomplished only when our status as God's
beloved sons and daughters comes to full revelation (8:18–27).
It is this restless, futurizing, dreaming hope aroused in Christians by the gift of the Holy Spirit which gives them indomita-
ble courage in the face of the enemy. Absolutely nothing,
"neither death nor life, no angel, no prince, nothing that exists,
nothing still to come, not any power or height or depth, nor
any created thing, can ever come between us and the love of
God made visible in Christ Jesus our Lord" (8:38–39). Such is
the power of the divine dream planted within the Church by
the risen Lord through his Spirit.

Notable in this New Testament eschatology of dreaming
hope is the role of the Spirit. In the last discourse of Jesus, the
primary accent was on the Spirit as agent of anamnesis; the
Spirit will teach by reminding the disciples of all that Jesus has
said to them (Jn 14:26). The passages in Acts typically show the
Spirit at work in the present outpouring of gifts, e.g., 2:17–21;
8:15–17; 10:46–48; 15:28; 19:5–6. Neither of these accents is
absent from Paul, but it seems to be the Spirit as orienting to
the future which he prefers to emphasize. There is a new
creation in the making and the Spirit leads us forward. What is
old must give way to what is new, and the dead letter must
yield to the life-giving Spirit (Rom 7:1–6; 8:1–4; 2 Cor 3:1–11;
5:16–17; Gal 5:1–6; Eph 2:15). Paul's prophetic gift is exercised
principally in resisting the efforts of the Judaizers to keep the
new vision imprisoned in the old ritualism. "When Christ
freed us, he meant us to remain free," he tells the Galatians
(5:1).

And so the rest of the New Testament contains the important facets of intuiting that we have seen in the ministry of
Jesus himself: dreaming hope, the prophetic call to alternative
ways, a focus on the future with the help of imagination,

soaring in freedom. It is also rich in the power of symbol, particularly of course in the Book of Revelation, about which we now want to say a word. Many Christians, accustomed to nourishing their faith with the Gospels and Epistles, don't quite know what to do with the Apocalypse, as we used to call it. They might do well to approach it in the light of the present chapter, letting its wild images work on their own imagination in freedom. It is important that they let the images and symbols flow without rationalistic interpretation. Societally, this book models for the Church today the necessity of bringing the power of holy imagination to bear on the struggle with principalities and powers in our own culture. What the Book of Revelation sought to do for early Christians who had to live counter-culturally in the Roman empire of Nero and Domitian needs also to be done by us in prophetic and apocalyptic forms suited to our own situation.

A Prophetic, Dreaming Church

We do not intend to describe the course of prophecy, eschatological hope, and symbolism through the centuries. Some readers may wish to explore this intriguing history, for example in Christian art and symbolism. Instead we will say a few ecclesiological and pastoral words relevant to the place of intuitive gifts in the life of the Church today.

As the Church is constituted by the grateful remembrance of Jesus Christ, so is it constituted by the dreaming hope of his coming again. "He will come again to judge the living and the dead" is an article of Christian faith, reaffirmed around the world by millions of Christians every Sunday. In our consciousness of his real presence among us, do we perhaps neglect that he is also, somehow, really absent? Otherwise, how could we "wait in joyful hope for the coming of our Savior, Jesus Christ," as we pray in each Eucharistic celebration after the Lord's Prayer? No less than memory, imagination is a constitutive element in the life of the Church. Were all Christians suddenly to be deprived of the power of imagination, the ability to yearn and to say "*marana tha*," there would literally be no

Church. Our community is defined as the community of this dreaming hope.

Even without our adverting to it, this dream of the second coming and of the world to come daily energizes the life of the Church. The celebration of the sacraments, particularly the Eucharist, is obviously central in the exercise of what we may call ecclesial intuition. This is true first of all because of the power of symbol contained in the basic sacramental gestures as well as in the accompanying ritual. In any good liturgical celebration we are invited to look beyond the bread we eat, to experience that water is water and yet somehow also the divine Spirit, to hear the reconciling word spoken by a fellow sinner as effectively reconciling us with the Trinity and with the whole of creation. Second, the sacraments are signs of a reality which is *not yet*, intimations of a future creation. To be so focused on the Eucharist as real presence or as a memorial supper that we miss its anticipatory showing forth of the heavenly banquet would be to deprive ourselves of life-giving energies from that future which is from God, which in truth *is* God.

When this eschatological sense, expressed and nourished in sacramental celebration, is taken by Christians into the communal and apostolic dimensions of their lives, it brings to all they touch a spirit of newness and hope. It is this ecclesial intuiting which gives to the prophetic Church remarkable resiliency and stamina in the face of the massive evil embedded in society and culture. "I beckon to the nations and hoist my signal for the peoples," says the Lord in a prophetic passage applied by Vatican II to the Church of all ages (Is 49:22; cf. 62:10; see the *Constitution on the Church*, nn. 9, 48). After several centuries of estrangement from Western society, the Roman Catholic Church has been consciously trying to be this standard of hope for the nations. Particularly in what has come to be called the ministry of peace and justice in the world is this prophetic stance at work. One of its most dramatic expressions took place in 1965 when Paul VI became the first Pope ever to address the United Nations. With a simplicity and power that thrilled all who heard it, he had the right word for the right occasion. "Let the weapons fall from your hands," he cried to the world leaders. "No more war! War never again!"[4] It was, of course, a Utopian utterance. It said nothing of the hard road by which the dream of peace had to journey in order to become a project and then an accomplishment. But we must first dream of peace and justice if there is to be a future of peace and justice.

The Church in our day increasingly feels a call to be prophetic. Christian ministers are growing in their realization that while peace is the work of justice—hence a contribution of the thinking function—it must also be *imagined* in itself and in the ways to its realization. Changing this or that political or economic structure will avail little unless the resources of imagination and the power of symbol are set free for the redemption of society and culture. It is no accident that we find a growing pastoral recourse to poetry, drama, and the arts, and particularly to the play of clowns and fools among Christian groups committed to peace and justice. The role of the court fool in past ages, notes Johannes Metz, was to represent that there were alternatives to the royal policies. So today, both in frolic and in vulnerable non-violent resistance to what is dehumanizing, Christians are once again learning to play the fool.

We bring this section to a close with two brief remarks. The first is that while the primary horizon of Christian dreaming is the kingdom in its fullness, the energies released by this absolute future become available for lesser dreams of the future within history. No specific political or economic scenario can be identified as *the* Christian society; nevertheless our energies are not directed to escaping from history but to rendering it more congruous with the final kingdom. And secondly, although we have dealt here primarily with ecclesial intuition in its societal aspect, comparable developments are possible with respect to the intrapersonal and interpersonal employ of the prophetic and symbolic imagination. The effort of individual Christians to grow in likeness to God through the development of the intuiting function, as well as their care to image God in their relationships, will have the same characteristics of dreaming hope, recourse to symbol and prophecy, and so forth, as we have described in the larger Church. We will have some suggestions on this score a little later, in discussing ways to develop the intuiting gift in its fullness. To that discussion we now turn.

III. DEVELOPING THE INTUITING GIFT

By now it will be clear that the remarks which follow are meant to be helpful to all readers, but particularly to those whose development has made sensing their dominant preference. This could be a good place for each reader, of whatever type, to create a scenario entitled, "The History of Intuiting in My Life." At which of the four periods, childhood or adolescence or early or later adulthood, did this side of my personality move forward to "do its thing"? Did this happen in an extraverted or introverted way? What were the specific manifestations of intuitive behavior? What tensions—particularly with sensing—were experienced? How would I now evaluate the quality of my creativity, my openness to unexplored possibilities? How does the future beckon me with respect to this gift?

I might want to pay special attention to the way in which this perceiving function has combined with my preferred judging function—feeling or thinking—at various periods of my life and at the present stage. What is characteristic of the rhythm of my living with respect to listening/responding, learning/speaking, contemplating/acting?

Each one will answer such a question, of course, not just in terms of belonging to one of sixteen developmental types, but also in terms of a unique history and call from God. In all such reflections, let it be said again, one should always trust one's experience, judgment, and call more than any general scheme devised by others. Still, it is remarkable how certain patterns of human growth repeat themselves in the lives of different people.

But let us direct our remarks now especially to dominant sensers, introverted or extraverted, particularly to those who find themselves at or near the "mid-life crisis." More than likely, the voice of intuition, faint or imperious, has been heard by them in recent years. They may be experiencing doubts or anxieties of a new kind, or a new dissatisfaction with life, without quite knowing where such movements are coming from or how they are to deal with them. Quite possibly this time of pain—even of crucifixion—represents also the biggest opportunity they will ever have for conversion and growth.

The general guideline of seeking development through exercise of the desired behavior with the help of models obtains here, as in the case of the other functions. If I live or work with one or more dominant intuiters I am blessed, whatever may be the resulting tensions. The witticism, "If you can't beat 'em, join 'em," has a wise application here. Let me, at least at times and within the limits of my growing toleration, play the intuiters' game and learn to deal with life as I see them do. I will do it rather badly at first. But I can learn, I can grow.

There are a number of specific strategies which can be helpful. Let me be wary of excessive neatness in my personal and relational life. It's quite possible, after all, that St. Joseph's carpenter shop was chaotic at times, especially when he wondered what was happening in his dream life. Dominant sensers who are developing their intuition will sometimes find themselves forgetful of detail and no longer in command of particulars. Their desk may become cluttered or the kitchen seem less orderly than they could formerly tolerate. If they can understand why such phenomena are appearing in their lives and how the emergence of the intuiting gift brings such limitations, they will be able to turn otherwise negative situations to fruitful purpose.

How I deal with space and time is also important. One broad strategy might be to encourage a greater feel for symbol in my shaping of life. Positioning my desk so that it looks out on the bell tower of the university where I have labored for twenty years, and stopping for an empty moment each evening at the fountain in the center of the campus, are examples of making space and time for symbolic moments.

There are, too, some ways of contemplating maps which

can modestly foster the yielding of the sensate to the intuitive. One can read a map with a view to the ability to situate every town and hamlet with accuracy, but one might also take some time with the same map to entertain what it would be like to drive through some of those exotic sounding places in Wyoming or New Mexico.

More generally, I can let myself spend a little more time in the world of the possible. Not every exploration of alternative ways unattached to present pragmatic reality is time wasted. Energies invested, for example, in an occasional dream of how I would spend a sabbatical or how I would deal with serious illness will not be wasted. Such exercises can deepen the dominant senser's readiness to respond to the surprises of life.

Intuitive Ways in Prayer

When it comes to making use of special times set aside for meditation and prayer, two quite opposite kinds of exercises can be helpful. One is simply to begin exercising the imagination, whether in fantasy or more pragmatically. The question "What would it be like if . . . ?" is a simple device for facilitating this kind of devout dreaming. What *would* it be like . . . if I took a *real* vacation this year, e.g., went back-packing with N. and N. in Maine or Colorado . . . if I were to ask for a sabbatical . . . if I changed from teaching to pastoral ministry, or vice versa . . . if I were Pope or President . . . etc.?

The opposite kind of exercise is one which is recommended by some psychologists on the basis of experiment and theory. When the senses are overloaded, there can take place at a certain point a spontaneous "flip" by which imagination is stimulated and set free to play. Sitting close to a waterfall and really listening to the particular sounds over a period of time, or doing something similar near a window which opens on a busy highway at rush hour, will, for some persons at least, provide the "trigger" which releases dreaming and fantasy.

The "process meditation" techniques of Ira Progoff's Intensive Journal, as well as some of the exercises listed by Anthony de Mello under "Fantasy" in *Sadhana: A Way to God,* may also be mentioned as examples of this approach to imaginative prayer. As was the case with the other three functions, there are traditional forms, both Christian and non-Christian, which have an affinity with intuiting. I may exercise devotional fantasy, for example, by spending a day in the woods with Jesus and Mary, creating some attractive natural setting, and dreaming of what the three of us might do and say over a period of several hours. In fantasy, too, I can be present to "the joys and the hopes, the griefs and the anxieties" (opening words of Vatican II's *Constitution on the Church in the Modern World*) of the several billion inhabitants of the planet, journeying in imagination to an infinite variety of scenes. Those who have made the *Spiritual Exercises* of St. Ignatius will recall the striking scenario in which the Trinity views and discusses the human plight—"some are white, some black; some in peace and some at war; some weeping, some laughing . . ." (n. 106); the scene then changes to disclose Mary at prayer, ready for the annunciation. Such "prayer of Christ's memories," which we mentioned in the chapter on feeling, can be a fruitful and enjoyable way of exercising both intuitive and feeling functions.

Praying with Symbols

Anthony de Mello points out that the use of fantasy in prayer can lead very naturally to prayer with symbols, and he offers some exercises to this end. The Fourth Gospel represents an especially rich source for such symbolic prayer. It can also be helpful to bring into prayer pictures, poems, music, and in general whatever invites to an attitude of unfocused wonder, of openness to undefined horizons. Where there is the opportunity, both the ocean and the mountains, and nature in general, can assist the development of intuition, provided the dominant sensers are willing to let go of their preferred posture of attending to things in and for themselves.

Groups Intuiting

When groups come together to pray and reflect, shared intuiting and dream should be an accepted thing. This is the moment for more sensate members of the family or community to let those who are considered dreaming types lead the way in common adventures into human spaces not yet experienced. Objects from nature—if a group is in a country setting—as well as photographs, personal treasures, symbolic passages of the Scriptures—just read or even acted out—the use of parable and of tales like *The Little Prince* and *Hope for the Flowers*, a set of slides with musical accompaniment—these are only a few of many possibilities.

In decision-making processes of groups or larger assemblies of people, it is important that there be regular times when participants are reflecting and relating in a dreaming, hope-filled posture. The same question "What would it be like if ... ?" which we recommended for individuals has been found to be extremely helpful in disengaging meetings from a plodding, pedestrian approach. When it is only the facts and their rational analysis which enter into the decision-making processes of a group or organization, only half of the available energies of people are being utilized.

Finally, though the point is obvious, we need to recall how much intuitive energy is contained in the sacraments of the Church, especially where the Eucharist is celebrated with attention to symbolic material and gesture. The rediscovery of the power and the role of the word in liturgy has been a blessing among Roman Catholics, thanks largely to the influence of dialogue with other Christian churches which have traditionally cherished the word of God to a greater degree. But this development of the past few decades has also occasioned in some circles a certain wordiness and excessively cognitive way of celebration. Now we seem to be returning to a fresh appreciation of how the flow of energy among all four functions can lead to a kind of empty silence, where minds and hearts are left free to soar to God under the movement of the Spirit.

"Soaring silence" might be a good phrase to end with. We would not want to leave readers, especially those with sensing preferences, with the misapprehension that intuiting prayer calls for a perpetual clicking of the shutter of the psychic camera. Intuitive prayer does differ sharply from sensate prayer, at least in its initial form. The former, as we have seen, is unfocused, whereas the latter tends to be sharply attentive. But contemplative prayer that is intuitive can, like the prayer of simple regard, lead to stillness, albeit a soaring stillness that moves ever beyond the now/here toward the no/where.

> Yonder,—What high as that? We follow, now we follow—
>   Yonder, yonder, yonder,
> Yonder.[5]

EXERCISES

A. *For the individual:*

1. Read Chapters 21 and 22 of the Book of Revelation. Then enter into the scene as a participant of life in the heavenly city.

2. Begin with the verse, "God loved the world so much that he gave his only Son" (Jn 3:16). Then imagine yourself as an angel (your name?) sent to be present contemplatively to places on the earth where people are, awake and asleep, laughing and weeping, loving and hating, etc. Where do you go? What do you see and hear?

3. Envisage yourself as living with greater freedom from what you consider to be your principal inordinate attachment. What would your prayer be like? Your relationships? Your engagement in ministry?

4. If the holy family were to be citizens of your city or town, what would they be like? Go through a typical day in their life. Imagine yourself being their neighbor.

5. Choose a symbol from nature—animal, vegetable, or mineral—expressive of what your life has been or of what you would like it to be.

B. *For groups:*

1. After some time for individual prayer, share with one another: (a) some dream each has had for herself or himself; (b) a dream for the group or community; (c) a dream for the Church, the country, humanity.

2. If you are in the country or at the shore, have people go off to find some object in nature expressive of a common theme, or of whatever theme the object itself symbolizes for them. Share the results, and incorporate the symbols into a Eucharistic or other celebration.

3. Let each member of the group, in solitary prayer, select for every other member of the group a verse or passage from Scripture which is expressive of that person's contribution to community life.

SCRIPTURE REFERENCES

1. Psalms: 8, 16, 24, 42, 43, 45, 48, 62, 63, 65, 72, 84, 85, 96, 98, 114, 115, 121, 122, 127.

2. Isaiah 2:1–5; 9:1–7; 11; 35:1–10; 40—66 passim; Jeremiah 23:1–8; 30—31; Ezekiel 1:4–28; 2:1–21; 34; 37:1–14; Daniel 4; 7—12; Zechariah 9—14.

3. John; 1 John; Revelation.

4. Romans 8; 11:25–36; 1 Corinthians 15; Ephesians 1; 3; Colossians 3:1–4.

NOTES

1. George J. Schemel, S.J. is the originator of the correlation of the four Jungian functions with the four philosophical transcendentals, *unum, verum, bonum, pulchrum* (the one, the true, the good, the beautiful).

2. "Only A Shadow," by Carey Landry. Copyright © by Rev. Carey Landry and North American Liturgy Resources, Phoenix, Arizona 85029.

3. Walter Brueggemann, *The Prophetic Imagination* (Philadelphia: Fortress, 1978).

4. Joseph Gremillion (ed.), *The Gospel of Peace and Justice: Catholic Social Teaching Since Pope John* (Maryknoll: Orbis, 1976), pp. 383–84.

5. Gerard Manley Hopkins, "The Leaden Echo and the Golden Echo," *Poems and Prose* (Middlesex: Penguin, 1953), p. 54.

CHAPTER 6
Fullness of Love

Individuation/Charity

St. Thérèse of Lisieux, who died at twenty-three, is an appropriate figure to introduce at the beginning of this final chapter. For one thing, she can help us to relativize the relative and to avoid turning the models we have employed into behavioral straitjackets. By God's grace, she did not have to celebrate her fiftieth birthday before achieving an extraordinary human and Christian wholeness. She became a saint without benefit of the mid-life crisis! And, again by God's grace, she was given to see, with a remarkable simplicity, that the wholeness we all seek consists in *love*.

In her autobiography Thérèse describes how she dealt with the consuming passion for greatness which marked her personality. Contemplating a world in which martyrs shed their blood for Christ, confessors proclaimed him, and bishops and priests ministered to their congregations, she wondered what was left for her. To contribute powerfully to the salvation of humanity while hidden behind cloister walls and leading a routine life of prayer, work, and companionship was the challenge that confronted her. She discovered that the secret was love:

> During my meditation, my desires caused me a veritable martyrdom, and I opened the Epistles of St. Paul to find some kind of answer. Chapters 12 and 13 of the First Epistle to the Corinthians fell under my eyes. I read there, in the first of these chapters, that all cannot be apostles, prophets, doctors, etc., that the Church is composed of different

members, and that the eye cannot be the hand at on
the same time. The answer was clear, but it did not ......
my desires, and gave me no peace. . . . Without becoming
discouraged, I continued my reading, and this sentence
consoled me: "Yet strive after the better gifts, and I point
out to you a yet more excellent way." And the apostle
explains how all the most perfect gifts are nothing without
love. That charity is the excellent way that leads most surely
to God.

I finally had rest. Considering the mystical body of the
Church, I had not recognized myself in any of the members
described by St. Paul, or rather I desired to see myself in
them all. Charity gave me the key to my vocation. I understood that if the Church had a body composed of different
members, the most necessary and most noble of all could
not be lacking to it, and so I understood that the Church had
a heart and that this heart was burning with love. I understood that it was love alone that made the Church's members act, that if love ever became extinct, apostles would not
preach the Gospel and martyrs would not shed their blood. I
understood that love comprised all vocations, that love was
everything, that it embraced all times and places . . . in a
word, that it was eternal.

Then, in the excess of my delirious joy, I cried out: O Jesus,
my love . . . my vocation, at last I have found it. . . . My
vocation is love![1]

Jung and Jesus

Where Jung spoke of *individuation,* Jesus spoke of *love.*
Both were thinking of the fullness of living to which we are all
called. Both saw this vocation in terms of likeness to God. For
Christians, to be like God is to love, for *God is love* (1 Jn 4:8).
The journey from image to likeness is consummated in love.
The transforming vision of God, in which we see God as God
truly is, as unlimited love, is what brings the created and
redeemed image of God in us to its full flowering in love (1 Jn
3:2).

As in the other chapters of this book, Jung can help us here to understand the Gospel more fully, and the Gospel in turn can throw a unique light on the journey toward the integration of personality. Let us examine now just how this is so, and then suggest some ways in which our development toward Godlikeness can be fostered.

I. THE JOURNEY TOWARD INDIVIDUATION

Human individuation or integration, as we conceive it according to the developmental typology employed in this book, may be described in six statements.

First, human beings come to wholeness in their life journey to the degree to which they develop the power or freedom to exercise *each* of the four functions in accordance with the call of each of life's situations.

Such a statement will be less abstract for us if we think of one or two persons, especially senior citizens, whom we would consider to be mature, truly free, holy. What are they like? Well, they are not without flaw. And they certainly have not lost their spontaneous behavioral preferences. But they have for the most part succeeded in developing their ability to exercise all four functions, particularly their less preferred ones, according to the requirements of each human situation. With a certain freedom they can listen when life calls for listening, even though their spontaneous preference may be to achieve or to respond. They are free to pay attention to the routine demands of the present, but also to let go of the present and to open themselves in order to create challenging alternatives. They are capable of showing sympathy for people in need, even when their natural bent inclines them more to letting the truth hang out, whatever the effects on others. In the technical language of Jungian typology, they have developed all four functions, even the so-called inferior function, to the point that they are free to employ each when life calls for it. To say this is not to suggest that their freedom is perfect, or that they are not still in need of further growth. But, though their physical energies may at this point be quite limited, they are psychically drawing on the energies of all four functions.

Second, human beings come to wholeness in their life journey to the degree to which all four of the functions are exercised in *harmony*, though not without an energizing *tension*.

Once again let us consider a mature person or two in whom the statement is notably verified. Here the key notion is harmony, reconciliation, peace. When we are just beginning our journey to wholeness, the opposites we carry within us tend to be at odds with one another. Our dominant intuiting, for example, may continually oppress our sensing and rarely permit us to draw energy from the perception of present concrete reality. At such a stage, our sensing may be able to do no more than submit to such oppression, with an occasional sortie into hostile or aggressive retaliation. As we grow, however, these contentious siblings, S and N, T and F, come slowly to appreciate each other and to learn that only in the acceptance of complementarity despite tension does the path to real life lie. Gradually the relationships between opposite functions, as well as between the attitudes of extraversion and introversion, and between perceiving and judging, can become one of mutual assertiveness. The dominant or preferred function, instead of jealously guarding its hegemony, can learn to let go and can experience, in pain but also in joy, that life must be shared if it is to be preserved, and that the empowerment of the weak is the noblest exercise of strength. When a dominant function yields to its weaker sibling, it eventually becomes itself more powerful. Without such sacrifice, this is not possible.

Third, human beings come to wholeness through four distinct stages of their life journey, and according to quite varied sequences of development of the functions in extraverted and introverted expressions.

This statement summarizes the working hypothesis of our developmental typology. We will not here repeat the detailed explanation of the theory of development we have sketched in Chapter 1; some readers may wish to review that description at this point. Our present focus on wholeness prompts two distinct remarks. The first is that, in the ordinary course of events, growth toward wholeness of personality is not like a balloon being inflated, at first small and then made larger and larger in a smooth and uniform expansion. It is rather, as we have said, like the "stick shift" and "clutch" mechanisms of some automobiles. One seems, from the age of six, to go through distinct and successive stages of development of each of the four facets of personal behavior. Each partial development, of sensing or intuiting, thinking or feeling, is carried as a gain into the next stage of growth. But in order that the later, and less favored, behavior may have its chance to emerge, the ones previously developed must, to some extent, be relativized, particularly when the opposite function is developing. This is especially true, as we have said several times, where there is question of the emergence of the inferior function, at about age thirty-five. This is a moment of life which calls for the apparent foolishness of letting go of the most preferred and usually best developed function. When one adds to this successive development of the four functions the further factor of the alternating attitudes of extraversion and introversion, the image of the journey to wholeness is seen as a dynamic and contrapuntal one. As we grow, we are continually called to a counterbalance (in Jungian language, to "compensation") and a rhythmic growth. For example, the boy or the girl of twelve who has spent childhood in developing introverted feeling will now be spontaneously drawn to develop extraverted sensing or intuiting. The shift here is from judging to perceiving and from introverted to extraverted behavior. Similar shifts at twenty and thirty-five are standard features of the journey to wholeness. Think of a sailboat approaching its goal not by a direct course but by tacking, maneuvering with sail and rudder first to one side, then to the other. Or think of a team of mountain climbers who scale a forbidding slope only diagonally, not straight up the vertical rock. It is by such indirection and accommodation, not head-on, that we move toward wholeness.

A second remark regarding our third statement is that it is important to emphasize the *variety* of patterns and sequences of growth toward wholeness, touching both the four functions and the introverted and extraverted attitudes. We have seen that there are no fewer than sixteen distinct patterns and sequences. Such a model will help to prevent too easy generalizations regarding the way in which human maturity is attained. It will, for one thing, keep us from misinterpreting Jung's celebrated remark about the second half of life bringing a call to interiority. There is a sense, for example, in which persons whose dominant function is introverted have been favoring interiority from childhood days. For such types the mid-life call may be to a fuller social engagement of their energies. At thirty-five, for instance, a personality of type INFP = FNST/*IEIE* may be given a call to enter more fully into a vigorous apostolic engagement in public affairs. Jung's remark is better understood in terms of transcendence than of introversion.

Fourth, human beings come to wholeness not in isolation, but within the environments created by groups and societies, whose preferences interact with those of individuals.

This statement brings us back to our model of solitude, friendship, and society, seen now from the perspective of wholeness. The character and the quality of each individual's growth at any stage, and especially during childhood and adolescence, will be profoundly affected by the consonance or dissonance between the individual personality and its current behavior, on the one hand, and the surrounding world, on the other. If, for example, I am attempting to develop in adolescence my gift of extraverted intuiting within a family which does not prize such behavior and offers no appealing model for it, my growth in that behavior may be significantly affected. Or if, as a child, my very feeling parents did not appreciate my preference for introverted thinking and, in their anxiety over my normalcy, did a kind of violence to me, the whole of my development will have to reckon with that unfortunate experience.

Here let us say that, while the Jungian functions and attitudes were constructed primarily for expressing the variety of personality traits of individuals, it seems clear that families and other groups can be analogously described in the same language. The same would appear to be true even of whole societies and cultures, which tend to reward certain types of behavior and discountenance others. We can all think of certain institutional settings, in Church or civil society, where the contribution of extraverted intuiting or feeling is a low priority compared with sensing or thinking. The societal climate called for in the space center at Houston is quite different from that of, say, an Egyptian bazaar. Like the behavior of individuals, group and societal behavior is subject to ethical evaluation and spiritual discernment. Ultimately, the criterion is human wholeness, the development of Godlikeness in persons, groups, and society as a whole.

These considerations are quite relevant and important for our understanding of human wholeness. Because human beings are called not to isolation but to communion, the wholeness we seek is not merely individual in character. Whole persons tend to build whole communities and whole societies, and these in turn provide climates favorable to the development of wholeness in persons.

Fifth, human beings do not *inevitably* come to wholeness. Inner and environmental factors can coalesce to hinder the fulfillment of the human potential.

This statement is aimed at views of human life which are blandly optimistic, which do not take into account the manifest occurrence of tragedy and failure in the three realms of solitude, friendship, and society. Jung himself felt that relatively few persevered in the journey to individuation. It is obvious that countless numbers never have a chance for the kind of fulfillment which he describes. Sometimes personal deficiencies are insuperable—brain damage at birth, for example, or social environments so dehumanizing as to render the exercise of genuine freedom all but impossible. There is also the possibility that, however well endowed, we will not use well the freedom which we have. While there is an element of givenness and grace in every coming to wholeness, it is also contingent on *choice*—we must *desire* wholeness, as a pearl of great price, and be willing to let go of everything else in order that we may gain it. Though the prodding to develop this or that function appears, according to the evidence we have, with a certain inevitability at its appointed time, this is no guarantee that we will hear and heed the call.

Sixth—and this final statement is a "nevertheless" to the preceding one—even the negativities of persons and their environments can become material for growth toward wholeness. Here we touch on a feature of the Jungian approach which has a special affinity with the basic Gospel paradox. Darkness as well as light, the flaws and failures no less than the gifts and successes, can be made to minister to enlightenment and liberation. If whatever is shadowy and adversarial in our psychic life—the realm of our humanity which is peculiarly vulnerable to assault from Satan (a Hebrew term meaning adversary)—is but recognized, acknowledged, and allowed to emerge into the light, its latent energies can be creatively turned to the pursuit of wholeness. Making friends with our shadow, as Jungians suggest, is an affirmation that God writes straight with crooked lines. Even on the behavioral level we should not be too ready to dismiss the power of weakness, the wisdom of foolishness. Perhaps wholeness is a mosaic, fashioned out of fragments.

II. THE GOSPEL JOURNEY TOWARD LOVE

Christianity has many names for individuation—the Christ, grace, fullness, salvation, peace, life, kingdom, etc. But the word which by general consensus seems to express the heart of the Gospel is *love*. "The whole of the law is summarized in a single command: 'Love your neighbor as yourself' " (Gal 5:14). "If you love your fellow men you have carried out your obligations" (Rom 13:8). "Love is the law in all its fullness" (Rom 13:10). "The greatest . . . is love" (1 Cor 13:13). "By this love you have for one another, everyone will know that you are my disciples" (Jn 13:35).

Unfortunately, the very universality of the acceptance of love as the heart of the Gospel tends in some fashion to blunt the sharpness of its radical call. And we can make the mistake of narrowing its scope to feeling and sentiment. That is why, as we now reflect on love as Gospel wholeness, we have recourse to Jesus' response to the scribe who asked him which was the first of all the commandments: "You must love the Lord your God with all your heart, with all your soul, with all your mind and with all your strength. . . . You must love your neighbor as yourself" (Mk 12:28–30); see Lk 10:25–28; Mt 22:34–40; Dt 6:5; Lev 19:18).

According to Mark's version and also Luke's—in the latter it is the scribe who gives the response—there is question of four aspects of love, whereas Matthew's rendition of the scene has only three. With very little distortion it is possible to correlate these four aspects with the four functions, and so to see the exercise of these as flowering in love. Before enlarging on this correspondence two preliminary remarks will help us to appreciate better what a rich understanding of love is contained in the Gospel.

Note first that in Jesus' response there are mentioned three recipients of love, although only two of them are made the object of an explicit command: God, self, other human beings. Let us suggest that the three are one, in the sense that it is impossible to love or to fail to love one of these three without, in the very act, loving or failing to love the other two. For God is truly in me and in my neighbor. Both the neighbor and I are in God. And I am in my neighbor and my neighbor is in me. Think of the mystery of love within the Trinity, where the Father is in the Son, and vice versa, and both Father and Son are in the Holy Spirit, and vice versa. The inseparability of love as it takes place among the divine persons helps us understand this mystery, the inseparability of our love for God, self, the neighbor.

A second thing to note is that while the explicit command of Jesus is to *love,* there is an implicit command, made explicit elsewhere in the New Testament, to *accept* love. Or, putting it a little differently, Jesus is commanding us to grow in a *mutual* relationship of love, in which God, our self, and the neighbor both *give* and *accept* love. Human love of its very nature is marked by mutuality. To profess to love others without being willing to receive love from them—sometimes a harder thing to do—is a contradiction. Often it is the unwillingness to *receive* love—from God, from the neighbor, or from the human sources of love within my very person—which is the primary hindrance to growth toward the fullness of love. Being closed to receiving the *gift* of love from the other constitutes the false autonomy which is at the heart of sin.

In what follows, then, let the reader understand that what we say of the four facets of love is to be understood of giving love/accepting love within the intertwined relationships of God, self, and the neighbor.

Loving with the Whole Mind

What does it mean to love with the whole *mind?* It is to engage in a mutual loving relationship with God, self, the neighbor, with a focus on acceptance of the *total present reality* of the beloved. The mind is given for knowing, and in the Bible to *know* someone is often synonymous with loving that person. When the psalmist says, "Yahweh, you . . . *know* me" (Ps 139:1), or when the prophet says of the time of fulfillment, "I will betroth you to myself forever . . . and you will come to *know* Yahweh" (Hos 4:21–22), there is question of a knowledge that is intimate and loving, marked especially by *acceptance.*

Such loving with the whole mind has the characteristics of sensing and simplicity. It is a love which is focused on the now/here reality of the beloved in its totality. It says, "I love you just as you are." The phrase made famous by the counseling method of Carl Rogers, "unconditioned positive regard," fits this aspect of love perfectly. When we love in this way, we accept the weakness as well as the strength, the poverty as well as the wealth, of the one we love. Francis of Assisi embracing the leper images this aspect of love.

When such a love is directed toward God, it lets God be God—as God is and chooses to be toward us. It is willing to let God love us in the same way. It has no anxiety to make itself presentable or more worthy of the divine spouse who knocks, because it knows that God's love is not conditioned on our being ready or worthy, but rather accepts and loves us just as we are, with a divine simplicity.

To the degree to which the mutuality of our love relationship with God has this knowing simplicity built into it, its natural dynamism is to draw us to love ourselves and the neighbor similarly with the whole mind. Self-acceptance is an obvious consequence. Loving ourselves with the whole mind means that we are willing to let our shadowy side emerge into the light of consciousness. Yes, I carry within myself some rather ugly baggage, bundles of anxiety and rage whose negative energies can be personally and socially destructive in their unaccepted state. But if I love myself with the whole mind, if I am willing to embrace the leper who dwells within, these energies can be transfigured into powerful currents of good. And to the degree to which I love myself with the whole mind, my capacity for loving the neighbor in the same way grows. For one thing, I am no longer constrained to project onto the neighbor the ugliness within myself, for I have known (loved) it within myself. In addition, I am more disposed to accept the ugliness which I experience in others, along with the beauty which I am now in a better position to see. Within the same dynamism of a sensing, simple love, I let down my guard and permit the neighbor to know me, in *my* ugliness, as well as in my beauty.

Such is the love to which we are called by the Lord's command, "You shall love with your whole mind."

Loving with All One's Strength

What does it mean to love with all one's *strength?* Strength and power, we have seen, are characteristic of the thinking function, and so this aspect of the Lord's command to love totally evokes all that we have said about that facet of God's image in us. When we love God, self, the neighbor with all our strength, we bring to bear on the relationship the assertiveness, the vigorous adherence to truth and justice, the capacity for ordering and structuring life, and all the other qualities which go with this majestic aspect of God's image in us. Thinking is a judging or responsive function, and so this aspect of love is focused on decision and deed. When we love God and let God love us in this way, we meet the divine partner on the road of great effort and enterprise. We are drawn to *deeds* of love, to the *labor* of love, recalling Augustine's beautiful saying, "Where there is love there is no labor, or if there is, it is a labor of love."

Jesus said, "My Father goes on working, and so do I" (Jn 5:18). This saying is orchestrated in the third point of St. Ignatius of Loyola's "Contemplation To Attain the Love of God." He bids the retreatant to "consider how God works and labors for me in all creatures upon the face of the earth, that is, he conducts himself as one who labors. Thus in the heavens, the elements, the plants, the fruits, the cattle, etc., he gives being, conserves them, confers life and sensation, etc. . . . Then I will reflect on myself." The reflection, of course, will deal with the appropriate response to the labors of divine love. What will be *my* labor of love for the One who labors for me in the groaning of the Holy Spirit within the groaning of the whole of creation (Rom 8:22–23)?

Our love for ourselves and for the neighbor, too, when it is Gospel love, will have thinking characteristics. There are times, for example, when our bodies, our psyches, need to be handled quite firmly, when coddling our biases or our laziness would represent a pseudo-love. And there are times when we need to listen to the assertive complaints of our inner citizens as they protest, for example, that we are being unfair to them by not giving them enough sleep or recreation, or that we are depriving them of needed vigor by harmful food or drug habits. Neglect of one's own health can come from being out of touch with the body, a proclivity of intuiting types. But it can also stem from a failure in the thinking aspect of love, which is careful to give each component of the person its due.

Love for the neighbor will likewise have thinking characteristics. Especially because of the tendency to sentimentalize love and reduce it to the scope of the feeling function, it is important to emphasize that genuine love for the neighbor will be assertive, truthful, just. Here Gandhi and other models of non-violent resistance to injustice have much to teach us about love. Alcoholics Anonymous likewise is our benefactor by teaching us the importance of speaking the truth in the face of the pain that comes to both lover and beloved when evasions are finally confronted. Especially if we are dominant feelers, a genuine love will challenge us to be receptive to those who, however awkwardly, insist on meeting us only within the sober light of truth. Even, or perhaps especially, in the more intimate human relationships, love must be truthful and just if we are really to love with all our strength.

This kind of love for the neighbor will show itself especially by perseverance in the face of ingratitude. As it is not motivated by the desire for affirmation by others but by the conviction that it is right that God's gifts should be effectively shared with others, it does good to others without asking whether they are pleased or grateful for the service of love.

Loving with the Whole Heart

What does it mean to love with one's whole *heart?* It means a relationship with God, our self, the neighbor, of mutual response characterized by benevolence (good will), familiarity, intimacy. It means saying—and hearing—"Thou" to and from the companion in love. It means bringing our most cherished values into the risk of relationship, and letting those values blend with the values of the companion. All that we have said in Chapter 4 of the feeling function is available for understanding this aspect of Gospel love. For it is through that function and gift, that aspect of God's image in us, that the energies of a heart-response to the command of love will be mediated.

Loving *God* with the whole heart means for most of us, perhaps, the need for a deep and lifelong conversion of being open to *receive* an infinitely gratuitous love. The distinctive mark of Christian asceticism is not the strenuous all-out effort at loving God, but rather the courageous letting down of the barriers to receiving that love, barriers which unbelief and lack of trust have erected. This is really the import of Paul's teaching on justification by faith and not by works, by grace and not according to merit. And it is epitomized in a verse of the First Letter of John, "We have to love, then, because he loved us first" (1 Jn 4:19). To the degree that we accept the offer of this undeserved love, a generous response will flow from the gratitude, joy and compunction generated by God's remembrance of that love. We will love even as we are loved.

Because, as sinners, we will fail and fail again in accepting and responding to God's call to intimacy, we will constantly need to be taken by that love back down the road of memory to the origins and to other peak moments of the relationship. There is nothing like holy remembrance for healing the wounds of infidelity. The prophet Hosea is a classic witness to the renewal of the covenant violated by infidelity. Yahweh says, "I am going to lure her and lead her out into the wilderness"—the desert where Israel first *knew* Yahweh as loving husband—"and speak to her heart" (2:16). And penitent Israel says, "Come, let us return to Yahweh . . ." (6:1). The feeling call to love is a call to shared remembrance.

So far as love of the self is concerned, it calls for a certain gentleness and compassion toward all the citizens of our inner city, especially the slum dwellers, the sick, the homeless. The same hostility or coldness that we sometimes show toward others who do not measure up to our standards can also be exhibited toward those facets of our own selves which do not meet our expectations. Do I have a poor memory? Or does my digestive system plague me with social embarrassment or with distraction in my work? If I learn to deal gently with these little and poor ones of my own inner household, I may be surprised at their response in love and growth.

Loving the neighbor with the whole heart is a theme so fully orchestrated in the Gospels as to need little elaboration. Forgiving seventy times seven times; letting God's patient compassion toward us be both model and stimulus for an unlimited readiness to show mercy; extending the circle of caring beyond the limits of natural intimacy, as in the parable of the good Samaritan—these are only a few of the guides to feeling love of neighbor available in the teaching of Jesus.

Something worth emphasizing here is the *mutuality* of Christian forgiveness. We are all pretty well aware that unwillingness to forgive separates us from God. But how many of us attend to our heart's readiness *to be forgiven* by others? We have already noted that while dominant feelers may find it hard to forgive, dominant thinkers often have difficulty in asking to be forgiven. There is at least as much humbling of self required by having to say "Please forgive me" as by "I forgive you." It may prove so difficult because asking for forgiveness involves entrusting ourselves to the free decision of another to grant—or not grant—what we desire and need, but cannot claim.

Loving with the Whole Soul (Spirit)

What, finally, does it mean to love with all our *soul?* The soul or spirit in us is that which perhaps has the closest affinity with the intuiting function. *Spirit* and *aspiration* have the same Latin root, which has to do with breathing. In Jungian psychology, the *anima/animus*—used more narrowly than *psyche*—lies deep in the personal unconscious, bordering on the collective unconscious; it has much to do with the images projected in dreams by night and by day. Loving with all our soul suggests, then, letting this aspiring aspect of God's image in us be drawn into the dance of love. Like loving with the whole mind, this is a perceptive or receptive side of love, more acted upon than acting, even though it is, like the other three facets of love, marked by mutuality. When we love in this way we let ourselves be *drawn* toward those we love through the intimations of beauty which lie between the lines of our concrete experience of them. To God, self, the neighbor, this aspect of love says, "I love you *as you can be,* beyond who and what you are now, in your boundless possibilities. I dream of you, for you, and with you toward a limitless future of love." In Gabriel Marcel's phrase it says, "I hope in you for us."

When this kind of dreaming, hope-filled love penetrates

our relationship with God, what happens is a mutual sharing of dreams. "Something beautiful for God," the oft-quoted phrase of Mother Teresa of Calcutta, admirably sums up this aspect of the saints' love for God. But can one speak of the infinitely perfect God as still having unrealized possibilities? What can one really do for a God who has everything, who is everything? This question has baffled theologians and enraptured mystics. Both have responded—and the Book of Psalms contains many glorious examples—"Praise God! Glorify God!" Do it with words of love but even more with deeds of love. Proclaim God's glory to all humanity, to the limits of the universe! This is the imaginative spark which makes the great apostles restless. Intuitive, dreaming love is not immediately an agent of the transformation of the world. It is, we have seen, a perceiving, receptive love. But it is nonetheless the generative force behind great apostolic achievements. Think of the adolescent ambition of Teresa of Avila to run off to martyrdom, or of Ignatius of Loyola's "for the *greater* glory of God." Both epitomize the passionate dreaming of the saints of endless ways of glorifying and praising God.

But, let us not forget, this facet of mutual love calls for letting *God* realize his dreams of love for, in, and through us. We have already quoted the song, "The dreams I have for you, my Lord, are only a shadow of your dreams for me...." The command of love involves a willingness to enter into God's own dreams, however wild and unrealistic they may appear. "How can this be?" is a frequent question in the Bible in the hearts of those whom God is inviting to some great adventure. It was Mary's question in the annunciation, and the grace of faith and trust given her was the grace to enter, with the full imagination and hope that inspired her *fiat,* into God's great dream of love for humanity.

Loving ourselves with the whole soul means loving ourselves in our potential for growth without limit. It means a love which is not optimism but hope. Especially as life advances, as physical and psychic resources begin to diminish, the temptation may come to many to conceive of old age as a time for relinquishing unrealized dreams, for shutting down, one after the other, the motors which have driven us in earlier decades. A love that is dreaming hope, however, knows how to create *new* garments out of the tattered remnants of the years. At sixty-five, a former Olympic star will never again do the hundred in record time. But she can discover a new joy in meditative walking, marveling perhaps for the first time in her life at the beauty of simple ambulatory motions. The retired soprano will never again reach for high C. But if she is willing to love dreamingly she can discover that humming can be a beautiful expression of deep union with God, humanity, and the universe. Loving oneself with the whole soul, then, means the continuous readiness to let limitation be transformed into enlargement, adversity into opportunity. To those who keep their eyes wide open in anticipation of good, life offers literally no end of surprising possibilities. Especially as we experience that this is the way that God loves us, such a love for self can energize the later decades of our earthly pilgrimage and prepare us—to the extent that it is possible—for the endless surprise of heaven.

It is similar with a whole-souled love of the neighbor. Here we think of Jean Vanier and others like him who, where nondreamers saw only tragedy and a social burden, had the imagination to see in the emotionally and physically handicapped rich possibilities for the enrichment of persons, groups, and society. Or think of doctors and scientists who refuse to accept the conventional wisdom regarding the "incurable" or "inevitable" fate of people variously afflicted. How much of what Mother Teresa and many others consider to be the most monstrous of injustices in our society, namely massive and facile recourse to abortion, is happening because our corporate love has not yet begun to imagine wildly and boldly enough?

Less dramatically, we are all familiar with stories of "incorrigible" or "neurotic" people who, when someone kept believing in them, finally were delivered. Here again we need to emphasize the mutuality of the commandment of love. How hard it is at times to let others' dreams for us make a dent in our often hidden despair. How we wish at times that a particular "do-gooder" would just leave us alone. The perversity of human pride is such that the loving hope of others for our growth and healing can at times constitute a major threat. But what a special kind of beauty is realized when pride finally yields to humility and we enter into the dream for us cherished by a loving dreamer who refused to give up.

Wholeness in Loving and the Cross

Such, then, is the light that can be thrown on the fourfold commandment of love when it is viewed from the standpoint of the four functions, and, conversely, the insight into the functions which can come from this interplay with the great commandment of love. Here are a few concluding observations on this correlation before we move on. It is important to see the four facets of love not only in their complementarity but in their tension. As perceiving/judging in general and sensing/intuiting and thinking/feeling specifically are opposites, so the effort to love integrally involves a great deal of tension. How, for example, can I at once accept and love people just as they are, and yet love them for what they can become? Or how can my love toward a wounded or alienated sister or brother be at once firm and gentle, steadfast and yielding? Well, what is impossible for sinful humans is possible for God. It is the power of God's Spirit in us which not only permits quite opposite energies to exist and flow simultaneously, but actually makes the friction of their encounter a fresh source of energy that would otherwise not be available. God does write straight with crooked lines. By divine providence the worst of times can become the best of times.

It is this fusion of the worst and the best which constitutes the paschal mystery. Our ability to marvel at it does not remove the pain and risk involved when it is we who are put on the cross. It would be absurd to offer ways by which the cross could become a place of comfort, free of confusion. But experience can offer a few hints for recognizing a genuine call to share the mystery of the cross. Generally speaking, the pain and risk will involve letting go of what is dominant and developed, so that what is "inferior" and weak may emerge. The *process* of letting go—and of letting come—constitutes the literal crux of the matter. Here our developmental typology counsels us to respect the *variety* of letting go/letting come experiences for different types of people and at different crucial points in life. The specific call of love may be very different for me and for my friend. For me at thirty-five the call may be to love with the whole heart, whereas for my friend it may be to love with the whole of one's strength. It is true that, in some fashion, all four facets of love are operative whenever we truly love. But generally only one, or perhaps two, facets are being strongly evoked at any one time by God's grace. As we grow in spontaneity, flexibility, and freedom of love, wholeness is more *given* than deliberately *chosen.* In the earlier periods of the journey, discerning choice will be more overt, reflective, deliberate. But the journey is always toward the fullness and wholeness of loving and being loved by God, oneself, and the neighbor.

Love's Body: The Church

The preceding reflection on Gospel love as wholeness has obviously centered on the first two members of the familiar triad, solitude, friendship, and society. But what of the third, the societal dimension of life, the world of structures and institutions? Is it somehow outside the dynamic of love, restricted perhaps to norms of a justice that is not formed by Gospel love? We think not. And when we turn again to the New Testament for light on the integral meaning of Gospel love, we are told, particularly in the Letters of Paul and in the Book of Revelation, that love has taken to itself a body, which is the Church. It is this ecclesial, sacramental, Eucharistic character of Gospel love that we now want to explore. We will do so within the framework of several ecclesial images, whose relation to one another is like that of different colored threads in a tapestry.

Paul says, first of all, that the Church is the *body of Christ* (Rom 12:4–8; 1 Cor 12:4–30; Eph 2:15; 4:1–16; 5:21–33; Col 1:8,

24; 2:9). We are the members of that body. Paul loves to celebrate the diversity of gifts within the common call. It is striking that when Isabel Briggs Myers came to the final paragraph and to the title of her book, she found it appropriate to employ the Pauline terminology, though the book itself is not professedly a spiritual one. *Gifts Differing* (see Rom 12:6) is how she summed up the fruit of a lifetime of creative research on personality types. And the Jungian functions and attitudes do provide a marvelous psycho-social rendition of the Pauline teaching on unity in diversity, harmony in tension.

What we have already said indicates how, within each person and within groups, there is both complementarity and tension between the contributions of different facets of human personality. Echoing Paul (1 Cor 12:21) we can ask: Can the intuitive feeler in the community say to the sensing thinker, "I have no need of you"? In the growth of persons and communities are there not moments which call for each of the gifts and combinations of gifts? And do we not find within our families and other groups those individuals who represent to a notable degree each of the gifts in question, and who therefore can serve, not as substitutes while others remain passive, but as models who evoke the needed behavior in the entire group?

It is even possible—and this is the pioneering contribution made by MDI—to use the framework of the functions and attitudes as basis for the analysis, evaluation, and transformation of organizational processes and structures.[2] Increasingly, the Church itself as an institution is being understood with the help of such models. Being love's human body, the Church does not cease, by the fact that it is the embodiment of divine mystery, to be within the scope of such understanding of whatever is human.

It would appear, then, that for the Church to grow to the *pleroma* intended by Christ, the discerning love of Christians must know just when and how to call forth, in individuals, groups, and institutions, the specific gifts needed at a particular moment, and also to keep the limitless resources of Christian energy flowing in a manner which builds, not enervates, love's body. Such a feat is, of course, beyond us. In fact, as sinners much of our actual behavior puts obstacles in the path of its achievement. But, Paul says, there is one body *and one Spirit* (Eph 4:4). It is the Holy Spirit, breathed forth by the crucified and risen Lord upon his Church (Jn 19:30; 20:21–23) and poured forth into our hearts in baptism (Rom 5:5), who makes possible the building up of that body throughout history, until the Lord Jesus himself returns.

Bride of Christ

Love's body is also love's bride, as Paul declares in Ephesians 5:31–33. He draws upon a key verse of Genesis (2:24) to describe both Christian marriage and the union of which it is the special sacrament, the wedding of Christ and his bride/body, the Church. This joining of metaphors to describe the mystery of the Church in its union with Christ, head and spouse, has the value of reducing a frequent dichotomy between the life of the Church as interpersonal communion of Christians and the life of the Church as societal structure. The *Constitution on the Church* (n. 8) of Vatican II insists that it is the one Church which is both communion and structure. Such is the power of the Spirit that the language of intimacy becomes appropriate to describe the union of head and members and of members among themselves, in a society of millions of human beings. When we Christians say with affection, "Our holy mother the Church," we are not designating a tiny sect or only a local gathering of Christians but the worldwide, agelong, institutionally structured society.

Children of such a marriage, we Christians become one family, one people, living in one house and sharing the same meal. Love's body/bride is thus revealed as a *Eucharistic* reality. In dealing with each of the four functions we have commented on how they are exercised in the Eucharistic liturgy. Now we are in a position to see both the wholeness and the rich variety which ought to characterize every celebration of the sacramental banquet. It is simultaneously a banquet of grateful remembrance (F), of dreaming, eschatological hope (N), of enjoyment of the real presence (S), and of the sacred, sacramental order (T). It is principally by the Eucharist that the Church is continually in process of being constituted as the body of Christ.

As we have already hinted, our Eucharistic celebrations will succeed in being, spiritually, pastorally and liturgically, powerful expressions and sources of Christian energy in the degree to which they enable all four streams of energy to flow from and to the individuals, groups, and larger assemblies which comprise the Church. Further, to the degree that the liturgical celebration of the paschal mystery really reflects and in turn enlivens every other aspect of the Church's life, the whole of Christian existence becomes Eucharistic. Though we cannot make the analysis here, there is no facet of Christian life—ministry, community, evangelization, spirituality, etc.—which cannot be set within the framework of the functions as they correlate with the Gospel. Love's body is a human body, called like all that is human to journey from image to likeness.

The Journey of the Pilgrim Body

Journey is the next image which helps us to appreciate love's body. The metaphor of the family of Christ and his bride gathered within the house of God at the one table needs to be modified in order to express the essentially pilgrim character of this family, as the final chapter of the *Constitution on the Church* sets forth. Introducing the metaphor of journey into our understanding of love's body at this point has the advantage of reminding us of the trap of tidiness which threatens every effort at correlation of human insight and God's revelation. Mobility, provisionality, and acceptance of insecurity characterize the life of the pilgrim. Between the sharp lines on a page of even the best of maps and the experienced reality of doubt and fallibility in the actual journey lies a distance which only discernment and trust can negotiate. There will always be critical points where the map will prove useless or even a distraction. The wise reader attempting to discern God's present call would do well to deal with this book and with the typology which it offers somewhat as a prudent traveler will deal with a map provided for a terrain still to be explored. There are times when the map needs to be laid aside and when walking in trust and discernment is all we can manage.

The City of God

The journey of the pilgrim body has a destination. We may call it wholeness, fullness, likeness to God, or name it with a whole host of other names, as the Bible does. But, in its societal character, which is our present focus, it is probably best imaged as the heavenly city of God described in the last chapters of the Book of Revelation. A myriad of converging images there portrays a humankind come to the fullness of its potential for imaging God. It is the wedding feast of the Lamb and the Bride, Christ and the Church (19:7–9; 21:2). It was for this consummation of love that the Spirit and the Bride have yearned throughout history with the ceaseless *Maranatha* (Come, Lord) of the Church's longing for the second coming (22:17, 20). The heavenly city, new Jerusalem, is the embodiment of a new creation (21:5), a new heaven and a new earth (21:1). God will become, in the fullest sense, God with us, Emmanuel (21:3), and will be effectively the Alpha and the Omega, the First and the Last, the Beginning and the End (22:13; see 1:8, 17). There will no longer be need of lamplight or sunlight, for God will be shining directly on the people (21:23; 22:5). God and the Lamb will rule from their thrones in the city (22:1, 3), and the life of the whole city will be nourished and healed by the Spirit, the divine river of life flowing crystal-clear from the throne of God and of the Lamb (22:1–2) down the middle of the city's street. It will be the wedding feast of the Lamb (19:9).

Such, in the very last pages of the Bible, is the description of journey's end, when God's image in humankind comes to its perfection of Godlikeness. God will truly be all in all (1 Cor 15:28). What we pray for daily in the Our Father, the kingdom in all its fullness, will have finally come.

III. GROWING IN GOSPEL LOVE

It will be obvious to readers from all that we have said in this book that a discerning and holistic feel for life is needed if we are to appreciate the dynamism of growth from image to likeness. These final remarks and the few exercises which follow them will seek, with some practicality, to help those who have walked with us to engage in the kind of practice which attends both to the rich variety and to the marvelous oneness of our human endowment. This reference to the one-and-many prompts a preliminary remark on an epigram of Pierre Teilhard de Chardin: *unity differentiates*. This terse distillation of his whole mysticism is a word of wisdom, at once psychological, social, and religious. Individuation, integration, the spiraling ascent to wholeness does not annihilate the reality of that which becomes whole. At the deepest level, our divinization is a reconstitution, not an abdication, of our humanity. This is true even and especially of what we have relinquished or relativized. Its moment will come again, more glorious than its prior moment. Within God, and within the mysterious processes of God's image within us, "the thing we freely forfeit is kept with fonder a care,/ Fonder a care kept than we could have kept it."[3] Unity differentiates—as in Paul's description of the body of Christ, the contribution of each remains irreplaceable—when there is question of the distinctive energies flowing from each of the functions. In a fully mature human being, it may be harder for the onlooker to sort out what is coming from one or other source, because the several functions and attitudes are in such harmony. Likewise, where true communion of persons takes place, the unique gift represented by each person is not swallowed up or dissolved in the whole. Teilhard's epigram, therefore, can help us to cherish each gift, and each member of the body that is being built.

A Consciousness Examen

But now we must ask what are some of the ways that one can go about growing, as we have described growth in this book. Let us respond within the pattern of what has come to be called a "consciousness examen," that is, a personal reflection on present, past, future, that is experiential and discerning. What is of primary importance is that this be done *in God's presence*. How absurd and tragic would it not be if, in our preoccupation with the specifics of human development, we were to forget the one who has called us to such growth and who alone can make it real. In all that follows, therefore, a prayerful faith and trust in God are presupposed.

An easy and appropriate place to begin is to take hold of the present moment of the journey by being in touch with our preferences right now. Whether or not we have made use of the MBTI or some other Jungian instrument, we might confidently set down the MBTI code letters which reflect our present self-understanding, and the corresponding code in the developmental typology of the present book. For this exercise the Appendices may be necessary or helpful. Then ask: What qualifications, if any, would I put on that code as a description of myself? What is clear and what is doubtful? I may have difficulty, for example, in surmising whether my introverted intuition or extraverted feeling is dominant. Or I may still have to struggle with my interpretation of introversion and extraversion, as I may tend to attach extraversion to my dominant preference simply because I sometimes talk a lot in company.

What is even more important is to discern what in my behavior is characterized by freedom, and what by a certain restraint or confinement. What kinds of activities come easily to me, or not? Running a party? Sitting alone gazing at the water? Working out a mathematical problem? Cooking a meal for my family or community? The point of this question is not merely to see whether I spontaneously prefer such activities, but whether my engagement in them, preferred or not, is marked by freedom, peace, presence to self and others, etc. Especially in what touches relationships with others, the traditionally honored virtues of purity of heart, detachment, and interior freedom are crucial spiritual qualities which can be understood from the standpoint of our developmental typology.

As I conclude this *sensing* phase of the consciousness examen wherein I focus on the present state of God's image in me, an appropriate posture is one of simple acceptance of myself as I am.

Next, taking whatever measure of understanding of my present self has been given, let me go next, through my *feeling*, to my personal history, from as early as I can remember in life's journey. Once again with the help of my code, let me be in touch with the kinds of behavior I seemed to favor in childhood, adolescence, and earlier in my adult life. Was the sequence indicated by the code actually the case in my own journey? Did I develop my dominant preference in childhood? And was there the alternation of extraversion/introversion in the successive periods? In any case, let me see how much clarity I can gain regarding the way I have developed up to now.

The review should touch not only on my preferences and the sequence of their development but on the factors—intrapersonal, interpersonal, and societal—which helped or impeded a healthy development. Especially at the "clutch points" of my life—at twelve, twenty, and thirty-five—how did persons, events, experiences affect what happened in a positive or negative way? Did the death of one of my parents, or their divorce, or the presence and influence of a grandparent make a notable difference? What fears and angers were deposited in my psyche, consciously or unconsciously, from such factors in my "personal salvation history"? As my interest is not merely psychological but moral and spiritual, I will observe what were the patterns of my Christian or un-Christian behavior at different periods. What role do I attribute both to my preferences and to environmental factors in establishing or modifying these patterns? Were there in my life outstanding conversion experiences? If so, how would I describe them from the standpoint of the developmental typology? Was I asked at some painful but privileged moment to let go of anything? Did something new—a new consciousness or a new freedom, perhaps—emerge at that point of my life?

One particular exercise within this retrieval of personal history might be to personify each of the functions, so that it can describe for me its experience of being part of me. Here the dialogue form of the Intensive Journal can be helpful. It is possible to spend a fruitful hour or two with one's sensing or intuiting, for example. I may be surprised or energized by the results.

Some such retrieval of my history can be more fruitful if it is shared with someone, a friend or perhaps an intimate group or a spiritual director. It will in most cases generate a good deal of feeling, particularly gratitude and compunction. Such feelings can be a beautiful grace, at once healing and energizing.

I may next choose to return to the present, but now as a moment of possibility, opportunity, potential. This phase of the reflection has an *intuiting* character. Quite spontaneously, perhaps, or by a deliberate disposing of myself, there will emerge out of being in touch with the present and the past a real call to the future. In terms of our typology it will be accented toward one or other function. Almost universally it will be heard as a call to let go, in moderate or more radical measure, of patterns of behavior and attitudes on which I have been excessively reliant. At the same time it will have to do with one or other of the deprived or neglected citizens of my interior city. It may have to do with work or leisure or both, with prayer or community or both, with bodily health, relationships, continuing education, etc. It is important that it be permitted to present itself in the dimensions of solitude, friendship, and society, with some feel for the interaction of the three. It is even more important that it be allowed to have at first the quality of a dream, a vision of the future, not of any set project or program. Let me not be in too much of a hurry to make resolutions, if I make resolutions at all. Emerging from the preceding steps, this intuiting phase can make me eager to move my vision toward execution.

Movement toward the practical is the fourth stage of the examen. It has to do with goals and objectives, strategies and tactics, and the exercise of prudent rationality—in a word, the *thinking* side of my personality, together with my *sensing* in its practical employ. My holistic sense will prompt me toward some kind of a flexible plan of life, even a weekly and daily order. I will be alert especially to the need to keep any facet of my life from becoming isolated. I know, for example, that if I stay up too late I will not pray well in the morning, and that my morning prayer is a key to the quality of my work and relationships throughout the day. Or the key decision may be the simple action of getting a health check-up for the first time in six years. In this phase, too, of the examen, the triad of solitude, friendship, and society can be a helpful framework for setting goals and objectives, establishing strategies and tactics, and taking first steps.

Groups and Organizations

We will not elaborate in detail as to how *groups* and *organizations* or institutions can engage in the kind of growth-oriented reflection which we have just described for individuals. The same basic framework and ingredients may be used, with appropriate modifications. Our own experience with a large religious health care corporation has confirmed us in our thinking that the analogy and interdependence of individual, group, and institution is a key assumption for the healing and growth of institutions. It is clear that institutional development, especially within our complex technological society, should not be approached naively or simplistically. One approach which would be naive would be to miss the way in which personhood, relationships, and structures mutually interact. Within any sound process of corporate renewal there needs to be space and time for each individual to be in touch with present personal reality, personal history, personal aspirations and goals. And a similar need exists for good interpersonal communication among the many individuals who constitute the membership of the organization. Any effort to improve structures and systems which disregards their mutual interdependence with the quality of persons and relationships is doomed to frustration. The model of solitude, friendship, and society is thus an almost indispensable tool for the renewal of institutions.

One of the great resources of any Christian individual, group, or institution in efforts at renewal and growth is to have available the model of the paschal mystery, especially as it is a mystery of death and resurrection. The language of growth, development, and evolution runs a perhaps necessary risk of blandness and unrealism with respect to what awaits any serious effort to improve human life. Often people in their enthusiasm will approach the building of a community or the reform of an institution without a deep consciousness of the place of the cross in human affairs. How often does disenchantment result as they come in touch with the negativities and discontinuities with which life is filled? It is a key point of affinity, we have found, between the basic Jungian and Christian approaches to human development that each recognizes that there is darkness and death present in the midst of life and light. And each view is convinced that the struggle with evil aims less at its annihilation than at its transfiguration, through the power, wisdom, and goodness of God who is at work through our human and cosmic dynamisms. This mysticism of *O felix culpa* (O happy fault) and of the cross of Christ becoming the flowering tree of a new creation is central to what we have attempted to say in this book.

EXERCISES

A. *For the individual:*

1. In prayerful imagination, sit in the living room or at the dining room table of your inner home with four members of your family, that is, the four functions with their unique characteristics as you have experienced them. Let each of them speak to you and to one another. You may wish to give each of

them a name, or ask them to name themselves. Let the conversation range from present relationships to past history to a sharing of aspirations and also of plans. If there are grievances, let them be aired, and let forgiveness be celebrated where necessary. See if the "family meeting" arrives at some kind of consensus statement, or even perhaps at a ritual celebration. This exercise might be made with the help of a dialogue exercise in the Intensive Journal.

B. *For groups:*

1. Have someone read aloud 1 Corinthians 12 or Ephesians 4:1–16. Then after a period of silent reflection let each member of the community be described by each of the other members in what they consider to be his or her special gift. Then, after a break, let each member of the community say which common climates, customs, etc. of the community are more supportive, and which ones create obstacles to growth for him or her.

SCRIPTURE REFERENCES

1. Psalms 23, 45, 72, 122, 126, 128, 132, 133, 148, 149, 150.

2. Songs of Songs (entire).

3. Isaiah 60–62; Ezekiel 47:1–12.

4. Mark 12:28–34; Matthew 22:22–40; Luke 10:25–28.

5. John 13–17; 21.

6. Romans 12; 1 Corinthians 11:17–34; 12–14; Ephesians (entire); Colossians 1:15–20.

7. 1 John (entire); Revelation 21–22.

NOTES

1. *Story of a Soul: The Autobiography of St. Thérèse of Lisieux* (Washington, D.C.: ICS Publications, 1975), pp. 193f.

2. See the reference in Appendix A to MDI (Management Design, Inc.).

3. Hopkins, *loc. cit.*

EPILOGUE
"The Way Has Come to Thee"

The short journey of this book is now ended, and we thank our readers for persevering with us on that road. In parting, there are just a few things we wish to say about the larger and longer journey from image to likeness which is life's task for all of us.

We have confidence in the value of the instruments we have used, the Jungian typology, the method of correlation between Jungian and Gospel categories, and the several models which we have offered. Our experience, especially in the R/W, has confirmed us in this confidence, and has broadened our appreciation of what human beings are like and how they grow.

At the same time we are conscious of the limitations contained in any effort at self-understanding, especially when that effort enters deeply into the human mystery as it meets the infinite mystery of God. As we close, then, we feel obliged to accent once again the limited and provisional character of the present endeavor.

First, the Jungian model does not say everything about our humanity, especially as it is realized in unique individuals. However obvious, it is important to repeat this statement, especially for the benefit of anyone who may have become enthusiastic in the course of reading this book. The very word type is hazardous, unless in speaking it we are conscious that no individual can even begin to be explained adequately by the categories of any system of thought. Jung's wariness of any effort to reduce his theory to a technical instrument for describing or predicting behavior can serve as a warning against stereotyping ourselves or others. We have frequently in the course of these chapters noted that other important factors besides personality preferences affect human behavior and development, and that two persons identical in type can be very different from each other. Both the complex environments within which they experienced the stages of their development and the diversity of their free choices within those environments contribute to making each personality utterly unique.

More specifically, there are two characteristic features of our book toward which we would encourage in readers a certain reserve, if not diffidence. The first is the hypothesis of a pattern and sequence of development of each of the functions through four life-stages in the alternating rhythm of extraversion and introversion. Our experience of its congruence for describing how people actually grow makes us think that it is a plausible hypothesis. But it has not yet been clinically validated. Nor do we consider it essential for the method of correlation of Jungian typology and Gospel themes which this book outlines. Any reader who does not recognize in any of the proposed schemas the pattern of his or her development from childhood on would do well simply to leave aside this aspect of our book and profit from the rest of it.

Second, we have spoken more optimistically about the possibility of developing the so-called inferior function than do most Jungian analysts and writers. For Jung himself and most of his distinguished disciples, very few individuals come to that degree of maturity in which the inferior function is so befriended that it emerges into the light of consciousness; and those who do come have generally been helped by a skilled analyst. The best that most people can expect, it is often implied, is to keep this shadow function from doing major damage to the personality.

This understandable reluctance to speak optimistically of individuation as a concrete possibility for the many is fed by Jungian practice and theory touching some central aspects of personality which have not been dealt with in this book. We refer here to such concepts as shadow, anima/animus, archetype, symbol, complex, projection, and the like. In any Jungian spirituality which would profess to be complete such facets of psychic life would need to be integrated with a discussion of the functions and types. We have made it clear, we think, that our approach is decidedly partial in this respect. It is far from our intent to suggest that growth to the wholeness which is holiness can take place without a profound interaction between conscious and unconscious levels of the personality. The lives of the great saints of all ages, who lived and died without benefit of modern psychological nomenclatures describing their struggle, testify to the radical nature of Christian conversion in its psychic as well as in its properly spiritual aspects.

And so we recognize the need to be sober in speaking of human development. But we are reluctant to acquiesce in any implied acceptance of mediocrity for the masses. What prompts us to this hopeful stance is partly the experience of meeting a good number of people of mature years and deep faith who have come to a relative but manifest wholeness and holiness. However we have also been influenced by the promises contained in the Gospel, promises of a dreaming God who looks beyond our fragility, a faithful God who always gives the means to achieve what is commanded. More specifically, we rely on the simple statement made by Jesus when his disciples were tempted to despair: "With man it is impossible, but with God all things are possible" (Mt 19:26).

To believe that with God all is possible is the very meaning of faith. Abraham went forth at the call of God without knowing where he was going (Heb 11:8). Mary spoke her *fiat* (let it be) without any foundation except the angel's word that God's Spirit and power had entered her life. And Jesus himself, in the great act of trust which has redeemed the whole of our humanity from a meaningless existence, became the prototype of those of whom he himself said, "Happy are those who have not seen and yet believe" (Jn 20:29). In the final analysis, Christian faith does not permit any one of us to doubt that God can make us whole.

Finally, our purpose has been to assist toward a deeper commitment to the mystery of life, not to encourage the illusion of escaping from mystery. For that dark venture into the mystery of God, the example, teaching, and power of Jesus are enough for the Christian journeying from image to likeness. As St. Augustine once wrote, in commenting on the words of Jesus, "I am the way, the truth, and the life" (Jn 14:6),

"I do not say to thee, 'Seek the way,'
The Way itself has come to thee.
Arise and walk!"[1]

NOTE

1. E. Przywara, *An Augustine Synthesis* (New York: Sheed & Ward, 1936), p. 198.

APPENDIX A
Resources

Note: The following list of resources is selective, and compiled with a view to helping readers who wish to pursue further what they have found in this book. More extensive references may be sought in many of the resources listed here.

A. *Jung and the Jungian Tradition*
   1. Carl Jung's classic work on types is *Psychological Types*, Princeton NJ: Princeton University Press, 1971. It was originally published in 1921. This edition of the English translation also contains one earlier and three later essays of Jung on his typology.
   2. A good general anthology and introduction to Jung will be found in Joseph Campbell (ed.), *The Portable Jung*, New York: Penguin, 1976.
   3. Two excellent essays, on the inferior function and the feeling function, respectively, will be found in Marie-Louise von Franz and James Hillman, *Jungian Typology*, Irving TX: Spring Publications, 1979.
   4. *Centerpoint* is an organization which promotes Jungian dialogue groups throughout the United States with the help of tapes, transcripts, and a book service; it also publishes a newsletter, *In Touch*, three times a year for $8.00. Address: Centerpoint, 22 Concord Street, Nashua NH 03060.

B. *Myers-Briggs Type Indicator*
   1. Shortly before her death Isabel Briggs Myers completed the book which gathers the fruit of her lifelong study of personality types, *Gifts Differing* (1980), available from Con-

sulting Psychologists Press, 577 College Avenue, Palo Alto CA 94306. This work in large part supplants her manual, *The Myers-Briggs Type Indicator,* Princeton NJ: Educational Testing Service, 1962. A revised manual is in preparation at CAPT (see next entry).

2. The *Center for Applications of Psychological Types* (CAPT), at 414 S.W. 7th Terrace, Gainesville FL 32601, under the direction of Mary H. McCaulley, has since 1975 been serving as center for education, research, and services connected with the MBTI. It publishes a quarterly newsletter, *MBTI News,* for users of the MBTI, and provides a wide variety of services, including the scoring of MBTI answer sheets, data analysis, bibliographies, etc. It has also sponsored workshops of MBTI users. But it does not sell MBTI test materials; for these, Consulting Psychologists Press, Inc. (above n. 1) is the source.

3. A help for teachers in identifying the learning styles and motivational patterns of their students is Gordon Lawrence, *People Types and Tiger Stripes* (1979), published by CAPT.

C. *Jung and the Gospel*

1. Among many authors who have dealt with Jung in relation to Christian faith, theology, and spirituality, we mention just a few:

a. Morton T. Kelsey, especially in *Transcend: A Guide to the Spiritual Quest,* New York: Crossroad, 1981 (pp. 121–130 deal with the types and meditation); and in *The Other Side of Silence,* New York: Paulist, 1976, which deals with the exercise of active imagination in prayer.

b. John Sanford, especially in *Healing and Wholeness,* New York: Paulist, 1977; *The Kingdom Within: A Study of the Inner Meaning of Jesus' Sayings,* Philadelphia: Lippincott, 1970; *The Invisible Partners,* New York: Paulist, 1980.

c. Victor White, *God and the Unconscious,* Chicago: Regnery, 1953.

d. Robert Doran, *Subject and Psyche: Ricoeur, Jung, and the Search for Foundations,* Washington DC: University Press, 1977; also "Jungian Psychology and Christian Spirituality," *Review for Religious* 38 (1979) 497–510; 742–752; 857–866.

e. Raymond Hostie, *Religion and the Psychology of Jung,* New York: Sheed and Ward, 1957.

f. John Welch, *Spiritual Pilgrims: Carl Jung and Teresa of Avila,* New York: Paulist, 1982.

g. Wallace B. Clift, *Jung and Christianity: The Challenge of Reconciliation,* New York: Crossroad, 1982.

2. Among efforts to relate the types to forms of prayer we mention:

a. Morton Kelsey in *Transcend* (see above).

b. Christopher Bryant, *Heart in Pilgrimage: Christian Guidelines for the Human Journey,* New York: Seabury, 1980 (pp. 182–195 are an appendix dealing with prayer and the types).

c. Robert Repicky, "Jungian Typology and Christian Spirituality," *Review for Religious* 40 (1981) 422–435.

d. At the Jesuit School of Theology in Berkeley, California, several dissertations have been written on the relationship of the types to prayer.

3. A number of spiritual centers offer programs dealing with Jungian spirituality in general, and with MBTI in particular. Among these are:

a. Kirkridge, R.D. 3, Bangor PA 18013.

b. Jesuit Center for Spiritual Growth, Wernersville PA 19565.

c. Loyola Retreat House, Guelph, Ontario N1H 6N6, Canada.

4. We have mentioned several times the little book of Anthony de Mello, *Sadhana: A Way to God,* St. Louis, Institute of Jesuit Sources, 1979. While not based on Jung, it does offer meditation exercises which broadly correspond to the functions of sensing, intuiting, and feeling.

D. *Management Design, Inc.* (MDI), 110 East 8th Street, Cincinnati OH 45202, is a consultant firm whose service to groups and organizations draws on Jungian theory and the MBTI.

APPENDIX B
Patterns of Type Development

The chapters of this book have discussed the Jungian typology as this has been encapsulated in the MBTI. It has also proposed the hypothesis of four periods of development of the functions in alternating attitudes of extraversion and introversion between the ages of six and fifty. The readers have been introduced to the respective codes which express the sixteen types in each approach, and to the correlation of MBTI and developmental codes. To complete the description of types we here present, first, a table which summarizes the correlation, and, second, a brief description of each of the types in each of the four periods of development.

SUMMARY OF DEVELOPMENTAL PATTERNS

		6–12 years	12–20 years	20–35 years	35–50 years
Sensing Types	ESTP	S (E)	T (I)	F (E)	N (I)
	ESFP	S (E)	F (I)	T (E)	N (I)
	ISTJ	S (I)	T (E)	F (I)	N (E)
	ISFJ	S (I)	F (E)	T (I)	N (E)
Thinking Types	ESTJ	T (E)	S (I)	N (E)	F (I)
	ENTJ	T (E)	N (I)	S (E)	F (I)
	ISTP	T (I)	S (E)	N (I)	F (E)
	INTP	T (I)	N (E)	S (I)	F (E)
Feeling Types	ESFJ	F (E)	S (I)	N (E)	T (I)
	ENFJ	F (E)	N (I)	S (E)	T (I)
	ISFP	F (I)	S (E)	N (I)	T (E)
	INFP	F (I)	N (E)	S (I)	T (E)
Intuiting Types	ENTP	N (E)	T (I)	F (E)	S (I)
	ENFP	N (E)	F (I)	T (E)	S (I)
	INTJ	N (I)	T (E)	F (I)	S (E)
	INFJ	N (I)	F (E)	T (I)	S (E)

Dominant Sensing Types

(a) Extraverted Sensing with Auxiliary Thinking—ESTP = STFN/*EIEI*

1st Period—6 to 12 years (Extraverted Sensing)

As a child you engaged in developing your sensing and were interested in everything and everyone around you. Facts and information were probably very important to you, and you wanted to share them with others. You may have collected and classified objects and become interested in sports, nature, gardening, or putting things together, preferring to engage in such activities with others. You needed a lot of stimulation and became easily bored. This may have led you into mischief through your curiosity and need for more information about people.

2nd Period—12 to 20 years (Introverted Thinking)

At twelve you found yourself turning inward. You began to be more logical in your decisions. You found yourself perhaps wanting to manage the groups in which you functioned, but in subtle and indirect ways. Frequently you reached conclusions which seemed reasonable to you, but because you did not share the reasoning process with others they may not have known where you were coming from. Your strong sense of honesty and truth may have led you to give a frank opinion when asked, producing at times some anger in those who were looking for a different answer.

3rd Period—20 to 35 years (Extraverted Feeling)

The fact that you now began to develop the function directly opposite the one you favored in adolescence possibly made this a difficult period of your life. Decisions you formerly made on the basis of logic now were shaped more by your feelings. You became more sensitive to the feelings of others and more sensitive in your own. You became somewhat sentimental and found yourself, to your embarrassment, sometimes close to tears. Your sense of compassion grew, and you became interested perhaps in ways of ministering to others. Your greater display of feeling may have made you more vulnerable to hurt, while at the same time others became more aware of the warmth of your expressed feelings.

4th Period—35 to 50 years (Introverted Intuition)

During this period you began to develop your shadow side. Having spent most of your life at home with your sensing, in tune with the present, and operating with efficiency, you now found yourself more interested in the future, and inclined to let go of the specific and the factual for the sake of the speculative. Given to daydreaming, you became more forgetful and felt less together than before; but you also felt rewarded by being less tied to detail and more able to disengage from tedious and useless worry. Your creativity increased and you began to see relationships with the help of your deductive rather than your inductive mind. Your best inspirations, you discovered, came when you were alone.

Dominant Sensing Types

(b) Extraverted Sensing with Auxiliary Feeling—ESFP = SFTN/*EIEI*

1st Period—6 to 12 years (Extraverted Sensing)

As a child you engaged in developing your sensing and were interested in everything and everyone around you. Facts and information were probably very important to you, and you wanted to share them with others. You may have collected and classified objects and become interested in sports, nature, gardening, or putting things together, preferring to engage in such activities not alone but with others. You needed a lot of stimulation and became easily bored. This may have led you into mischief through your curiosity and need for more information about people.

2nd Period—12 to 20 years (Introverted Feeling)

During this period you became more inclined to develop your feelings and compassion, though you were not inclined to show these to others. But you were interested in helping others, and perhaps joined a few groups committed to the needy. Being yourself sensitive to hurt, you were sensitive to the pain of others. You found it difficult to say no to a request, and avoided at all cost offending others; you would sacrifice your real wishes so as to gain appreciation or avoid displeasing others. Generally speaking, others were not aware of the depth of your feelings, and so at times they seemed to you to be brushing those feelings aside.

3rd Period—20 to 35 years (Extraverted Thinking)

Having developed your feelings and experienced them more fully, now something in you told you that you needed to look out for yourself and be true to your own needs by becoming more assertive in the face of unreasonable demands by others. Having had little experience of such behavior, it was difficult for you to avoid hostility and aggressiveness as you gradually learned not to do things just because others would think well of you. You found yourself at times feeling guilty when people accustomed to your former submissiveness expressed surprise or displeasure at your new behavior. But you began to enjoy a new sense of being in charge of yourself and free to be what you wanted to be.

4th Period—35 to 50 years (Introverted Intuiting)

Now you began to develop your shadow side. Having spent most of your life being at home with your sensing, in tune with the present, and operating with efficiency, you now found yourself more interested in the future, and inclined to let go of the specific and the factual for the sake of the speculative. Given to daydreaming, you became more forgetful and felt less together than before; but you also felt rewarded by being less tied to detail and better able to disengage from tedious and useless worry. Your creativity increased and you began to seek relationships with the help of your deductive rather than your inductive side. Your best inspirations, you discovered, came when you were alone.

Dominant Sensing Types

(c) Introverted Sensing with Auxiliary Thinking—ISTJ = STFN/*IEIE*

1st Period—6 to 12 years (Introverted Sensing)

As a child you found delight in listening, watching, and touching as you developed your sense life. But for the most part you kept this delight to yourself, and were not interested in sharing with others the discoveries you made as you explored nature's resources, collecting and classifying items of interest to you. Or you may have enjoyed sports, playing a musical instrument, or working with your hands in carpentry, sewing, arts and crafts. Rooted in the present, you were practical, attentive, and dependable, remembering facts and information and using them in sensible pursuits.

2nd Period—12 to 20 years (Extraverted Thinking)

As you reached adolescence you began to develop your thinking, and to find enjoyment in organizing things, making your choices on the basis of logic, analysis, and truth. Justice was of primary importance, and your sense of fair play together with your ability to reason in an emotionally detached way enabled you to assume roles of responsibility. You were interested in working with others in projects, yet were able to keep your emotional cool in times of crisis. Your ability to handle difficult matters with an orderly objectivity impressed and sometimes surprised your peers, some of whom assumed you to be without feelings simply because you preferred not to express them.

3rd period—20 to 35 years (Introverted Feeling)

In direct contrast to the previous period, now you felt impelled to explore the world of feeling, becoming more sensitive to the feelings of others, more compassionate, but also more easily offended. Decisions which in adolescence had been made on the basis of reason and logic now came to be based on personal values and sensitivity to persons. The inner world of feeling assumed more importance for you as you attempted to learn more about your true identity. As your developing life of feeling was directed inward, others were generally unaware of the depth of your emotions, though they would come into contact with your compassion indirectly in the decision-making process.

4th period—35 to 50 years (Extraverted Intuiting)

Now your shadow side began to come to the fore, and to exercise itself socially, so that the presence of others enriched its quality and encouraged its struggling development. You showed more interest in future possibilities, and were better able to let go of the details of your daily experience. You may have found a new creativity, an ability to dream and plan, along with others, with more facility and zest. Your ability to let go of specifics diminished some of the worry you had experienced in the past. At the same time your newfound ability to dream may have brought some forgetfulness of important details, and this, in view of your having been known for dependability and efficiency, may have been disconcerting both to you and to others.

Dominant Sensing Types

(d) Introverted Sensing with Auxiliary Feeling—ISFJ = SFTN/*IEIE*

1st period—6 to 12 years (Introverted Sensing)

As a child you found delight in listening, watching, and touching as you developed your sense life. But for the most part you kept this delight to yourself, and were not interested in sharing with others the discoveries you made as you explored nature's resources, collecting and classifying items of interest to you. Or you may have enjoyed sports, playing a musical instrument, or working with your hands in carpentry, sewing, arts and crafts. Rooted in the present, you were practical, attentive, and dependable, remembering facts and information and using them in sensible pursuits.

2nd period—12 to 20 years (Extraverted Feeling)

As you reached the age of twelve you felt the need to extend your interests to wide relationships, becoming more outgoing and more conscious of the attraction of group activities. You became more conscious of the needs of others and more anxious to help them. Your compassion grew, together with your desire to please. When you failed to please others you may have felt guilty and blamed yourself. At the same time your growing empathy for others may have attracted them to confide in you.

3rd period—20 to 35 years (Introverted Thinking)

In strong contrast to your now developed feeling life, you began to make decisions in a more logical and analytical way. You became more protective of your own interests, and felt more free to deny requests which made demands on your time. Your new freedom possibly surprised and even dismayed those who had taken your compliance for granted, and you yourself wondered at times if your heart had not become hardened. And your exercise of this freedom was halting and sometimes harsh or grating. Yet the knowledge that you were now able to be yourself and make sound decisions was a new satisfaction. This was a period, too, in which you turned to the world within for a grasp of your true self. You preferred to share the results with a few friends rather than with many. You may have found yourself taking little on faith and insisting on verifying claims and reasons before acting on them.

4th period—35 to 50 years (Extraverted Intuiting)

Development of your shadow function, intuition, took place during this period as once again you turned to the outer world of people and things. Your growing preference for imagination and creativity, therefore, was exercised socially; it was the suggestions and comments of others which stimulated you to new ideas. This new interest in the possible and the future resulted in a letting go of your rootedness in the present; you found speculation and daydreaming more to your liking. But, especially in the early years of this period, you found yourself, in sharp contrast to your earlier behavior, distracted to the point of forgetting important matters and at times losing or misplacing things. However you took a new satisfaction in realizing that your outlook had become more expansive, and that you were able to put aside some of the persistent worries which earlier your tenacious memory would have clung to.

Dominant Thinking Types

(a) Extraverted Thinking with Auxiliary Sensing—ESTJ = TSNF/*EIEI*

1st period—6 to 12 years (Extraverted Thinking)

You were probably an outgoing, inquisitive child who sought reasons for the directives given you, and you were reluctant to follow them without an understanding of why they were given. Once given an explanation you found it less difficult to obey. Your decisions, small as they may have been, were based on logical analysis free from the desire to please anyone. Fairness was a paramount importance to you. Rarely did you do something which you did not want to do, even though your sense of reason and fair play convinced you to do the right thing even when it was unpleasant.

2nd period—12 to 20 years (Introverted Sensing)

It is likely that as you moved into adolescence you found interest in such things as collecting and classifying things, sewing, playing a musical instrument, and engaging in crafts or sports. Facts and figures became more important as you yourself became more practical and dependable. You were able to give your full attention to the task at hand without distraction. During this period you turned your attention to the world inside you, and you preferred to exercise your newly discovered life of the senses in solitude, or at most with one or two close friends.

3rd period—20 to 35 years (Extraverted Intuiting)

As you began to develop the function directly opposite to the one you had developed in adolescence, you may have found it difficult to understand your growing tendency to break away from the present and spend time daydreaming and speculating about the future. You may have been surprised and chagrined by your occasional forgetfulness. But you took pleasure in realizing that your creativity was coming to the fore, and that in groups you were frequently the one to come up with fresh ideas. These ideas in fact came to you for the most part through stimulation from discussion with others, rather than in solitary moments.

4th period—35 to 50 years (Introverted Feeling)

At thirty-five you turned to the development of your feeling. Since it involved the side of yourself directly opposite to your dominant thinking, this was a period when you probably had difficulty understanding yourself. You found yourself making decisions on the basis of personal feelings, and at first you yourself and others found these decisions to be often moody and arbitrary, not subject to logical analysis. The primary arena for this struggle to let feeling have its place was within you. There also you discovered a new kind of compassion and sensitivity to the feelings of others, together with a greater susceptibility to being hurt by others.

Dominant Thinking Types

(b) Extraverted Thinking with Auxiliary Intuiting—ENTJ = TSNF/*EIEI*

1st period—6 to 12 years (Extraverted Thinking)

You were probably an outgoing, inquisitive child who sought reasons for the directives given you, and you were reluctant to follow them without an understanding of why they were given. Once provided with an explanation you found it less difficult to obey. Your decisions, small as they may have been, were based on logical analysis free from the desire to please anyone. Fairness was of paramount importance to you. Rarely did you do something which you didn't want to do, even though your sense of reason and fair play convinced you to do the right thing even when it was unpleasant.

2nd period—12 to 20 years (Introverted Intuiting)

As you reached adolescence your interests would have turned to the development of your intuitive function, which now began to express itself through an expansion of your imagination. At the same time your former concern for managing the outer world of people and things was put aside for a new interest in exploring the inner world of ideas. With your enhanced imagination you found yourself prone to daydreaming. Off by yourself you found yourself conceiving all kinds of plans and proposals for the future, which you subsequently shared with others. To some, even to yourself, you may have appeared to be scattered, forgetful, and impractical, but you often came up with ideas and solutions to problems which surprised those who were more down to earth. Rather than remember facts and details you were more likely to recall the substance of an event. Your ability to let go of specifics may have diminished the amount of worry you experienced.

3rd period—20 to 35 years (Extraverted Sensing)

At this point of your life you may have surprised yourself by shifting from a future-oriented disposition to one focused on the present, from the inner employment of imagination to the exercise of your external senses. As new interests developed—sports, handcrafts, a musical instrument, enjoyment of nature—you were led to share them with others. A new concern for tidiness, accuracy, and punctuality—formerly the bane of your existence—expressed itself awkwardly at first, puzzling both yourself and others, but gradually blended in with other traits of your developing personality.

4th period—35 to 50 years (Introverted Feeling)

At thirty-five you turned to the development of your feeling. Since it involved the side of yourself directly opposite to your dominant thinking, this was a period when you probably had difficulty understanding yourself. You found yourself making decisions on the basis of personal feelings, and at first you yourself and others found these decisions to be often moody and arbitrary, not subject to logical analysis. The primary arena for this struggle to let feeling have its place was within you. There also you discovered a new kind of compassion and sensitivity to the feelings of others, together with a greater susceptibility to being hurt by others.

Dominant Thinking Types

(c) Introverted Thinking with Auxiliary Sensing—ISTP = TSNF/*IEIE*

1st period—6 to 12 years (Introverted Thinking)

Your dominant function, thinking, developed from the time you were six, operating within yourself as you organized your internal world. You tended to share your well-considered thoughts with a special few or not at all. You wanted to know the reason for everything even when you did not ask directly, and you paid serious attention to explanations of life that were logical, consistent, analytical. If you were expected to abide by rules you wanted them to be clear and fair; otherwise you found compliance difficult, or you refused to comply.

2nd period—12 to 20 years (Extraverted Sensing)

As you reached the age of twelve you began to experience a new enjoyment in such activities as collecting and classifying things, performing tasks which you could do with your hands such as sewing and carpentry, playing a musical instrument, appreciating nature, getting involved in sports. As you lost some of your earlier shyness you preferred to share such activities with others. Your growing interest and skill in handling the practical may have led you to responsibilities for keeping things efficiently operating. You were able to fulfill these responsibilities without yielding to distractions, but tended at times to be worrisome about them.

3rd period—20 to 35 years (Introverted Intuiting)

At twenty you may have experienced a readiness for creative inner experience. Your developing imagination led you to explore future possibilities, sometimes in bizarre fashion. This development was accompanied by your being more forgetful, less attentive to details, and more interested in the potential than in the actual. This exercise of creativity was not contingent on stimulating discussions with others, though you were ready to bring the results of your inner probings to others who might be interested. You often found yourself daydreaming, previously a rare practice in your life. And your former need to keep things in precise order gave way somewhat under the pressure of your focus on the future.

4th period—35 to 50 years (Extraverted Feeling)

At thirty-five your shadow side began to make itself felt, and the logical analysis which you had been accustomed to use for making your decisions yielded to a new sensitivity to persons and to personal values. This was, especially at first, a strange new experience, and others may have noticed something strange happening in you, especially since the development was taking place in the social forum. This sometimes brought embarrassment both to you and to them. But you gradually learned both to express your own compassion and to enjoy emotional expression on the part of others which would have previously made you quite uncomfortable. You found yourself accepting that not everything in human relationships and society was or needed to be rational.

Dominant Thinking Types

(d) Introverted Thinking with Auxiliary Intuiting—INTP = TNSF/*IEIE*

1st period—6 to 12 years (Introverted Thinking)

Your dominant function, thinking, developed from the time you were six, operating within yourself as you organized your internal world. You tended to share your well-considered thoughts with a special few or not at all. You wanted to know the reason for everything even when you did not ask directly, and you paid serious attention to explanations of life that were logical, consistent, and analytical. If you were expected to abide by rules you wanted them to be clear and fair; otherwise you found compliance difficult, or you refused to comply.

2nd period—12 to 20 years (Extraverted Intuiting)

During this period you developed your intuitional life, especially perhaps through an expansion of your imagination. This took place in an outgoing manner, contrasting with the way you developed your thinking in childhood; you received your best ideas from your interacting with others in discussion. More generally, though you retained your deep tendency toward cherished time alone, you found more satisfaction than before in your participation in group activities. Your developing creativity led you frequently toward considering new possibilities, finding more imaginative ways of doing things, and planning for the future. You may have found yourself daydreaming, forgetful and disinterested with regard to details, and more concerned with the essence of things than with their simple actuality. You may also have found it difficult to keep your things in precise order, although when necessary you were able to retrieve them at random and to your own satisfaction.

3rd period—20 to 35 years (Introverted Sensing)

At twenty you began to feel ready for and even excited about dealing with the world of the senses, something which had never interested you very much. This development took place through a flow of energy toward the interior, in contrast to the way that your imagination developed in adolescence. For example, you enjoyed the world of nature without having to share it with someone else. Your interest was in the life of the senses, for example making things with your hands, playing a musical instrument, listening to music with quiet attentiveness to each bar, note, and instrument, or collecting and classifying things. Facts assumed more importance for you than heretofore. Your image before others became more important to you, and you became more conscious of how others saw you and of how you yourself related to them.

4th period—35 to 50 years (Extraverted Feeling)

At thirty-five your shadow side began to make itself felt, and the logical analysis which you had been accustomed to use for making your decisions yielded to a new sensitivity to persons and to personal values. This was, especially at first, a strange new experience, and others may have noticed something happening in you, especially since the development was taking place in the social forum. This sometimes brought embarrassment both to you and to them. But you gradually learned both to express your own compassion and to enjoy emotional expression on the part of others which would previously have made you quite uncomfortable. You found yourself now accepting that not everything in human relationships and society was or needed to be rational.

Dominant Feeling Types

(a) Extraverted Feeling with Auxiliary Sensing—ESFJ = FSNT/*EIEI*

1st period—6 to 12 years (Extraverted Feeling)

During this period you were probably a friendly, outgoing, and loving child, wishing to please those around you, especially your parents and others in authority. You were sensitive to the needs of others and perhaps vulnerable in your own feelings. You may have assumed responsibility for others and their actions simply because you felt it was expected of you. Any infraction of rules by you brought feelings of guilt, and any resentment or anger toward those you loved or felt obliged to love may have resulted in a good deal of self-blame. Your strong desire was to keep everyone happy and to see that life ran smoothly for all around you. When you were not feeling the weight of responsibility you were inclined to express outwardly the sheer joy of being alive.

2nd period—12 to 20 years (Introverted Sensing)

As you approached adolescence your interest in the outer world made way for a new interest in the inner world, and you possibly became less interested in group activities, preferring to be alone or with one or two intimates. You developed interest in pursuits that related to your senses—playing a musical instrument, engaging in physical exercise, collecting and classifying objects, working with your hands, all of which you could enjoy by yourself without the need for others to share them with you. Keenness of observation, accuracy in your work, and attention to detail became important for you.

3rd period—20 to 35 years (Extraverted Intuiting)

During this period you may have once again become interested in the outer world, which you now viewed more creatively, seeing all kinds of possibilities in people and things where formerly you experienced them as commonplace. As your imagination developed you may have found yourself, to your chagrin, becoming less rooted in the present and more likely to become distracted, forgetful, and absent-minded. But this would possibly have diminished the amount of worry in your life as you let the worrisome things slip away in favor of alternative solutions to problems. Group discussions rather than time spent alone were more likely to provide the spark of these creative ideas.

4th period—35 to 50 years (Introverted Thinking)

During this period you faced the shadow side of your personality. You began to experience a strong inclination to assert yourself, something that you may have begun to develop previously but not with the same urgency. Requests to which you would have readily acceded in an earlier period you now often chose to refuse. Your decisions became more logical, rational, and analytical, and you were less inclined to yield to unsubstantiated arguments just for the sake of harmony. Because this development was taking place in the inner world, you probably had difficulty in getting others to see the logic of your position. And the contrast between your former willingness to be imposed upon and your somewhat awkward efforts to become assertive may have caused others to judge you less benevolently. Despite the pain of this you experienced a new peace from knowing that you were free to *choose* to be generous on the basis of clearly perceived reasons.

Dominant Feeling Types

(b) Extraverted Feeling with Auxiliary Intuiting—ENFJ = FNST/*EIEI*

1st period—6 to 12 years (Extraverted Feeling)

During this period you were probably a friendly, outgoing, and loving child, wishing to please those around you, especially your parents and others in authority. You were sensitive to the needs of others and perhaps vulnerable in your own feelings. You may have assumed responsibility for others and their actions simply because you felt it was expected of you. Any infraction of rules by you brought feelings of guilt, and any resentment or anger toward those you loved or felt obliged to love may have resulted in a good deal of self-blame. Your strong desire was to keep everyone happy and to see that life ran smoothly for all around you. When you were not feeling the weight of responsibility you were inclined to express outwardly the sheer joy of being alive.

2nd period—12 to 20 years (Introverted Intuiting)

As you reached adolescence your interest turned to the exercise of your imagination. Your earlier concern to foster harmony in the outer world of people and things was put aside in favor of a new interest in the inner world of ideas. You found yourself prone to daydreaming, and when off by yourself you tended to conceive all kinds of plans and proposals for the future. To some others and perhaps to yourself you may have appeared as scattered, forgetful, and impractical, but you often came up with ideas and solutions to problems which surprised those who were more down to earth. Rather than remembering facts and details you were more likely to recall the substance of an event, the total picture, the ambiance, and you worried little or not at all about losing touch with the particulars.

3rd period—20 to 35 years (Extraverted Sensing)

Now you experienced a desire to shift from orientation to the future to interest in the present. You became interested about facts, information, and specifics, and wanted to share this interest with others. Group activities such as sports, the appreciation of music, and hiking now attracted you. You also became more concerned with tidiness, accuracy, and punctuality, things which had been previously the bane of your existence. As these behaviors were for you new and unpracticed, it was only gradually that you acquired ease and skill in them. And, in the long run, they did not displace your basic preference for the world of inner dreaming.

4th period—35 to 50 years (Introverted Thinking)

During this period you faced the shadow side of your personality. You began to experience a strong inclination to assert yourself, something that you may have begun to develop previously but not with the same urgency. Requests to which you would have readily acceded in an earlier period you now often chose to refuse. Your decisions became more logical, rational, and analytical, and you were less inclined to yield to unsubstantiated arguments just for the sake of harmony. Because this development was taking place in the inner world, you probably had difficulty in getting others to see the logic of your position. And the contrast between your former willingness to be imposed upon and your somewhat awkward efforts to become assertive may have caused others to judge you less benevolently. Despite the pain of this you experienced a new peace from knowing that you were free to *choose* to be generous on the basis of clearly perceived reasons.

Dominant Feeling Types

(c) Introverted Feeling with Auxiliary Sensing—ISFP = FSNT/*IEIE*

1st period—6 to 12 years (Introverted Feeling)

As a small child you were intent on pleasing others, and you were probably an obedient and considerate member of the family. Since your feelings were directed toward the inner world, you were likely shy and inclined to spend time by yourself. Your desire to be helpful may have led you to disregard your own interests simply to be of service and to win praise. You may have developed a delicate conscience, leading perhaps to feelings of guilt over inconsequential matters. And you may have felt an obligation to keep harmony in the family, taking responsibility for any failure to maintain it.

2nd period—12 to 20 years (Extraverted Sensing)

As you came to adolescence you began to experience pleasure in such activities as collecting and classifying things, performing tasks which you could do with your hands, sewing, playing a musical instrument, enjoying nature, engaging in sports. You were inclined to share such activities with others, and you lost some of your former shyness. Your new interest in the practical may have led to your accepting responsibility for keeping things efficiently operating. You were able to focus on such things perseveringly and without distraction.

3rd period—20 to 35 years (Introverted Intuiting)

As you reached adult life you experienced a readiness to move from an outgoing engagement of the senses to an accent on inner exploration through your imagination. The future and its possibilities now began to attract you, and especially at the beginning of this development you found yourself somewhat forgetful and unable to handle details. You were not very dependent on social interaction for this growing in creativity; your best dreams came when you were by yourself. In fact you spent a good deal of time in daydreaming, as your former need for efficiency took a back seat to concocting schemes for the future.

4th period—35 to 50 years (Extraverted Thinking)

Now you began a discomforting and awkward period, as you were drawn despite yourself toward assertive behavior. Because for the greater part of your life your feelings had taken primary responsibility for your decisions, it was somewhat unsettling to deal with life with more detachment and not from any desire to please or to create harmony around you. You yourself and others were sometimes surprised when your hostile or aggressive behavior signaled your slow ascent to assertiveness. At times you may have experienced rebelliousness and resentment over your previous submission to domination by others. You were determined to withstand threats to your new freedom, even though you were not entirely happy about the vigor with which you did this. This was also a period of questioning in your life, as you became less vulnerable to the criticism of others and more forthright in expressing your own. Your new attitudes were manifest to others.

Dominant Feeling Types

(d) Introverted Feeling with Auxiliary Intuiting—INFP = FNST/*IEIE*

1st period—6 to 12 years (Introverted Feeling)

As a small child you were intent on pleasing others, and you were probably an obedient and considerate member of the family. Since your feelings were directed toward the inner world, you were likely shy and inclined to spend time by yourself. Your desire to be helpful may have led you to disregard your own interests simply to be of service and to win praise. You may have developed a delicate conscience, leading perhaps to feelings of guilt over inconsequential matters. And you may have felt an obligation to keep harmony in the family, taking responsibility for any failure to maintain it.

2nd period—12 to 20 years (Extraverted Intuiting)

About the age of twelve you turned to the life of imagination, which you tended to exercise in the company of others, where your best ideas came to you. Though you still retained the deep tendency to spend time alone, particularly in the cultivation of your feelings, during adolescence you found more satisfaction than before in being with others, especially when something exciting was in prospect. Your developing creativity led you to conceive ever new possibilities, more imaginative ways of doing things, and shaping plans for the future. You probably found yourself daydreaming, forgetful of details, disinterested in specifics, but more concerned for the essence and the potential of things than for their actuality. You may have found it difficult to be efficient and precise in handling your belongings, though you may have been able to keep enough in touch with the practical for the pursuit of your projects.

3rd period—20 to 35 years (Introverted Sensing)

At twenty you felt ready for and even excited about dealing with the world of the senses in new ways. Having made your excursion into the outer world during the preceding period, you now turned within yourself for this cultivation of the sense life. You enjoyed the world of nature without having to share it with others. You may have become interested in making things with your hands, listening to music, collecting and classifying objects. Facts may have assumed more importance to you than before. Your own image in the outside world became more important to you, and you were more sensitive to how others saw you and how you related to them.

4th period— 35 to 50 years (Extraverted Thinking)

Now you began a discomforting and awkward period, as you were drawn despite yourself toward assertive behavior. Because for the greater part of your life your feelings had taken primary responsibility for your decisions, it was somewhat unsettling to deal with life with more detachment and not from any desire to please or to create harmony around you. You yourself and others were sometimes surprised when your hostile or aggressive behavior signaled your slow ascent to assertiveness. At times you may have experienced rebelliousness and resentment over your previous submission to domination by others. You were determined to withstand threats to your new freedom, even though you were not entirely happy about the vigor with which you did this. This was also a period of questioning in your life, as you became less vulnerable to the criticisms of others and more forthright in expressing your own. Your new attitudes were manifest to others.

Dominant Intuiting Types

(a) Extraverted Intuiting with Auxiliary Thinking—ENTP = NTFS/*EIEI*

1st period—6 to 12 years (Extraverted Intuiting)

Your first period of development found you absorbed in the life of the imagination, not so much in solitary as in social situations. If you were an only child, for example, you may have invented a playmate and chatted away with her or him in the presence of your amused parents. In playing with other children you were the one who came up with new and exciting things to do, and you became easily bored with routines of play or work or study. Often your parents and teachers had to call you back to the world of the concrete, or scolded you for not paying attention. You found it hard to keep your room tidy, and were quite at home in disordered social situations. Today's task found you dreaming of what tomorrow would bring.

2nd period—12 to 20 years (Introverted Thinking)

Now you found yourself looking within in a new way, and becoming more reflective and logical. You wanted your schemes to manage the groups in which you functioned, but in an indirect fashion. Often others had difficulty seeing the logic of your suggestions because you had difficulty communicating that logic to them. When asked your opinion you usually gave it in frank, objective terms, sometimes offending those who were looking for a more sensitive response. You developed a strong sense of fairness.

3rd period—20 to 35 years (Extraverted Feeling)

Now you began to find yourself, to your own surprise and that of others, behaving more subjectively and with more feeling in social situations, in contrast to your previous detached manner and cool logic. In the early years of this period you even found yourself acting on the basis of whim instead of following your previous well-considered patterns of behavior. Sudden emotional reactions which you earlier would have considered too sentimental also became characteristic. At the same time people noticed that you were showing more warmth, tenderness, and compassion in relating to them.

4th period—35 to 50 years (Introverted Sensing)

Now you felt a call to develop the least acknowledged part of your personality, the life of the senses, exterior and interior. Your earlier years had seen you so engrossed in the world of the possible that you did not care to notice the details of the world around you or within you. Now you began to take pleasure, for example, in doing things with your hands, sewing, taking up a craft, learning to play a musical instrument. You became more concerned with having all the facts and accurate information before making your decisions. And punctuality, neatness, and simplicity became more important for you. All of these new kinds of behavior you preferred to savor with a certain solitude which contrasted with your long-standing attraction to the excitement of being with others. This major transition of your life was far from being a smooth path, and your exercise of the newly discovered life of the senses may have demonstrated immaturity.

Dominant Intuiting Types

(b) Extraverted Intuiting with Auxiliary Feeling—ENFP = NFTS/*EIEI*

1st period—6 to 12 years (Extraverted Intuiting)

Your first period of development found you absorbed in the life of the imagination, not so much in solitary as in social situations. If you were an only child, for example, you may have invented a playmate and chatted away with her or him in the presence of your amused parents. In playing with other children you were the one who came up with new and exciting things to do, and you became easily bored with the routines of play or work or study. Often your parents or teachers had to call you back to the world of the concrete, or scolded you for not paying attention. You found it hard to keep your room tidy, and were quite at home in disordered social situations. Today's task found you dreaming of what tomorrow might bring.

2nd period—12 to 20 years (Introverted Feeling)

If your childhood found you removed from other people while being in their midst, adolescence was a time of a different kind of disengagement, as you moved within yourself to cultivate your feeling life. Compassion began to develop, and your interests turned to helping others; you may have joined efforts to help underprivileged and deprived groups. Your religious commitment may have become more important. You found yourself becoming more sensitive to the criticism of others. As you considered possible careers you gave high priority to professions that were service-oriented.

3rd period—20 to 35 years (Extraverted Thinking)

At twenty you found yourself asking whether your life had not been too much shaped by the desires of others, and you began to shape it yourself on the basis of your own strongly held convictions. Because this development was taking place in the social dimensions of your life, and because it was in contrast with the more introverted nature of your adolescent development, it brought you some uneasiness and self-doubt and made others wonder what was taking place in you. At the same time you began to feel good about becoming more assertive, and to be more secure in your right to have convictions and to make your own decisions. You realized that your occasional ineptness in this new behavior caused some hard feeling in others, but were convinced that the answer was in going forward toward assertiveness, not back to your earlier submissiveness.

4th period—35 to 50 years (Introverted Sensing)

Now you felt a call to develop the least acknowledged part of your personality, the life of the senses, exterior and interior. Your earlier years had seen you so engrossed in the world of the possible that you did not care to notice the details of the world around you or within you. Now you began to take pleasure, for example, in doing things with your hands, sewing, taking up a craft, learning to play a musical instrument. You became more concerned about making your decisions only after having all the facts and accurate information. Punctuality, neatness, and simplicity became more important for you. All of these new kinds of behavior you preferred to savor with a certain solitude which contrasted with your long-standing attraction to the excitement of being with others. This major transition of your life was far from being a smooth path, and your exercise of the newly discovered life of the senses may have demonstrated immaturity.

Dominant Intuiting Types

(c) Introverted Intuiting with Auxiliary Thinking—INTJ = NTFS/*IEIE*

1st period—6 to 12 years (Introverted Intuiting)

By innate preference you were drawn in childhood to develop your imagination and creativity. Perhaps you created an imaginary play-mate, or several, with whom you secretly lived while your parents wondered about your dreamy silence. Only a favorite friend or two, or a wise and gentle parent, was permitted to share your world of make-believe. Teachers frequently had to remind you that you were not paying attention. It is hard for you to remember the details of this period, especially as details did not engage your interest. But you do recall the general atmosphere, whether of happiness, sadness, pain, or pleasure.

2nd period—12 to 20 years (Extraverted Thinking)

As you reached adolescence you turned to developing your thinking, and began to find enjoyment in managing and directing groups and projects in an orderly, logical fashion. Justice was of primary impor-tance, and your sense of fair play together with your reasoning ability and detachment from emotional involvements made it natural for you to assume roles of responsibility. In times of crisis you were able to work with others in a cool, unemotional way.

3rd period—20 to 35 years (Introverted Feeling)

You now found yourself, somewhat surprisingly, basing your decisions on the personal values and the feelings of yourself and others. You began to express your emotions with greater freedom, at least with a few trusted friends. Because this development of feeling life was taking place within yourself, it was only indirectly accessible to oth-ers. Many would be unaware, for example, of your developing com-passion and sensitivity.

4th period—35 to 50 years (Extraverted Sensing)

At this point you began to experience a call to develop your least acknowledged gift, your sensing. Now you began to notice the details of life around you which previously, in your basic preference for exploring the possible, had not engaged your interest. As if for the first time you took pleasure in the exercise of some or all of your senses. You probably became keenly interested in doing things with your hands, playing a musical instrument, taking up a craft, or collecting and classifying objects; and you engaged in this type of activity with a precision which contrasted strongly with your previous vagueness about the life of the senses. Now in fact you became somewhat impatient with inexactitude, daydreaming, and disorder in yourself and others. Your preference now was for engaging in the newly found life of the senses in company with others, not in solitude. You liked to have someone with you as you attended concerts or visited museums; and your companions were struck with your attentiveness to the fine details of artistic creation.

Dominant Intuiting Types

(d) Introverted Intuiting with Auxiliary Thinking—INFJ = NFTS/*IEIE*

1st period—6 to 12 years (Introverted Intuiting)

By innate preference you were drawn in childhood to develop your imagination and creativity. Perhaps you created an imaginary play-mate, or several, with whom you secretly lived while your parents wondered about your dreamy silence. Only a favorite friend or two, or a wise and gentle parent, was permitted to share your world of make-believe. Teachers frequently had to remind you that you were not paying attention. It is hard for you to remember the details of this period, especially as details did not engage your interest. But you do recall the general atmosphere, whether of happiness, sadness, pain, or pleasure.

2nd period—12 to 20 years (Extraverted Feeling)

While continuing to perceive in a predominantly intuitive way, you now became aware of a desire to give expression to your life of feeling. Sensitivity to your own feelings and compassion for others became characteristic of you, and because you were led to manifest these qualities others came to know you predominantly through them. You perhaps surprised yourself by becoming more outgoing, in contrast to your previous shyness. You became more aware of ways in which you could help others, especially the poor, the suffering, the underdog, and you may have joined groups committed to the service of others. You may have found it difficult to find time for yourself in the process of obliging others.

3rd period—20 to 35 years (Introverted Thinking)

At twenty you experienced a tendency to become more independent, more your own person, and became critical of your previous habits of submission to the wishes of others. Because this development was taking place in an introverted way, you were not fully able to explain to others your new determination to become more autonomous; hence others may have been offended or baffled by the change in you. At the beginning of this period you probably felt you were handling the transition badly, but your conviction that it was right helped you to persevere and grow. The solution to your occasional ineptness was, you believed, in going forward toward assertiveness, not back to your earlier submissiveness.

4th period—35 to 50 years (Extraverted Sensing)

At this point you began to experience a call to develop your least acknowledged gift, your sensing. Now you began to notice the details of life around you which previously, in your basic preference for exploring the possible, had not engaged your interest. As if for the first time you took pleasure in the exercise of some or all of your senses. You probably became keenly interested in such things as doing things with your hands, playing a musical instrument, taking up a craft, or collecting and classifying objects; and you engaged in this type of activity with a precision which contrasted strongly with your previous vagueness about the life of the senses. Now in fact you became somewhat impatient with inexactitude, daydreaming, and disorder in yourself and in others. Your preference now was for engaging in the newly found life of the senses in company with others, not in solitude. You liked to have someone with you as you attended concerts or visited museums; and your companions were struck with your attentiveness to the fine details of artistic creation.

© Grant, Thompson, Clark, *From Image to Likeness*, 1983.

A concluding observation or two may be helpful. With the incipient development at thirty-five of your inferior function, whichever one it was, you may have come to a time of crisis, even of impasse and a certain kind of crucifixion or dark night. What then ensued hinged on a number of factors: how well you had developed the first three functions; whether you now recognized what was happening in you and soundly interpreted it as a crisis of growth, not a total disintegration; whether you had available, in friends, community, a spiritual director, Scripture, or elsewhere some models and supports which encouraged you to let go of your previous strengths so that your weaker side might carry you toward wholeness. To the degree to which such graces were present and received your positive response, you experienced a certain wholeness. And you came to see that your basic preferences were abiding, even though you had been wisely willing to set them aside for a while so that God's image in you might grow toward Godlikeness. In a much more limited way, something similar might be said about the two previous transition points, your entry into adolescence and into adult life.

Biographical Data

W. HAROLD GRANT is Director of the Missionary Cenacle Volunteers. He is an Associate in the Missionary Cenacle Apostolate, a community of lay missionaries, which he currently serves as Custodian General. He received the bachelor's degree from Auburn University and the doctorate from Columbia and did post-doctoral studies at Stanford University in the behavioral sciences. He served in faculty and administrative positions at Cornell, Michigan State and Auburn Universities and was president of the American College Personnel Association in 1974–75. He is the editor of *Theories of Counseling* (McGraw-Hill, 1971) and has authored several articles and chapters. Married with four children, he lives with his family in Waverly, Alabama.

MAGDALA THOMPSON, R.S.M. is a Sister of Mercy of the Baltimore Province. Currently director of Career Development Services at Auburn University and a marriage and family therapist in private practice, she has served in administrative posts at Mount Saint Agnes and Loyola Colleges and Michigan State University. She received her Ph.D. from Michigan State University. She has co-authored two books and a number of articles on higher education. She has also served as a consultant for groups in higher education and Church ministry.

THOMAS E. CLARKE, S.J. (S.T.D. Gregorian University) is a Jesuit priest, writer and lecturer residing in New York City. He was formerly a professor of systematic theology at Woodstock College, a Jesuit seminary, staff member of Gonzaga Center for Renewal, and research associate of the Woodstock Theological Center. He is an associate editor of *The Way* and an editorial consultant for *Concilium* and *Hospital Progress*. He has contributed to many periodicals and journals and is the author of several books, including *New Pentecost or New Passion?* (Paulist, 1973) and *Above Every Name: The Lordship of Christ and Social Systems* (Paulist, 1980). He has given retreats, lectures and workshops in North America, Asia and Rome.